JN325526

"Working Together" for Peace and Prosperity of Southeast Asia, 1945-1968

The Birth of the ASEAN Way

Kazuhisa Shimada

大学教育出版

For Elisa

CONTENTS

ABBREVIATIONS	*iii*
FIGURES	*iii*

INTRODUCTION — 1
   The history of international relations in Southeast Asia — 1
   About the book — 3
   The structure of the book — 4

1 THE ASEAN WAY – HOW HAS IT BEEN IDENTIFIED? — 6
   The ASEAN Way — 6
   Scholarly discussion of the ASEAN Way — 8
   (i) The principle of non-interference — 8
   (ii) Face-saving behaviour — 11
   (iii) Consultations — 12
   (iv) Informality — 13
   (v) The spirit of working together — 13
   The influence of Southeast Asian cultures on the ASEAN Way — 14
   ASEAN and its precursors: The origin of the ASEAN Way — 16
   Concluding remarks — 17

2 AN AWAKENING OF REGIONAL CONSCIOUSNESS — 19
   Southeast Asia after the Japanese surrender — 19
   The advent of the Cold War — 19
   Towards self-reliance — 25
   The birth of regional consciousness — 28
   The political situation in Indonesia — 29
   The development of the plan — 33
   The significance of the establishment of the ASA — 34
   Concluding remarks — 35

3 THE ATTEMPT TO FIND A REGIONAL SOLUTION TO A REGIONAL PROBLEM — 36
   The declaration of the Malaysia plan — 36
   The regional situation in a broader context — 39
   The reaction from potential claimants — 40
   Starting the verbal war — 45
   Seeking peaceful coexistence — 50
   The beginning of discord — 59
   The significance of the Manila agreements and Maphilindo — 65
   Concluding remarks — 68

4 THE SETTLEMENT OF THE REGIONAL PROBLEM AND THE FORMATION OF ASEAN — **70**

- The Malaysia issue after the establishment of Malaysia — 70
- Suharto's rise to power — 73
- Indonesia's new foreign policy — 74
- Towards reconciliation — 78
- Post-Bangkok talks — 82
- Towards regional cooperation — 84
- From 'antagonising each other' to 'working together' — 90
- Concluding remarks — 94

5 THE CORREGIDOR AFFAIR — **95**

- The killings in the Corregidor Island — 95
- Reaction from Kuala Lumpur — 96
- Tempering an international dispute — 97
- Bangkok talks — 98
- The Jakarta agreement — 98
- The Annexation Law and the further deterioration of relations — 100
- Towards re-establishing the Jakarta agreement — 101
- The significance of the Corregidor affair — 103
- Concluding remarks — 105

6 THE NATURE OF THE ASEAN WAY — **107**

- The ASEAN Way and traditional culture — 107
- The ASEAN Way and the principle of non-interference — 109
- What is the ASEAN Way? — 111
- Four conventions for 'working together beyond difference' — 114
- The formation process of the ASEAN Way — 116
- ASEAN, the ASEAN Way and the goal of ASEAN — 118
- Concluding remarks — 121

CONCLUSION — **123**

BIBLIOGRAPHY — **125**

INDEX — **153**

ABBREVIATIONS

AMDA	Anglo-Malayan Defence Agreement
AMM	ASEAN Ministerial Meeting
ASEAN	Association of Southeast Asian Nations
ASA	Association of Southeast Asia
ASAS	Association of South East Asian State
ASPAC	Asian and Pacific Council
CAB	The British Cabinet
CO	The British Colonial Office
DC	The British Defence Committee
ECAFE	The United Nations Economic Commission for Asia and the Far East
FCO	The British Foreign and Commonwealth Office
FO	The British Foreign Office
ICJ	International Court of Justice
KOGAM	Crush Malaysia Command
MCEDSEA	Ministerial Conference on Economic Development in Southeast Asia
MCP	Malayan Communist Party
MPRS	Indonesia's Provisional People's Consultative Assembly
NKKU	Unitary State of North Borneo
PKI	Indonesian Communist Party
PMO	The British Prime Minister's Office
PRRI	Revolutionary Government of the Republic of Indonesia
SEAFET	Southeast Asian Friendship and Economic Treaty
SEATO	Southeast Asia Treaty Organisation
TAC	Treaty of Amity and Cooperation
TR	The British Treasury
TUNK	North Borneo National Army

FIGURES

Fig. 1   The ASEAN Way (Concept and conventions)
Fig. 2   ASEAN, the ASEAN Way and the goal of ASEAN

INTRODUCTION

This book looks at the origins of the Association of Southeast Asian Nations (ASEAN) and, specifically, of the ASEAN Way in the period 1945-1968. The periodisation is significant because it encapsulates the decolonisation of many of the Southeast Asian states, the subsequent search for stability in the region, and, beyond that, for a broadly acceptable working method in maintaining good relations between economically and politically diverse states. The period is also a momentous one, given the range of political upheavals that characterised it. The end of the war brought processes of decolonisation to both Malaya and Indonesia, but very different ones. Malaya adopted a more moderate approach, maintaining close relations with the former metropolitan power there, Britain. Indonesia, on the other hand, broke its colonial ties in a violent, troubled way. Partly as a result of this, these two neighbouring states quickly entered into a period of confrontation, known as *Konfrontasi*. As scholars such as Leifer observe of the latter, 'ASEAN was a primary product of the termination of Indonesia's campaign of "Confrontation"'.[1]

But the end of *Konfrontasi* was not the only catalyst, nor was ASEAN the sole regional organisation created in that period. The earlier organisations, the Association of Southeast Asia (ASA) and the Southeast Asia Treaty Organisation (SEATO), did not work well enough, and provided neither a broad enough base for confidence-building in the region, nor sufficiently workable platforms for conflict resolution. And while scholars such as Leifer interpret *Konfrontasi* as a watershed, they pay less attention to the immensely troubling Indochinese conflicts,[2] and to the territorial disputes evident in the period. At its heart, this book argues that this all-important period of diplomatic innovation, together with the urgency of resolving tensions, diplomatic rows and conflicts in the region gradually, and through earlier attempts for regional cooperation, gave rise to the idea of forming an ASEAN-like regional organisation. Its emergence was, however, very much contingent upon evolving a working method, coming to be known as the ASEAN Way. Elements of the latter are visible in the course of the conflicts and processes of conflict-resolution, attempted severally and collectively by Southeast Asian states. With the emergence of the overarching notion of 'working together', a number of formal and informal diplomatic methods gave body to that principle.

While the book argues that many of the rudiments of regional cooperation had existed a decade or more before the establishment of ASEAN; setting down philosophical continuity for regional cooperation in the region, this longer history has been largely overlooked by existing scholarship, which focuses on a particular event or crisis as a watershed in the development of ASEAN and the ASEAN Way. The book therefore suggests a need to revise existing approaches to the subject. In examining the period, the work makes extensive use of official documents from Japan and Britain; both countries being strongly interested in contributing to stability in the Southeast Asian region. Japanese foreign ministry documents are especially interesting in this regard, as they have hitherto never been used in work on the formation of ASEAN.

The history of international relations in Southeast Asia
The Second World War finally ended with the Japan's surrender. In the wake of this surrender, colonies in Southeast Asia began to press for independence, a process which in some cases con-

---

[1] Michael Leifer, 'The ASEAN peace process: a category mistake', *The Pacific Review*, 12/1 (1999), pp. 26-27.
[2] These were proxy wars between the Eastern and the Western blocs in the Cold War structure.

tinued for a period of nearly 40 years.[3] The Cold War began just after the end of the war, and the two opposing blocs divided Southeast Asia into spheres of influence and client states. For example, in Vietnam, communist pressure at first focussed on the overthrow of French colonial rule, but after a cease-fire was agreed upon in 1954, Communist power continued to expand across Indochina, backed as it was by the Soviet Union and Communist China. Perhaps in anticipation of this, the West pressed for the creation of SEATO. Formed in the same year as the cease-fire in Vietnam, the defence organisation was intended as a bulwark against the emerging Communist threat. And while foreign policy changes in the Soviet Union gave rise to détente in Europe in mid 1950s and after, the armed conflict between East and West continued to smoulder in Southeast Asia, and notably in Indochina. In the first half of 1960s, Communist power gained some momentum, with anti-American leaders' governments seizing power in Laos and Cambodia. Furthermore, while Burma maintained an isolationist policy, it was one that showed a very strong independent socialist line. Internally, this country remained highly politically unstable, and therefore quite vulnerable.

In this insecure regional environment, the ASA, the first regional organisation, was established in 1961, through the initiative of Malaya, the Philippines and Thailand, its founding members. However, Indonesia, Malaya and the Philippines descended into conflict in 1963 over the formation of Malaysia, resulting in further regional instability. As a result of these pressures, the ASA became dysfunctional just two years after its establishment. A series of Manila agreements were signed in mid-1963 between Indonesia, Malaya and the Philippines for the second regional cooperation (Maphilindo), aiming at peaceful settlement of the tripartite dispute. The agreements themselves brought into being some significant concepts for regional cooperation. However, Maphilindo soon collapsed too, and the three-way dispute continued for another two years. After the abortive coup against him on 30 September 1965, Indonesian President Sukarno lost his power and General Suharto came to office. The latter changed the policy direction of Indonesia, which brought the regional disturbances to a sudden end. In parallel with this process, a new regional cooperation plan was sought by countries in the region in order to realise peace and stability in Southeast Asia. In this way, the third regional cooperation scheme, ASEAN, was established in 1967 by Indonesia, Malaysia, the Philippines, Singapore and Thailand.

ASEAN came into existence at an important juncture in regional history while the political situation was going to be chaotic in Indochina. The US heightened its military presence and activities in Vietnam, particularly after the Gulf of Tonkin incident in August 1964. The increased conflict there brought no quick solution, which resulted in a strategic impasse. The British announcement of the withdrawal of troops from East of Suez in 1967 cast a further shadow over regional security in Southeast Asia. Two years later, the American President, Richard Nixon, announced the so-called Guam doctrine, which proposed: first, that allied countries in Asia should share the responsibility for their regional security and, second, that US troops should begin to withdraw from Vietnam. The Americans withdrew completely from Vietnam, after the signing of the Paris Peace Agreement in January 1973. However, the war did not cease: the Communist-controlled North Vietnam occupied South Vietnam. In the rest of Indochina, Pol Pot and his Khmer Rouge came to power in Cambodia, and Pathet Lao seized Laos.[4] In this way, all of Indochina fell into the hands of the Communists.

At the end of 1978, when Vietnam, backed by the Soviet Union, invaded Cambodia, ASEAN had its first opportunity to contribute to extra-regional peace. From 1979, ASEAN continuously submitted motions to the United Nations, repeatedly denouncing the Vietnamese for their invasion of Cambodia. The Association also played a mediator's role between the parties concerned in the Cambodian situation. Although the Vietnamese withdrawal from Cambodia in

---

[3] The first county to gain independence was the Philippines in 1946, and the last one was Brunei in 1984.
[4] Both historical events occurred in 1975.

1991 was not directly brought about by ASEAN's political activities,[5] its moderator's role should not be underestimated.[6]

By contrast with the highly volatile situation in Indochina, in the rest of Southeast Asia, ASEAN had steadily attracted international attention with its notable economic growth. In addition, it received considerable praise for its international efforts to influence the situation in Cambodia. However, this praise did not last, as with the end of the Cold War, new international paradigms emerged, such as human rights and democratisation. These replaced the conventional ideological antagonism between the East and the West; this is the so-called Asian values debate.[7]

In addition to the Asian values debate, two notable developments occurred in ASEAN during 1990s. Firstly, the Association's membership expanded sharply after 1995, when Vietnam joined the Association. This expansion continued until Cambodia became a member in 1999, and, with that, all ten countries in Southeast Asia had become members of ASEAN.[8] Secondly, ASEAN's extra-regional role became a reality when ASEAN Regional Forum (ARF) was set up in 1994, including the US, Canada, Japan, Australia and New Zealand. In addition to the ARF, the Association created foundations for non-binding political cooperation in East Asia through the East Asia Summit, the latter involving countries such as China, Japan, India and Australia.

In this way, ASEAN countries increased their international status and learned how to work together peacefully, and did so through a distinctive form of organisational cooperation. It is noteworthy that no major armed conflict has occurred in the ASEAN region in the forty years since its formation. Part of the reason for this has been, of course, the impetus for socio-economic development there; itself based to a degree on the adoption of the ASEAN Way, as it will be argued in the book. To this end, there is a specific code of practices in place in ASEAN for maintaining cooperation for peace and stability, the sum total of which are now known collectively as the ASEAN Way. The latter has, indeed, been expanded into the work ASEAN carries out in international forums, such as the ARF.

About the book

The book argues that ASEAN and the ASEAN Way work in a comprehensive fashion. It addresses three aspects of the organisation and its approach to confidence-building. Firstly, the importance of the history of locally-generated regional cooperation in post-War Southeast Asia is examined. Secondly, the book identifies the specific practices for establishing and maintaining regional cooperation. Thirdly, it vivifies from a novel perspective the role of the ASEAN Way in ASEAN itself.

Although the ASEAN Way has been frequently referred to and examined in scholarly and broader contexts, its actual nature has until now remained vague. This, it can be argued, is because too much attention has been paid to the structural aspects of ASEAN, and that these have

---

[5] It was triggered by the change in international circumstances, and notably the end of the Cold War.
[6] Yoneji Kuroyanagi, *ASEAN 35 Nen no Kiseki: 'ASEAN Way' no Koyo to Genkai [The trajectory for 35 years of ASEAN:Tthe Good and the Limit of the 'ASEAN Way']* (Tokyo: Yushindo Kobun Sha, 2003), p. 95.
[7] Western countries began to criticise ASEAN countries for the unsatisfactory domestic conditions in human rights and democratisation. ASEAN countries, having great confidence in their international reputation, opposed this criticism by presenting a new thesis: the Asian Way, in which they argued that there was a specific way of national development in Asia. However, this new axis of antagonism between Asia and the West disappeared when ASEAN countries became inward-looking in response to as a result of the Asian financial crisis in late 1990s.
[8] Brunei became an ASEAN member after its independence in 1984, whereas Myanmar and Laos joined the Association in 1997.

often been found to be weak.[9] Little work has been done on the ideology underpinning the association, and so by examining the origins of the ASEAN Way, a more refined understanding of ASEAN itself should be developed. The book argues that the ASA and Maphilindo are forerunners of ASEAN and that there is a considerable ideological continuity between these organisations. Existing scholarly literature pays little attention to this factor.[10] In addition to these landmark formations in the pre-history of ASEAN,[11] are the all-important matters of dispute resolution between member states in less formal and fluid contexts.[12] In exploring this further, and most important, dimension, one other dispute-resolution process occurred in 1968, and in significant ways crystallised ASEAN work as an association; the so-called Corregidor affair.

The structure of the book

Chapter One outlines the nature of the ASEAN Way through an examination of the existing literature, and sets the broader themes of this book. The first part focuses on exploring statements given by ASEAN leaders and reviewing existing scholarly discussions; then attempts to draw the silhouette of the ASEAN Way. The second part sets forth the importance of cultural influence in the region, and presents the significance of ideological impact from ASEAN's precursors, the ASA and Maphilindo.

Chapter Two explores the formation process of the ASA. In particular, it focuses on the region's leaders and their perspectives on regional cooperation. The chapter pays particular attention to the fact that the formation of these perspectives came at a very early stage in the nation-building processes of these states, and Southeast Asia as a whole. This period was also the beginning of the Cold War, which, to a lesser or greater extent, affected the whole Southeast Asia. The chapter depicts how, through complex initiatives, the states involved came to form the first regional organisation (the ASA).[13] Although the ASA is significant in terms of regional cooperation, its formation process has been neglected.[14] The chapter argues that the ASA was an important staging post for the formation of ASEAN, and that its history deserves far more attention in this regard.

---

[9] The critical view of ASEAN varies from scholar to scholar. For sharp criticism, see David Martin Jones and Michael L. R. Smith, 'ASEAN's Imitation Community', *Orbis*, 46/1 (Winter 2002), pp. 93-109. For sympathetic criticism, see Simon S. C. Tay, 'Institutions and Process: Dilemmas and Possibilities', in Simon S. C. Tay, Jesus P. Estanislao and Hadi Soesastro (eds.), *Reinventing ASEAN* (Singapore: Institute of Southeast Asian Studies, 2001), pp. 243-272.

[10] Exceptions are: Estrella D. Solidum, *Towards a Southeast Asian Community* (Quezon City: University of the Philippines Press, 1974); Susumu Yamakage, *ASEAN: Shinboru kara Shisutemu he [ASEAN: From Symbol to System]* (Tokyo: Tokyo Daigaku Syuppankai [University of Tokyo Press], 1991); Amitav Acharya, *Constructing a Security Community in Southeast Asia: ASEAN and the problem of regional order* (London: Routledge, 2001); and Jurgen Haacke, *ASEAN's Diplomatic and Security Culture: Origins, development and prospects* (London and New York: Routledge Curzon, 2003).

[11] The ASA was launched in 1961whereas Maphilindo was formed in 1963.

[12] Indonesia, Malaysia and the Philippines worked on solving the tripartite dispute in 1966, on the eve of ASEAN's formation.

[13] There were some regional conferences led by Asian countries in order to establish the framework of regional cooperation, such as the Asian Relations Conference in New Delhi in 1947 and the Baguio Conference in the Philippines in 1950. For the details, see Estrella D. Solidum, *Towards a Southeast Asian Community*, pp. 19-25. However, these attempts were transient and, in addition, they did not hold any clear objectives. In this context, the ASA can be said to be the first regional cooperation, established by a regional initiative.

[14] For examples of intellectual discussions about the ASA, see Bernard K. Gordon, *The Dimensions of Conflict in Southeast Asia* (Englewood Cliffs, N.J.: Prentice-Hall, 1966), PP. 162-187; Arnfinn Jorgensen-Dahl, *Regional Organization and Order on South-East Asia* (London and Basingstoke: Macmillan Press, 1982), pp. 9-44; Susumu Yamakage, *ASEAN*, pp. 23-51; Vincent K. Pollard, 'ASA and ASEAN, 1961-1967: Southeast Asian Regionalism', *Asian Survey*, 10/3 (March 1970), pp. 244-255; and Nicholas Tarling, *Regionalism in Southeast Asia: To Foster the Political Will* (Oxford: Routledge, 2006), pp. 95-140.

Chapter Three examines the formation process of a series of agreements – the Manila agreements – in 1963, which were concluded during the three-way conflict over the incorporation of British territories in Southeast Asia into Malaysia. Indonesia and the Philippines strenuously opposed the formation of a British-influenced Malaysia. Indonesia objected to the Malaysia plan because the latter was drafted without respecting the right of self-determination in the British Borneo territories, which were to be incorporated into Malaysia[15]. The Philippines, on the other hand, raised a territorial claim to Sabah, and therefore threatened to undermine the building of the new state. Maphilindo was formed after the three leaders signed the Manila agreements at a Summit conference in August 1963. However, Maphilindo as well as the agreements collapsed within a month, and the three countries subsequently descended into deep discord. Nevertheless, the idea underlying Maphilindo provided an important foundation for the ASEAN Declaration. Therefore, the formation process of the Manila agreements is a significant area to look at in order to deepen our understanding of the philosophy behind ASEAN cooperation.

Maphilindo too has attracted little attention from scholars. In particular, few works have examined how the idea of regional cooperation was *built up*, and how the idea of regionalism was shaped.[16] This chapter argues that Maphilindo, contrary to received opinion, was an important precursor of ASEAN.[17]

Chapter Four looks at the resolution of the dispute over the formation of Malaysia. After Suharto took power from Sukarno, Indonesia showed its renewed desire for reconciliation with Malaysia. The mood for peace also quickly drew in the Philippines, which resumed bilateral relations with Malaysia without further reference to the Sabah problem. As a result, regional disturbances, arising from this episode, were quickly settled. The chapter also deals with the formation of ASEAN.

Chapter Five focuses on the settlement process of a bilateral territorial dispute between Malaysia and the Philippines, the so-called Corregidor affair. This chapter examines how ASEAN members maintained harmonious relations and successfully saved their new association from an early collapse. The affair had its origin in the recurrent territorial dispute between Malaysia and the Philippines over Sabah. Although this threatened to plunge ASEAN into a state of terminal dysfunction, member countries successfully overcame difficulties through the holding of secret consultations. Some scholars point out the importance of the Corregidor affair in terms of the emergence of the ASEAN Way. However, most of them do not describe the details of the settlement process, and therefore do not wholly clarify the formation process of the ASEAN Way.

Chapter Six draws together the nature of the ASEAN Way. It is, as discussed above, an examination that clarifies the ideological background of ASEAN itself. In this context, the chapter identifies the factors directly/indirectly affecting the establishment of ASEAN throughout the post-war period of the region. It also examines the particular practices contained in the ASEAN Way, and the fashion in which these manage ASEAN's behaviour as a grouping of states.

---

[15] In addition, Indonesia also posed the question regarding its national security and, in a sense, regional security in Southeast Asia as a whole.
[16] Exceptions are J. A. C. Mackie, *Konfrontasi: The Indonesia-Malaysia Dispute, 1963-1966* (Kuala Lumpur: Oxford University Press, 1974); and Susumu Yamakage, *ASEAN*.
[17] In addition, it was not the historical cul-de-sac that it has frequently been seen as.

1 THE ASEAN WAY
HOW HAS IT BEEN IDENTIFIED?

The leaders of the Association of Southeast Asian Nations (ASEAN) have often used the term the 'ASEAN Way' in their speeches or statements. However, the Association itself has never stated its official definition and seldom uses the term in its official documents. On the other hand, active discussion about the specific aspects of the ASEAN Way has been done among scholars. This chapter first looks at statements delivered by the leaders of ASEAN states, and draws the outline of the ASEAN Way. Then, it reviews scholarly works, and picks up and argues the specificity of the components of the ASEAN Way. Furthermore, this chapter reviews discussions about its origin by looking at ASEAN's precursors, the Association of Southeast Asia (ASA) and Maphilindo.

The ASEAN Way
Although the Association rarely refers formally to the term the ASEAN Way, the Hanoi Declaration of 1998 employed the term in the following way: 'We shall endeavour to resolve outstanding problems and prevent the emergence of disputes in the *ASEAN way* and in accordance with international law and practice'.[1] Although there is no definition of it in the Declaration itself, the ASEAN Way is clearly significant in addressing problems or disputes among member countries. It is quite different from international law and practice, which, so to say, was the accumulation of diplomatic practice of Western countries.

It is unclear when the term the ASEAN Way was used for the first time. Two high-ranking politicians made mention of it in their speeches at the formative period of ASEAN. In particular, a speech from Thai Foreign Minister Thanat Khoman was the first one in which the term was mentioned.[2] On 25 June 1968, ten months after the establishment of ASEAN, Thanat gave an opening address at the First Meeting of the Ad hoc Committee on Civil Aviation of ASEAN in Bangkok:

> I would not dwell on these activities…, except to highlight the significance of ASEAN cooperation and to emphasize the earnestness with which the Association has been awakened by the new spirit of neighbourly partnership and mutually beneficial cooperation. This is what all of us believe to be the path to peace, progress and prosperity. Such is the *ASEAN way* to preserve our national independence and regional integrity.[3]

Considering the fact that the meeting was held in Bangkok at the same time as the reconciliation talks between Malaysia and the Philippines over the Sabah issue,[4] it is not difficult to imagine that Thanat was indirectly expressing his wish for a peaceful settlement of the dispute. In his speech, the ASEAN Way is presented as a mode of dispute settlement based on neighbourliness and mutual benefit for the sake of peace and prosperity in the ASEAN region.

---

[1] Hanoi Declaration, 16 December 1998. Italics added.
[2] Amitav Acharya, a leading academic of ASEAN studies, made a brief reference in his book of Ali Murtopo's speech in 1974 as one of the oldest ones. See his book, *Constructing a Security Community in Southeast Asia*, p. 63. However, this book identifies Thanat's speech as the oldest one in which the term of the ASEAN Way was used.
[3] Thanat Khoman, Opening address of The First Meeting of the Ad hoc Committee on Civil Aviation of ASEAN, 25 June 1968, in *Foreign Affairs Bulletin*, 7/6 (June-July 1968), pp. 540-541. Italics added.
[4] The so-called Corregidor affair, which is to be discussed in Chapter 5.

Six years after Thanat's speech, Lieutenant General Ali Murtopo,[5] an advisor of the Indonesian President, used the term the 'ASEAN Way' in a speech he gave as an opening address to the First Conference of ASEAN Students of Regional Affairs in Jakarta on 22 October 1974:

> [M]any observers overseas see the ASEAN as a success, among other things, because of the system of consultations that has marked much of its work, what I may call the *ASEAN way* of dealing with a variety of problems confronting its member nations'.[6]

In Murtopo's speech, the term became more specific in its nature: the ASEAN Way is a specific mode of addressing problems or disputes among member countries using consultations.

In the late 1990s,[7] the definition of the ASEAN Way became even narrower. By that time, there had been a considerable accumulation of practice in its application. The Indonesian Foreign Minister, Ali Alatas, defined it in the following way in 1998:

> The ASEAN Way is to 'discuss within ourselves without adopting a confrontational approach and not putting to shame or embarrassing the other party. If we make official statements, it can result in people becoming displeased, and give rise to tension'.[8]

It can be said, therefore, that the ASEAN Way became defined as an amicable process of discussion, incorporating the additional practice of face-saving. By this, member countries do not criticise one another in public. In other words, losing face should be strictly avoided in order to maintain friendly relations between the countries concerned. Thai Foreign Minister Surin Phitsuwan gave an opening address at the ASEAN Ministerial Meeting (AMM) in 1999:

> To be sure, tremendous success has been achieved over the past 30 years by what some people called the "ASEAN Way" – a process of consultation, engagement and consensus-building that has not only managed to keep the peace in the region, but has also contributed to regional cooperation.[9]

It can be clearly seen from this that the ASEAN Way also includes consensus-building, employing as it does a consultative process.

---

[5] Murtopo was the foreign affairs advisor of President Mohamed Suharto. Before this, he first served Suharto in 1950s when the latter was the Commander of the Central Java Diponegoro division. Then he served Suharto again as a senior member of Kostrad (*Komando Cadangan Strategis Angkatan Darat*: Army Strategic Reserve Command) as a head of its affiliated intelligence agency, Opsus (*Operasi Khusus*: Special Operations). In August 1966, Murtopo became a member of Spri (Staf pribadi: Personal Staff), which Suharto established, and dealt with political affairs. The Spri had a stronger influence on Indonesian politics than the existing Cabinet and was called the 'invisible government'. (Harold Crouch, *The Army and Politics in Indonesia* (Ithaca, NY: Cornell University Press, 1978), p.243.) Murtopo was also the architect of Suharto's political philosophy and became a co-founder of the Centre for Strategic and International Studies (CSIS) in Indonesia in 1971.

[6] Ali Murtopo, Opening Address at the First Conference of ASEAN Students of Regional Affairs (ASEAN I), Jakarta, 22 October 1974, in Centre for Strategic and International Studies (ed.), *Regionalism in Southeast Asia, Papers Presented at the Fist Conference of ASEAN Students of Regional Affairs (ASEAN I), 22-25 October 1974, Jakarta* (Jakarta, 1975), pp. 11-16. Italics added.

[7] It was during the period of the argument over the usefulness of the so-called ASEAN principle of 'non-interference'. The argument was first given by Anwar bin Ibrahim, the then Deputy Prime Minister of Malaysia, and he proposed the new principle of 'flexible engagement' to be involved in domestic issues in other member countries.

[8] *Asiaweek*, 28 July 1998.

[9] Surin Phitsuwan, *BBC Monitoring Service: Asia-Pacific*, 26 July 1999. The term of 'engagement' was used in his speech as Surin Phituswan was one of ardent proponents of introducing flexible engagement into ASEAN practice.

Thus, the cumulative profile of the ASEAN Way, as depicted in speeches by ASEAN leaders in the span of thirty years, can be defined as a distinctive way in which ASEAN countries cooperate and harmonise the process of maintaining peace, and especially so when differences, problems or disputes arise between them. More specifically, it can be identified as consensus-building through a friendly process of consultation, and incorporated into this is the facility of face-saving practice for the parties involved.

Scholarly discussion of the ASEAN Way
The ASEAN Way has often been referred to in scholarly studies, and particularly so since the 1990s.[10] However, definitions vary, and there is no definitive rendition of it to date. Based on the discussions in existing literature, the characteristics of the ASEAN Way can be categorised as: (i) the principle of non-interference, (ii) face-saving behaviour, (iii) consultations, (iv) informality and (v) the spirit of working together.

(i) The principle of non-interference
Many of the discussions which argue the limitations of the ASEAN Way employ the question of the principle of non-interference. While this principle comes from the international law, as articulated in the United Nations Charter, it is argued that the principle lies 'at the heart of the approach adopted by ASEAN members'.[11] The important question here is why such universally-applied principle can have a unique manifestation in the context of ASEAN. Kuroyanagi sets out the principle of non-interference as a core element of the ASEAN Way. The other elements observed in international relations between countries in the region, such as: (1) ambiguity, (2) sensitivity towards sovereignty, national interest and face-saving, (3) evolution (mutual understanding through a continuous dialogue), (4) avoidance (shelving a problem) and (5) neighbourliness, are in complete harmony with this principle, and therefore he regards it as a key feature of the ASEAN Way.[12]

Acharya offers a different, more formalistic, definition of the ASEAN Way:

> The 'ASEAN Way' consists of a code of conduct for inter-state behaviour as well as a decision-making process based on consultations and consensus. The code of conduct incorporates a set of well-known principles, e.g. non-interference in the domestic affairs of each other, non-use of force, pacific settlement of disputes, respect for the sovereignty and territorial

---

[10] See, for example, Amitav Acharya, *Constructing a Security Community in Southeast Asia*; Zakaria Haji Ahmad, 'The World of ASEAN Decision-makers: A Study of Bureaucratic Elite Perceptions in Malaysia, the Philippines and Singapore', *Contemporary Southeast Asia*, 8/3 (1986), pp. 192-212; Jose T. Almonte, 'Ensuring Security the "ASEAN Way"', *Survival*, 39/4 (Winter 1997), pp. 80-92; Michael Antolik, *ASEAN and the Diplomacy of Accommodation* (Armonk, NY: M. E. Sharpe, 1990); Mely Caballero-Anthony, *Regional Security in Southeast Asia: Beyond the ASEAN Way* (Singapore: Institute of Southeast Asian Studies, 2005); Jurgen Haacke, *ASEAN's Diplomatic and Security Culture*; Timo Kivimaki, 'The Long Peace of ASEAN', *Journal of Peace Research*, 38/1 (2001), pp. 5-25; Yoneji Kuroyanagi, *ASEAN 35 Nen no Kiseki*; Shaun Narine, "ASEAN and ARF: The Limits of the "ASEAN Way"', *Asian Survey*, 37/10 (October 1997), pp. 961-978; Estrella D. Solidum, *Towards a Southeast Asian Community*; Richard Stubbs, 'ASEAN: Building Regional Cooperation', in Mark Beeson (ed.), *Contemporary Southeast Asia: Regional Dynamics, National Differences* (Basingstoke; New York: Palgrave Macmillan, 2004), pp. 222-224; and Susumu Yamakage, *ASEAN*.

[11] Alan Collins, 'Mitigating the Security Dilemma, the ASEAN Way', *Pacifica Review*, 11/2 (June 1999), p. 106. The same view is in Amitav Acharya, *Constructing a Security Community in Southeast Asia*, pp. 57-60.

[12] Yoneji Kuroyanagi, *ASEAN 35 Nen no Kiseki*, p. 155. For the same view, see Kay Moller, 'Cambodia and Burma', pp. 1087-1088.

integrity of member states, that can be found in the Charter of the United Nations as well as regional political and security organisations elsewhere in the world.[13]

He argues that the inter-state relations based on international law itself are 'hardly unique'.[14] The characteristic of the ASEAN Way is a process in which international law (such as non-interference or sovereign equality) was implemented throughout the specific practices in the region. He continues, 'To this extent, the "ASEAN Way" is not an unusual construct. But where it can claim a certain amount of uniqueness is the manner in which these norms are operationalised into a framework of regional interaction'.[15] Acharya lists specific regional elements such as, 'discreetness, informality, pragmatism, expediency, consensus-building, and non-confrontational bargaining style'.[16]

Tay finds the background of the principle of non-interference in ASEAN in the post-World War II history of the region, and in particular, independence, nation-building and the influence of the Cold War:

> The ASEAN emphasis on this principle [of non-interference] can be seen against the background of its historical development: the colonial history of the region; continuing interventions by the great powers during the Cold War; the relatively fragile nation-states that emerged, with disputed boundaries and cross-border ethnicities; the internal problems of different states, such as communist insurgencies and separatist tendencies; the lack of a uniting principle of integral governance, such as democracy, and the coexistence of regimes with differing bases and levels of legitimacy.[17]

There is some difference among member countries over the role of external powers. As Acharya points out, 'One of the major points of contention and constraints on regionalism in Southeast Asia since the Second World War had to do with the dependence of the regional countries on extra-regional powers for protection against internal as well as external threats'.[18] Indeed, ASEAN members have had mixed feelings with regard to the maintenance of regional security (in the context of the principle of non-interference). On one hand, four of five original members have relied on Western powers for their defence. The Philippines and Thailand are members of Southeast Asia Treaty Organisation (SEATO), while Malaysia and Singapore have been members of the Five Power Defence Arrangement with Britain, Australia and New Zealand. Indonesia, on the other hand, adopted a non-aligned position without having any defence agreements with external powers.[19] Nevertheless, all of ASEAN countries display great sensitivity to the importance of sovereignty or the principle of non-interference. At the same time, they are entirely sympathetic to the particularity and the repeatedly iterated words, 'Asian solutions to Asian problems'.

This is because ASEAN states gradually realised that the diplomatic principles of international relations in the region were different from those in Western countries. They developed a regional consciousness in the process to seek to 'solve their own problems in their own way, rather than inviting Western countries to proffer advice about policies concerning national development and international conflict'.[20] The sense of regional self-reliance was increased by

---

[13] Amitav Acharya, *Regionalism and Multilateralism: Essays on Cooperative Security in the Asia-Pacific* (2nd edn., Singapore: Eastern Universities Press, 2003), pp. 253-254.
[14] Amitav Acharya, *Constructing a Security Community in Southeast Asia*, p. 63.
[15] Amitav Acharya, *Regionalism and Multilateralism*, pp. 253-254.
[16] Ibid, p. 254
[17] Simon S. C. Tay, 'Institutions and Process', p. 251.
[18] Amitav Acharya, *Constructing a Security Community in Southeast Asia*, p. 51.
[19] Mohammad Hatta, 'Indonesia's Foreign Policy', *Foreign Affairs*, 31/3 (April 1953), p. 449.
[20] Michael Haas, *The Asian Way to Peace: A Story of Regional Cooperation*, New York: Praeger Publishers, 1989, p. 5.

two major factors. In 1967, Britain announced its decision to withdraw its forces from East of Suez by the mid-1970s. Then, in1969, American President Nixon declared a new US doctrine, phasing out its military involvement in Asian security.[21] The idea of regional responsibility for regional issues therefore provided a strong impetus for the formation of regional cooperative frameworks such as the ASA, Maphilindo and ASEAN.[22]

The principle of non-interference 'was intended to apply not only to interference by extra-regional powers...but also by Southeast Asian countries in the affairs of their own neighbours'.[23] Indeed, Soesastro points out that the principle of non-interference was seen as 'a significant factor which made it possible for member countries to avoid conflicts, thus allowing their governments to concentrate on the primary task of putting one's house in order as a basis of regime legitimacy'.[24]

To this, Kraft adds that '[the principle of non-interference] has been a major factor in sustaining ASEAN solidarity over the years'.[25] At the same time, however, non-interference 'has become a stumbling block to ASEAN's potential for pushing social transformation in the region' over the issue of the membership expansion in late 1990s.[26] In this regard, ASEAN's obstinate adherence to the principle of non-interference has, of course, led to considerable criticism.[27] This was especially so when ASEAN could not, or would not, take any action on human rights abuses in Myanmar in 1990s. The Association admitted that 'acceding to sanctions would not only be tantamount to intervening in the internal politics of Myanmar, it would also signify consent to interference from external powers in regional affairs'.[28] Namely, ASEAN countries recognised that if they interfere in the internal affairs of other countries, they themselves would potentially be laid open to external intervention.

In looking at this aspect of the Association, Moller argues that the widening of its membership in the mid- to late-1990s did not involve a commensurate deepening of its administrative and political 'machinery'.[29] In particular, he points out that it is problematic to widen the membership without partially transferring sovereignty of member countries (transferring a state's sovereignty to a regional organisation, inevitably reduces a member's right to advocate the principle of non-interference, because member states involve in their interfering each other in order to justify the organisation's raison d'être).[30] Tay points out, however, that the principle of non-interference 'does not mean that ASEAN members do not or have not become involved in each other's affairs'.[31] Indeed, the Association had been actively engaged in the matter of the Vietnamese invasion of Cambodia (1979-1991), both as a mediator holding the peace talks, and also as a protester against the Vietnamese action, bringing a resolution to the United Nations.[32]

---

[21] Amitav Acharya, *Constructing a Security Community in Southeast Asia*, pp. 52-53.

[22] Michael Haas, *The Asian Way to Peace*, p. 15.

[23] Amitav Acharya, *Constructing a Security Community in Southeast Asia*, p. 57.

[24] Hadi Soesastro, 'ASEAN in 2030: The Long View', in Simon S. C. Tay, Jesus P. Estanislao and Hadi Soesastro (eds.), *Reinventing ASEAN* (Singapore: Institute of Southeast Asian Studies, 2001), p. 282.

[25] Herman Joseph S. Kraft, 'ASEAN and Intra-ASEAN relations: Weathering the Storm?', *The Pacific Review*, 13/3 (2000), p. 462.

[26] Ibid.

[27] Ibid, pp. 462-463.

[28] Ibid, p. 463.

[29] Kay Moller, 'Cambodia and Burma', p. 1104.

[30] Ibid.

[31] Simon S. C. Tay, 'Institutions and Process', p. 251.

[32] ASEAN's response to the Cambodian issue has been widely argued. See for example, Mely Caballero-Anthony, *Regional security in Southeast Asia*, pp. 83-112; Michael Leifer, 'The ASEAN Peace Process', pp. 30-31; and Yoneji Kuroyanagi, *ASEAN 35 Nen no Kiseki*, pp. 81-99. For more critical view on ASEAN in Cambodia, see for example, Kay Moller, 'Cambodia and Burma', pp.1087-1104; and Samuel Sharpe, 'An ASEAN Way to Security Cooperation in Southeast Asia?', *The Pacific Review*, 16/2 (2003), pp.231-250.

Goh adds to this that 'the "ASEAN Way" is much more than the principle of non-intervention'.[33]

(ii) Face-saving behaviour

When a debate arose over flexible engagement,[34] the new proposition challenging ASEAN's long-iterated tenet of non-interference, the Filipino Secretary of Foreign Affairs, Domingo Siazon, said in 1998, 'Times have changed. After 31 years, we are now adults and should be able to discuss problems frankly'.[35] The ASEAN Secretary-General, Rodolfo Severino, sent a similar message in 1998: 'As the ASEAN family, we should be free to talk frankly'.[36] These statements are evidence that ASEAN countries had refrained from mentioning issues occurring in other countries. This practice can also be interpreted as non-interference in other countries' business. But at the same time, it shows a face-saving attitude. In particular, the principle of non-interference in newly-independent countries allows them to be involved in their own affairs without losing face. This is because an emerging country is inexperienced in managing its government, and has weak political foundations. In such a situation, criticism from other countries will affront its dignity. Therefore, in such contexts, it is important to behave in a face-saving manner and employ low-key diplomacy between member states.[37] In this regard, Pushpa Thambipillai et al. point out that face-saving has been prominently exercised in the consensus formation process: '[N]egotiations and decision-making are also conducted in a manner to "save face" and maintain a conciliatory relationship among the participants'.[38] Behind-the-scenes activities are a derivative of face-saving behaviour, and they take place as consultations by '"sending out feelers" to the member countries'.[39]

The practice of saving face takes various modes. For example, an issue on which compromise cannot be achieved is shelved in order to avoid highlighting the parties as 'winners' and 'losers'.[40] Making an issue that has occurred opaque, and therefore neutralising the controversial point, is also an important dimension of this element.[41] Caballero-Anthony points out that if 'a consensus cannot be reached, the members agree to put off a decision, or agree to disagree'.[42]

---

[33] Gillian Goh, 'The "ASEAN Way": Non-intervention and ASEAN's Role in Conflict Management', *Stanford Journal of East Asian Affairs*, 3/1 (Spring 2003), p. 118.

[34] For discussions about the principle of non-interference versus a counter-proposal of flexible engagement, see, for example, Jurgen Haacke, 'The concept of flexible engagement and the practice of enhanced interaction: Intramural challenges to the "ASEAN way"', *The Pacific Review*, 12/4 (1999), pp. 581-611; and Erik Martinez Kuhonta, 'Walking a tightrope: democracy versus sovereignty in ASEAN's illiberal peace', *The Pacific Review*, 19/3 (2006), pp. 337-358.

[35] *The Sun*, 12 December 1998.

[36] *Asiaweek*, 28 July 1998.

[37] Solidum sees the customs, such as restraint and face-saving, are common in Asia as a whole. She recognises that 'problems in Asia should be solved only by those who are from the region. Only Asian solutions which contain Asian values are legitimate…the Asian Way of solving a problem involves very low-key diplomacy and avoids fanfare before an agreement is achieved'. See Estrella D. Solidum, ''The Role of Certain Sectors in Shaping and Articulating the ASEAN Way', in R. P. Anand and Purificacion V. Quisumbing (eds.), *ASEAN: Identity, Development and Culture* (Quezon City: University of the Philippines Law Centre and Honolulu: East-West Centre Culture Leaning Institute, 1981), p. 136. Michael Haas takes the same view. See his work, *The Asian Way to Peace*, pp. 2-3.

[38] Pushpa Thambipillai and J. Saravanamuttu, *ASEAN Negotiations: Two Insights* (Singapore: Institute of Southeast Asian Studies, 1985), p. 13.

[39] Ibid, p. 14.

[40] 'Adjournment of the problem' is another expression of it. (Alan Collins, 'Mitigating the Security Dilemma', pp. 107-108.) The good example of shelving the uncompromisable issue can be seen in the territorial dispute between Malaysia and the Philippines (the Corregidor affair). For the details, see Chapter 5.

[41] Susumu Yamakage, *ASEAN*, p. 275.

[42] Mely Caballero-Anthony, 'Mechanisms of Dispute Settlement: The ASEAN Experience', *Contemporary Southeast Asia*, 20/1 (April 1998), p. 58.

This is 'quite a salient feature' of the ASEAN Way.[43] To agree to disagree 'allows for "acceptance time" whereby states will be able, perhaps over a longer time-frame, to adjust their positions and eventually reach agreement'.[44] In addition, disagreement is 'rarely stated openly'.[45] This mechanism can be categorised as face-saving.

Haacke points out that ASEAN, in comparison with previous forms of regional cooperation, pays 'much greater attention to the exercise of restraint and respect for national sensitivities'.[46] Narine interprets this specific feature as a product of 'a sense of mutual weakness' in ASEAN.[47] Indeed, ASEAN members would not want a full resolution of issues 'when this comes at the expense of maintaining stable inter-state relations'.[48]

(iii) Consultations

Because of the great social and political diversity in the region during ASEAN's formative years, a lot of problems against their cooperation were expected between the member countries. Therefore, '[f]requent contacts or communication among the political elite help to crystallise a community of sentiments'.[49] Indeed, face-to-face conversation of an amicable sort is important to remove any sense of suspicion between states. Leifer recognises that frequent consultation in the informal working group largely contributed to develop common norms among countries.[50] Lengthy consultations will be held informally so that consensus can be reached.[51] In the frequent consultation process,

> ASEAN members get to know one another, learn about each other's interests and sensitivities, and explore possibilities for expanded co-operation. Additionally, officials at different levels are encouraged to contact one another and establish personal relationships so that in the event of crisis they can pick up the telephone and call each other, thus increasing the possibility of containing any dispute.[52]

In this context, the ASEAN Ministerial Meeting (AMM) provides an effective place of 'continuous consultation and repeated deliberations'.[53] Soesastro states that the AMM and its preparatory meetings hold four functions: (1) They serve as a 'useful vehicle by which ASEAN high officials become more acquainted with one another', (2) constitute 'a forum for the institutionalisation of a habit of dialogues among member states', (3) provide 'a venue for consultation and exchange of views over bilateral and regional problems', and (4) play 'a central role as a forum for regional confidence-building measures'.[54] After time-consuming consensus building through informal talks, 'more formal ties are frequently established'.[55] Indeed, peace and stability in the region have been maintained by precisely such 'intra-mural dialogue and consultation'.[56]

---

[43] Ibid, p. 60.
[44] Ibid, pp. 60-61.
[45] Ibid, p. 58.
[46] Jurgen Haacke, *ASEAN's Diplomatic and Security Culture*, p. 50.
[47] Shaun Narine, 'ASEAN and ARF', pp. 974-975.
[48] Ramses Amer, 'Conflict Management and Constructive Engagement in ASEAN's Expansion', *Third World Quarterly*, 20/5 (1999), p. 1036.
[49] Estrella D. Solidum, *Towards a Southeast Asian Community*, p. 205.
[50] Michael Leifer, 'The ASEAN Peace Process', p. 28.
[51] Mely Caballero-Anthony, 'Mechanisms of Dispute Settlement', p. 58.
[52] Hoang Anh Tuan, 'ASEAN Dispute Management: Implications for Vietnam and an Expanded ASEAN', *Contemporary Southeast Asia*, 18/1 (June 1996), p. 67.
[53] Michael Antolik, *ASEAN and the Diplomacy of Accommodation*, p. 91.
[54] Hadi Soesastro, 'ASEAN in 2030', p. 282.
[55] Timo Kivimaki, 'The Long Peace of ASEAN', p. 17.
[56] Michael Leifer, 'The ASEAN Peace Process', p. 28.

Many scholars argue that ASEAN employs the Malay practices of *musyawarah* (consultation) and *mufakat* (consensus).[57] The reason why member states emphasise *musyawarah* as the principle of decision-making in ASEAN is 'not only to realise the importance of the mechanism of consensus-building itself, but also to regard consultation as the most important custom in the Association'.[58] These states frequently refer to themselves as one family, friends or neighbourhoods, and this helps to establish a custom of consultation or working together. In this respect, Kurus argues that 'ASEAN has gradually fostered a family feeling of togetherness and shared interests among a group of states that had very little in common to begin with'.[59]

(iv) Informality

ASEAN's preference to informality has been pointed out by a number of scholars, such as Caballero-Anthony.[60] Informality has two aspects. The first one is related to the institutional structure. Suffice it to say here that an ASEAN Summit Meeting was not held until 1976, nine years after the organisation was established. In addition, fewer hard rules can be found in official documents issued by ASEAN than in the case of other international organisations, such as the European Union. This practice originated in the ASA, which was finally materialised as a loose association of states rather than a formal treaty-based organisation. It is often pointed out that the foundation document of ASEAN, the ASEAN Declaration, was just that: a 'declaration', not a constitution or a charter.[61] Additionally, the rule of decision-making (majority or unanimous decision) is not formally stipulated in any official documents. The second point of informality is in the communication style between ASEAN leaders. They prefer to employ informal talks over golf, breakfast and so on which lead to formal negotiations. It is important to note that in this context, informal talks are more important than formal ones, and a decision is often reached well before the formal talks take place.

(v) The spirit of working together

The slogan of 'working together' has encouraged ASEAN to maintain cooperative relations to overcome difference among member countries. When ASEAN members refer to 'working together' in ASEAN, the term strengthens cooperation and works as if it has long been a common value held between them. As Almonte points out, 'The basic lesson ASEAN teaches is that dif-

---

[57] See, for example, Amitav Acharya, "Ideas, Identity and Institution-building: the "Asia-Pacific Way"", *The Pacific Review*, 10/3 (1997), p. 330; Tobias Ingo Nischalke, 'Insights from ASEAN's Foreign Policy Co-operation', p. 90; Michael Leifer, *The ASEAN Regional Forum* (Adelphi Papers, London: Oxford University Press, 1996), p. 40; Mely Caballero-Anthony, 'Mechanisms of Dispute Settlement', p. 58; Rajshree Jetly, 'Conflict Management Strategies in ASEAN: Perspectives for SAARC', *The Pacific Review*, 16/1 (2003), p. 57, Hoang Anh Tuan, 'ASEAN Dispute Management', pp. 66-67; Pushpa Thambipillai and J. Saravanamuttu, *ASEAN Negotiations*, p. 11; Jose T. Almonte, 'Ensuring Security the "ASEAN Way"', p. 81; Miles Kahler, 'Legalization as Strategy: The Asia-Pacific Case', *International Organization*, 54/3 (Summer 2000), p. 552; Ramses Amer, 'Conflict Management and Constructive Engagement in ASEAN's Expansion', p. 1036; and Arnfinn Jorgensen-Dahl, *Regional Organization and Order on South-East Asia*, p. 166.

[58] Susumu Yamakage, *ASEAN*, p. 274. Author's translation.

[59] Bilson Kurus, 'The ASEAN Triad: National Interest, Consensus-seeking, and Economic Co-operation', *The Contemporary Southeast Asia*, 16/4 (1995), p. 825.

[60] Caballero-Anthony deals with it largely in her work. See Mely Caballero-Anthony, *Regional Security in Southeast Asia*, pp. 64-78. See also Amitav Acharya, *Constructing a Security Community in Southeast Asia*, pp. 64-67; Rodolfo C. Severino, *Southeast Asia in Search of an ASEAN Community: Insights from the Former ASEAN Secretary-General* (Singapore: Institute of Southeast Asian Studies, 2006), pp. 11-18; Michael Leifer, *The ASEAN Regional Forum*, p. 40; Michael Haas, *The Asian Way to Peace*, pp. 7-9; Kusuma Snitwongse, 'Thirty Years of ASEAN: Achievements through Political Cooperation', *The Pacific Review*, 11/2 (1998), p. 184; Samuel Sharpe, 'An ASEAN Way to Security Cooperation in Southeast Asia?', p. 232; and Miles Kahler, 'Legalisation as Strategy', p. 552.

[61] Michael Leifer, *ASEAN and the Security of Southeast Asia* (London: Routledge, 1989), p. 24.

ferences or even disputes should not stop countries from promoting mutually beneficial relationship – because the very act of sitting down together can begin to build mutual trust and confidence'.[62]

Susilo Bambang Yudhoyono, the current Indonesian President, in 2007 stated that: 'The formation of ASEAN was regarded as the last chance for the nations of Southeast Asia to achieve some kind of unity'.[63] ASEAN members believe that if they break the all-important foundations of the Association, then the region would become insecure. Such sentiment encourages member countries to work together for the sake of ASEAN's longevity, and cooperate through frequent consultation. Snitwongse recognises that the reason why members were willing to work together, she says, is that '[few] demands were made on members and the resulting peaceful relations served both their national and regime interests' on the basis of the lowest common denominator.[64] Indeed, ASEAN countries believe that working together is the most important philosophy to overcome any existing, or potential rifts between them.[65] In this respect, Ahmad suggests that there is a basic concept of cooperation in ASEAN, which gave birth to a series of conventions. He lists three specific elements: 'solidarity', 'consensus' and 'the primacy of ASEAN', and points out that these elements are linked together under one concept of 'working together'.[66] However, his novel definition has not been further developed by other scholars, or even by himself.

The influence of Southeast Asian cultures on the ASEAN Way
Some scholars emphasise the importance of the cultural component in the ASEAN Way. It is pointed out that ASEAN uses the earlier-mentioned Malay practices, *musyawarah* and *mufakat*, which are culturally dominant in the region (including Indonesian Village politics, and to some extent those of Malaysia and the Philippines too).[67] In particular, behind-the-scene mediation, face-saving behaviour, and furthering a conciliatory relationship during the negotiation process, are specific features of *musyawarah* and *mufakat*, and this distinguishes the ASEAN Way from other negotiation styles.[68] Askandar et al. point out that traditional values in the decision-making process: respecting consultation and consensus, 'play a significant role' when a dispute happens in ASEAN.[69] Solidum recognises an important dimension of cultural similarity amongst the member states, therefore recognises culture as one of constitutional factors of the ASEAN Way.[70]

Peter Boyce points out that *musyawarah* and *mufakat* prevailed even in non-Malay countries, such as Thailand and Singapore:

---

[62] Jose T. Almonte, 'Ensuring Security the "ASEAN Way"', p. 81.
[63] Susilo Bambang Yudhoyono, Keynote Speech by H.E. Susilo Bambang Yudhoyono President of Indonesia at the ASEAN Regional Forum: Rethinking ASEAN Towards the ASEAN Community 2015, Jakarta, 7 August 2007, <http://www.aseansec.org/20812.htm>, accessed 26 October 2008.
[64] Kusuma Snitwongse, 'Thirty Years of ASEAN', p. 184. In particular, excluding bilateral issues from the agenda of ASEAN helped to work together among member countries. (Ibid, p. 185.)
[65] Pushpa Thambipillai, 'The ASEAN growth areas: Sustaining the dynamism', *The Pacific Review*, 11/2 (1998), p. 250.
[66] Zakaria Haji Ahmad, 'The World of ASEAN Decision-makers', p. 203.
[67] Pushpa Thambipillai and J. Saravanamuttu, *ASEAN Negotiations*, p. 11. Mely Caballero-Anthony gives the same view. See her book, *Regional security in Southeast Asia*, pp. 72-74. She also points out that the negotiation process by *musyawarah* and *mufakat* would take long time and explained the reason why such 'tedious practice' have prevailed: 'in most ASEAN states, decision-making was highly centralised and almost always limited to a small number of political elites'. (Ibid., p. 74)
[68] Thambipillai, Pushpa and J. Saravanamuttu, *ASEAN Negotiations*, pp. 12-13.
[69] Kamarulzaman Askandar, Jacob Bercovitch and Mikio Oishi, 'The ASEAN Way of Conflict Management: Old Patterns and New Trends', *Asian Journal of Political Science*, 10/2 (December 2002), pp. 23-24.
[70] Estrella D. Solidum, 'The Role of Certain Sectors in Shaping and Articulating the ASEAN Way', p. 134.

It seems that all ASEAN governments are familiar with *musyawarah* and accept its implications for diplomacy. For the Thais and for the three ASEAN states inhabited principally by Malays, *musyawarah* or something akin to it (such as the Filipino *pulong*) is apparently an indigenous tool, and even the predominantly Chinese leadership of Singapore seems to have adjusted to it.[71]

Given the fact that the consensus-building process stemmed from Malay culture, how did Thailand and Singapore come to accept, and indeed embody, that value? Callister et al. observe that harmony and face-saving are both conflict-resolution techniques and core values in Thailand.[72] This is also applicable to Singapore.[73] Indeed, such a shared attitude towards conflict-resolution in the region is what Trood and Booth conclude might be regarded as strategic distinctiveness of the region: Asian strategic culture to manage conflict.[74]

Acharya, on the other hand, raises the issue of relevance of a broader cultural aspect: '[T]he cultural underpinnings of the ASEAN Way of managing disputes and advancing security cooperation could be overstated',[75] he writes, '[t]he ASEAN Way itself resulted not so much from preordained cultural sources, Javanese or otherwise, but from incremental socialisation'.[76] Haacke supports this view because frequent consultations were the product of two key international norms (sovereign equality and mutual respect) rather than the loan of the existing indigenous practice.[77] Kurus says, ASEAN members became 'more attuned and sensitive to each other's interest' and this created a common sense of togetherness.[78] 'At a deeper level, he concludes, ASEAN has afforded the member states a vehicle to identify with the region'.[79]

Caballero-Anthony gives a different, and more functional, explanation for this question: ASEAN leaders are able to forge consensus because decision-making is centralised in leaders themselves: '[I]n most ASEAN states, decision-making is highly centralised, and almost always limited to a small number of elites. The political set-up of most states does not really require political leaders to explain to their respective populations why certain decisions have been

---

[71] Peter Boyce, 'The Machinery of Southeast Asian Regional Diplomacy', in Lau Teik Soon (ed.), *New Directions in the International Relations of Southeast Asia: Global Powers and Southeast Asia* (Singapore: Singapore University Press, 1973), p. 176. Hoang Anh Tuan takes the same view that the Malay cultural practice has been accommodated to ASEAN members. See Hoang Anh Tuan, 'ASEAN Dispute Management', p. 67. Haas employs the view more broadly, and points out, 'Despite geographic and historical diversity, the peoples of Asia share a common culture in regard to international relations'. He views that Malay practice of *musyawarah* and *mufakat* was accepted by all over Asia although he sees the Asian style of international relations 'developed in the year after World War II'. (Michael Haas, *The Asian Way to Peace*, p. 3.)

[72] Ronda Roberts Callister and James A. Wall Jr., 'Thai and U.S. Community Mediation', *Journal of Conflict Resolution*, 48/4 (August 2004), p. 582.

[73] Edith Yuen Chi-Ching, 'Social-Cultural Context of Perceptions and Approaches to Conflict: The Case of Singapore', in Kwok Leung and Dean Tjosvold (eds.), *Conflict Management in the Asia Pacific: Assumptions and Approaches in Diverse Cultures* (Singapore: John Wiley and Sons (Asia), 1998), p. 139.

[74] Russell Trood and Ken Booth, 'Strategic Culture and Conflict Management in the Asia-Pacific', in Ken Booth and Russell Trood (eds.), *Strategic Cultures in the Asia-Pacific Region* (London: Macmillan Press, 1999), pp. 342-348.

[75] Amitav Acharya, *Constructing a Security Community in Southeast Asia*, p. 64. Yamakage takes the same position. See Susumu Yamakage, 'Tenkanki no ASEAN: Kakudai, Shinka, Aratana Kadai [ASEAN in the Turning Point: Expansion, Deepening and New Issues]', in Susumu Yamakage (ed.), *Tenkanki no ASEAN: Aratana Kadai heno Cyousen [ASEAN in the Turning Point: The Challenge for New Issues]* (Tokyo: Nihon Kokusai Mondai Kenkyujyo [The Japan Institute of International Affairs], 2001), p. 7.

[76] Amitav Acharya, *Constructing a Security Community in Southeast Asia*, p. 71.

[77] Jurgen Haacke, *ASEAN's Diplomatic and Security Culture*, p.7.

[78] Bilson Kurus, 'Understanding ASEAN', p. 825.

[79] Ibid.

reached'.[80] She also argues that another related, but no less important, feature of this can be found in the significance of personal connections between leaders and bureaucrats.[81]

ASEAN and its precursors: The origin of the ASEAN Way
Despite the preceding discussion about the components of the ASEAN Way in the existing literature, there is nonetheless little discussion on its origin, and this stands in stark contrast to the literature devoted to its definition. Indeed, as Haacke puts it: 'Dating the origins of the "ASEAN Way" is an endeavour fraught with difficulty'.[82] Therefore, commentators have steered clear of tackling the issue. In this context, endeavour to trace the origin of the ASEAN Way to ASEAN's precursors, the ASA and Maphilindo, has produced limited results. Although the details of the formation process of the ASA are described by such authors as Jorgensen-Dahl, Gordon and Yamakage, these descriptions did not refer to the origin of the ASEAN Way.[83] In addition, from their perspectives, the ASA suddenly emerged without any ideological accumulation towards regional cooperation among the leaders in Southeast Asia. They do not examine the reason why the Philippines and Thailand were not satisfied with the Southeast Asia Treaty Organisation (SEATO) led by the US, and why they developed the first local-made regional organisation instead.

Some scholars argue that ASEAN took over the Malay custom of *musyawarah* and *mufakat* from Maphilindo.[84] Modelski points out Indonesia's ideological influence on Maphilindo. He sees that its ideology was 'derived from the concepts guiding Indonesian foreign policy'.[85] Peter Boyce further argues such a view in his own work:

> *Musyawarah* diplomacy seems to have been adopted, for publicly purposes at least, as a central and distinctive element in the *inter se* relations of ASEAN states. Promulgated by Sukarno as the basis of his Guided Democracy, it was adopted by him and by other Southeast Asian leaders as an instrument of diplomacy during the 1960s, notably from the first ministerial discussions on ASA (which did not include Indonesia) in 1961 and the first heads-of-government meetings on Maphilindo at Manila in mid-1963.[86]

Tamaki, on the other hand, directly seeks the philosophical basis of the ASEAN Way in Indonesia's ideology, *Pancasila*.[87] *Pancasila*, or the five principles of Indonesia, was announced by Sukarno before the Investigating Committee of Preparation for Independence in June 1945.[88] It was basically the ideology of a new Indonesia, engaged in nation-building, and directed to the

---

[80] Mely Caballero-Anthony, 'Mechanisms of Dispute Settlement', p. 59.
[81] Ibid, p. 60.
[82] Jurgen Haacke, *ASEAN's Diplomatic and Security Culture*, p. 16.
[83] Arnfinn Jorgensen-Dahl, *Regional Organization and Order on South-East Asia*; Bernard K Gordon, *The Dimensions of Conflict in Southeast Asia*; and Susumu Yamakage, *ASEAN*.
[84] The same view can be seen in Susumu Yamakage, *ASEAN*, pp. 273-275; and Gillian Goh, 'The "ASEAN Way"', p. 114.
[85] George Modelski, *The New Emerging Forces: Documents on the ideology of Indonesian foreign policy* (Canberra, Department of International Relations, Research School of Pacific Studies, Institute of Advanced Studies, The Australian National University, 1963), p. 74. He further develops the argument by saying that 'The text of the Manila Declaration (one of the three documents approved by the Summit Meeting) shows the influence of Indonesian ideas'. (Ibid)
[86] Peter Boyce, 'The Machinery of Southeast Asian Regionl Diplomacy', p. 176.
[87] Kazunori Tamaki, 'ARF Kouiki Anzen Hosyou, ASEAN Way no Kanousei [The ARF, Expanding Regional Security Cooperation: The Possibility of Introducing the ASEAN Way]', in Yoneji Kuroyanagi (ed.), *Ajia Chiiki Chitsujyo to ASEAN no Tyōsen: 'Higashi Ajia Kyoudoutai' wo Mezashite [Regional order in Asia and the Challenge of ASEAN: 'Seeking the East Asia Community']* (Tokyo: Akashi Syoten, 2005), p. 253.
[88] Sukarno was a member of the Committee organised by the Japanese military.

necessary harmonisation of a broad range of ethnic and religious groups in the country.[89] Its third principle is consensus decision-making by consultation: 'unanimity arising out of deliberation amongst representatives',[90] which is supposed to be originated in *musyawarah* and *mufakat* in Indonesian village politics.[91]

Haacke, on the other hand, sees that the ASEAN Way has its roots in the common history of the region, rather than in traditional culture.[92] According to such an approach, the ASEAN Way is based on the historical background of shared colonial experience, struggle for independence, and the origins of intra-regional disputes. Countries in the region encountered Westphalian principles, such as sovereign equality, non-interference and the non-use of force in the colonial period.[93] Consequently, and with the exception of Thailand, they awoke to such ideas as independence, nationalism and sovereignty that were strongly linked to Western perceptions.[94] In large part because of the uncompromising factors associated with such an outlook (and political method), after independence, a three-sided struggle broke out between Indonesia, Malaysia and the Philippines in 1963. Haacke's conclusion is that the ASEAN Way was created in the course of these historical interactions. This perspective, while being valuable, does not fully explain the origin or the formation process of the ASEAN Way.

In this regard, but also in a limited fashion, Acharya is the only scholar who has alluded to a broader process from which the ASEAN Way emerged. He recognises that the main body of the ASEAN Way was socially constructed by member countries. But even he somewhat limits the scope of his investigation by arguing that the appearance of the ASEAN Way was attributable, finally, to a single event: the Corregidor affair of 1968 (a territorial dispute between the Philippines and Malaysia over Sabah). He points out in this regard that the ASEAN Way was 'indicative' in the dispute settlement process.[95]

Concluding remarks

This book argues that the origin of the ASEAN Way should be traced not only in accordance with the uses and features of the concept, but also by paying attention to the crises and conflicts that they were applied to, and, to some extent, emerged from. Most of commentators who refer to the origin of the ASEAN Way do not identify the specific events from which the ASEAN Way emerged. In addition, none of these does examine the interactions between states during conflicts. This book focuses on this significant, but largely underexplored, element in the existing scholarship, while also specifying important factors for regional cooperation.

None of the authors surveyed here provides a holistic approach to the creation of the ASEAN Way. This is because they limit their attention to separate key factors or events in constructing this concept. This book will go on to explain that a number of important processes were at work in the gestation period of the ASEAN Way, and none was by itself responsible for this birth. In

---

[89] *Pancasila* is regarded as Indonesian ideology unifying ethnic and religious diversity for peaceful coexistence. It was announced by Sukarno in his speech, 'Birth of Pancasila', on 1 June 1945 before the Investigating Committee of Preparation for Independence. Five principles are, (i) nationalism, (ii) internationalism, (iii) 'unanimity arising out of deliberation amongst representatives', (iv) 'equality in the economic field', and (v) 'belief in God with mutual respect for one another'. For more details, see his speech, 'Speech before the Investigating Committee for the Preparation of Independence', 1 June 1945, in Herbert Feith and Lance Castles (eds.), *Indonesian Political Thinking, 1945-1965* (Ithaca and London: Cornell University Press, 1970), pp. 40-49.
[90] Ibid.
[91] Kazunori Tamaki, 'ARF Kouiki Anzen Hosyou, ASEAN Way no Kanousei', p. 253.
[92] Jurgen Haacke, *ASEAN's Diplomatic and Security Culture*, pp. 16-51.
[93] Shaun Narine, 'State Sovereignty, Political Legitimacy and Regional Institutionalism in the Asia-Pacific', *The Pacific Review*, 17/3 (2005), p. 426.
[94] Mark Beeson, 'Sovereignty under Siege: Globalisation and the State in Southeast Asia', *Third World Quarterly*, 24/2 (2003), p. 364.
[95] Amitav Acharya, *Constructing a Security Community in Southeast Asia*, p. 50.

addition, broad historical processes were also at play, and these were encouraging states in the region to seek a working method that was not reliant on an imperfect Western approach to diplomacy and conflict-resolution. There was, however, every urgency in seeing such a method emerge, as the tightly framed nature of the Southeast Asian region after the end of World War II (and the attendant process of decolonisation coming with it) would not allow comfortable political cohabitation without such a working method in the area of international relations.

2 AN AWAKENING OF REGIONAL CONSCIOUSNESS

This chapter explores historical influences on the ASEAN Way, encompassing the 15 years between the end of World War II and the establishment of the Association of Southeast Asia (ASA). The premise of the argument in this chapter is that ASEAN's foundation philosophy was deeply impacted upon by the history of the countries in the region. Firstly, it describes the processes of achieving independence and nation-building in these countries after the war. In this regard, it pays particular attention to their different views of nation-building. Secondly, and building on this, it argues that at the core are their different attitudes towards the Cold War antagonism. It also explores how Western-made regional organisations, such as Southeast Asia Treaty Organisation (SEATO) and the Colombo Plan, influenced the shaping of the politics of the region. Lastly, it analyses the reason why countries in the region agreed to establish the first locally-made regional organisation, the ASA, by taking some distance from existing regional organisations provided by Western countries, and in particular SEATO. The analysis teases out the specific features of locally-formed regional cooperation, and clarifies the background of the formation of the ASA itself.

Southeast Asia after the Japanese surrender
In Asia, the end of World War II was marked by Japan's acceptance of the Potsdam Declaration on 15 August 1945. Various relations were created between Southeast Asian countries and Western countries after the withdrawal of the Japanese. The first country in Southeast Asia to achieve independence was the Philippines, which maintained close bilateral relations with the United States after its peaceful withdrawal in July 1946. The Federation of Malaya, replacing the former British colony of Malaya in February 1948, suffered from continual disturbances (the Malayan Emergency) generated by the Malayan Communist Party (MCP). Its independence was not realised until 1957.[1] In Indonesia, Sukarno and Mohammad Hatta declared independence from the Netherlands, establishing the Republic of Indonesia on 17 August 1945. However, this was not recognised by the Dutch, thus plunging the country into four years of fierce struggle. Indonesia finally became independent in December 1949, when the Hague Agreement was reached through American mediation.[2] Indonesia's suspicion and distrust of the Netherlands (and, in a sense, Western power as a whole) ultimately resulted in the creation of an independent foreign policy.[3] In Thailand, the only country in Southeast Asia which had no colonial experience, the army had been in power since the replacement of the absolute monarchy in 1932.

The advent of the Cold War
Soon after the end of the Second World War, the rapid growth of Communist power brought on armed conflicts with the 'free world' in Europe and Asia, thereby creating the bipolar system,

---

[1] The MCP, which was composed of the Chinese Malayan, opposed the privileges of the Malayan population in the proposed Malay-favoured federation. The British diplomat, Harold MacMichael, initially proposed the Malay Union in 1946 where all ethnic groups would have equal rights. However, the proposal was withdrawn because of strong opposition from the Malay. Instead, the Malay-favoured Federation was launched. The Chinese Malay's anger has been directed toward the British in Malaya since June 1948.
[2] Herbert Feith, 'Indonesia', in George McT. Kahin (ed.), *Governments and Politics of Southeast Asia* (2nd edn., Ithaca, NY: Cornell University Press, 1964), p. 203.
[3] Mohammad Hatta, 'Indonesia's Foreign Policy', p. 444.

which lasted for over four decades. In Asia, military action occurred in the Korean and Indochina Peninsulas, backed by the two major blocs of the Cold War. The Democratic People's Republic of Korea (North Korea), supported by the Soviet Union and Communist China,[4] went to war in 1950 against the Republic of Korea (South Korea), which was backed by the United States and the United Nations. The battle came to a standstill, and an armistice was signed in July 1953 in the presence of the UN, North Korea and China.

In Vietnam, several days after Japan's surrender, Ho Chi Minh, the Communist leader, forced Emperor Bao Dai to step down and created the Democratic Republic of Vietnam (North Vietnam) in Hanoi. However, the French government did not recognise it and restored Cochin China (its puppet government) in southern Vietnam in March 1946. In December, France attacked North Vietnam, and the First Indochina War began. In March 1949, the French government established the State of Vietnam (South Vietnam) led by Emperor Bao Dai in Saigon. In January 1950, the Soviet Union and Communist China recognised North Vietnam and began providing it with military assistance. The US, on the other hand, recognised South Vietnam in February. By then, the conflict in Vietnam had become an international issue backed by the two blocs.

Soon after the end of the Second World War, most of the countries in Southeast Asia, and in particular Malaya and the Philippines, suffered from anti-government actions by Communist groups, which mostly developed from the anti-Japanese resistance during wartime. Malaya and its metropolitan government, Britain, had been annoyed by the rioting and troubles generated by the MCP for over 12 years since 1948.[5] Thus, the country was tense with guerrilla warfare and the 'primary task was restoration of law and order' in Malaya.[6] The rebellion was at its height when Sir Henry Gurney, the British High Commissioner, was assassinated on 6 October 1951 while travelling through the winding road to the government house in Frayser's Hill. In the Philippines, the Hukbalahap movement, which originated from the People's Anti-Japanese Liberation Army, was conducting anti-government military activities throughout the country since its independence ten years earlier.

The West tried to protect Southeast Asia from the Communists' infiltration by launching two regional forms of cooperation: the Colombo Plan launched by Britain, and SEATO led by the US.[7] These regional organisations contrasted sharply: the Colombo Plan focused on socio-economic development, whereas SEATO gave considerable weight to military defence.[8] However, in reality, since 'small nations, particularly the countries of South East Asia, do not have many policy choices',[9] they eventually continued their relations with external powers on the basis of historical ties. The Philippines joined SEATO, whereas Malaya became a member of the Colombo Plan. Thailand joined SEATO because it received aid for its post-war reconstruction from the US. Indonesia, on the other hand, adopted a non-aligned position.

The Colombo Plan originated from the conference of Ministers of the Commonwealth countries, Britain, Canada, Australia, New Zealand, Ceylon, India and Pakistan, at Colombo, Ceylon

---

[4] China was established in 1949.

[5] It is noted that the MCP had cooperated with the British government during the wartime to resist the Japanese occupation.

[6] *Federation of Malaya, Annual Report, 1952* (London: Her Majesty's Stationery Office, 1954), p. 3.

[7] The Economic Commission for Asia and the Far East (ECAFE) was another distinctive regional cooperation established by the United Nations on 28 March 1947. Including geographically distant countries from Japan to Iran, the ECAFE was composed of 24 members, such as Federation of Malaya, Indonesia, the Philippines, Singapore (the associate member) and Thailand as well as their former colonisers. It promoted economic development by exchanging views and technology and collecting statistical data rather than by providing financial aid and assistance.

[8] SEATO was also supposed to contribute to economic and technical fields as well as defence. See Manila Pact, 8 September 1954.

[9] Thanat Khoman, 'A Policy of Regional Cooperation', *Foreign Affairs Bulletin*, 8/1 (August-September 1968), p. 1.

in January 1950.[10] They 'agreed upon the vital importance of the economic development of South and South-East Asia in the maintenance of the political stability of the countries in that area'[11] as '[t]he present state of development in South and South-East Asia is probably as low as anywhere in the world'.[12] The main purpose of the Colombo Plan was to build up strong nations that could resist Communist infiltration, and this was to be achieved through financial aid and technical assistance.[13] In launching the Plan, the British were required 'to persuade the people of the region that their true interests are best served by continued association with the free world'.[14] The Plan originally focused on Commonwealth countries in South and Southeast Asia, but it later opened associate status to other countries in the region.[15] Indonesia joined in 1953, and Thailand and the Philippines did in 1954.[16]

SEATO was established on 8 September 1954 in Manila through, as stated earlier, a US initiative.[17] There were eight signatories (Australia, Britain, France, New Zealand, Pakistan, the Philippines, Thailand and the United States) and three protocol states (Cambodia, Laos and South Vietnam). It had three main purposes: defence cooperation, economic aid and technical assistance. Through these, SEATO could 'strengthen the fabric of peace and freedom' and 'promote the economic well-being and development' in the treaty area.[18] However, its main function was to form an anti-Communist military alliance, particularly against Communist China, which was growing in influence in the region, and to avoid the '"falling domino" principle' of Indochina.[19] At the inaugural conference of SEATO in Manila, John Foster Dulles, the American Secretary of State, stated,

> We are confronted by those who believe in the power of intimidation by violence. The Korean Armistice negotiations reached their climax to the accompaniment of suicidal assaults by

---

[10] Ceylon is present-day Sri Lanka.

[11] CAB 134/226, EPC(50)105, October 1950 (Final Report of the Commonwealth Consultative Committee on South and South-East Asia about co-operative economic development), paragraph 9.

[12] Ibid., paragraph 4.

[13] It was launched on 1 July 1951 with 7 countries and has expanded to 26 countries. Britain was not concerned about the establishment of Communist China. (Evelyn Colvert, *Southeast Asia in International Politics, 1941-1956* (Ithaca, NY: Cornell University Press, 1977), p. 143.)

[14] CAB 129/48, C(51)51, 20 December 1951 (Joint Cabinet Note by Mr. Eden, Mr Butler, Lord Ismay and Mr Lennox-Boyd), paragraph 2.

[15] The US joined the Colombo plan in 1951 and became a major aid donor. The British government recognised that '[w]ithout it [the US's participation], there is no hope for the non-Commonwealth countries – Burma, Indonesia, Indo-China and Siam – and the Commonwealth countries would probably have to do less economic development than they are doing now, rather than more'. (CAB134/225, EPC(50)40, 22 March 1950 (Joint Memorandum for Cabinet Economic Policy Committee by the Working Parties on the Sterling Area and on Development in South and South-East Asia on 18 March 1950), paragraph 16.)

[16] Subsequently, the status gap between the commonwealth members and the associate members caused a problem. See Daniel Wolfstone, 'Colombo Plan Issues', *Far Eastern Economic Review*, 2 November 1961, pp. 267-268.

[17] John Foster Dulles, the Secretary of State of the United States, was the principal architect of SEATO. SEATO dissolved on 30 June 1977.

[18] Manila Pact, 8 September 1954. The US regarded the Geneva Conference (21 July 1954) as 'a defeat for the West', and took the initiative of the formation of SEATO against its previous policy on Southeast Asia: 'regional organization must stem from regional initiative'. (Evelyn Colvert, *Southeast Asia in International Politics*, p. 291)

[19] Dwight D. Eisenhower, The President's News Conference, 7 April 1954. President Eisenhower emphasised the importance of Indochina in his message to Winston Churchill, the British Prime Minister: If 'Indochina passes into the hands of the Communists, the ultimate effect on our and your global strategic position with the consequent shift in the power ratio throughout Asia and the Pacific could be disastrous and, I know, unacceptable to you and me'. See Dwight D. Eisenhower, Cable to Winston Spencer Churchill, 4 April 1954.

the red Chinese and North Korean forces. The Geneva Conference on Indochina was accompanied by violent Communist military activity in that area.[20]

In Southeast Asia, the policies towards Communism varied from country to country. As Pye puts it, 'the politics of all the countries are strongly influenced by the question of how best to deal with the realities of Communism in Asia'.[21] The Philippines and Thailand were engaged in Cold War politics by fully supporting the American security policy of 'containment'. They sent troops to South Korea and South Vietnam.[22] Indeed, Philippine President Elpidio Quirino said in 1950 that 'he was anxious to keep Philippine policies attuned to that of the U.S.'[23] In 1951, the Mutual Security Act of 1951 was passed in the US Congress. It allowed much larger military aid to favoured Asian countries so that America could reinforce its defence function in Asia to withstand Communist aggression.[24] Although Thailand was very fearful of Communist infiltration, it did not have a bilateral defence treaty with the US. Therefore, Thailand 'welcomed the more formal commitment provided by SEATO'.[25] The Philippines, on the other hand, did not seem more concerned about the Communist infiltration than Thailand; however, its attitude towards Communist China remained resistant.[26] Both SEATO ally countries, the Philippines and Thailand, inevitably brought most attention to military defence rather than nation-building.

Malaya was suffering from the Malayan Emergency and held a strong sense of threat from Communist activities. However, it did not join SEATO, but rather focused on national development, in line with the Colombo Plan. Malaya fully enjoyed the British 'benevolent tutelage' in national security, as well as socio-economic development.[27] It believed that the most effective strategy in withstanding Communist expansion was to raise its standards of living.[28] Malaya did not send its troops outside of the country. Although British forces successfully suppressed Communist riots during the Emergency, Tunku Abdul Rahman, the Malayan Prime Minister, later expressed his view that 'no amount of British arms would by itself ever rid Malaya of the menace of Communism. The solution could not come about by military means alone; it was essential to win the minds and hearts of the people, to satisfy their aspirations, and thus draw them away from the enticements of Communism'.[29]

When the People's Republic of China was established in 1949, Indonesia was quick to recognise it. In domestic politics, the Indonesian government tried to keep a balance between political groups on the basis of *Pancasila*.[30] In his address to the Constituent Assembly in April 1959, Indonesian President Sukarno said, 'Independent Indonesia is a golden bridge on which

---

[20] John Foster Dulles, Statement in the Closing Session at the Southeast Asia Conference at Manila, 8 September 1954.

[21] Lucian W. Pye, 'Southeast Asia', in Robert E. Ward and Roy C. Macridis (eds.), *Modern Political Systems: Asia* (Englewood Cliffs, NJ: Prentice-Hall, 1963), p. 298.

[22] Thailand was the first Asian country which sent troops (4,000 personnel) to South Korea.

[23] 'Meeting, The White House, February 4, 1950', Memorandum of Conversation, Department of State, 4 February 1950.

[24] Aurelius Morgner, 'The American Foreign Aid Program: Costs, Accomplishments, Alternatives?', *The Review of Politics*, 28/4 (October 1966), p. 66.

[25] Evelyn Colbert, *Southeast Asia in International Politics*, p. 306. However, it was 'equivocal about stationing SEATO forces on its own territory'. (Ibid, p. 307)

[26] Mariano Cuneco, President of the Senate in the Philippines, said in April 1951 that the US policy in the Far East was 'erroneous' as it 'leaned toward appeasement of Communist China'. See 'Chronology of Principal Events Relating to the Korean Conflict, Research Project No. 244, April 1951'.

[27] Michael Leifer, *The Foreign Relations of the New States* (Camberwell, Vic: Longman Australia, 1974), p. 57.

[28] Bernard K. Gordon, *The Dimensions of Conflict in Southeast Asia*, p. 166.

[29] Tunku Abdul Rahman, 'Malaysia: Key Area in Southeast Asia', *Foreign Affairs*, 43/4 (July 1965), p. 660.

[30] For the details of *Pancasila*, see Chapter 1.

we should not push each other, or elbow each other aside, because this golden bridge is our collective possession'.[31] The sense of tolerance characterising *Pancasila* shaped the 'independent and active foreign policy' and let Indonesia keep away from the Cold War antagonism.[32] Indonesia declared that it would play 'no favourites between the two opposed blocs and follow its own path' because joining the either bloc 'would merely create new suspicions and new enmities'.[33] However, in terms of foreign aid, Indonesia relied on Western countries (mainly the US) for its economy as '[o]nly the West at this time was prepared to provide such assistance'.[34]

Two incidents in mid-1950s gave rise to a change in the security environment in Southeast Asia. Firstly, Nikita S. Khrushchev, the successor of Joseph Stalin, became the First Secretary of the Communist Party of the Soviet Union in 1953. He presented the new Soviet strategy of 'peaceful competition' with the free world by saying, '[L]et us compete without war'.[35] His new strategy was to expand Communist power by financial aid and technical assistance towards the non-Communist countries, while '[p]reviously Soviet leaders had made it abundantly clear that they couldn't care less about the progress of the newly developing areas'.[36] The Soviet Union was particularly keen to connect the leading forces of the non-aligned Third World, such as Indonesia and Burma.[37] Russia became increasingly confident in the exercise of its economic influence on outside of the countries: Communist's economic power 'will help … to consolidate world peace'.[38] Khrushchev's policy reduced the imminent threat of nuclear war between the two opposing blocs.[39]

A second factor was the cease-fire in Vietnam. After the French lost the battle of Dien Bien Phu in northern Vietnam in March 1954, peace talks were initiated in Geneva in April. On 21 July, both sides signed the Geneva accord, which stated that the country should be divided into two at the 17th parallel; and thus the First Indochina War ended.

With the new policy of Khrushchev and the end of the First Indochina War, a need for change in the American policy towards Southeast Asia was called for within the US. In 1954, the former US Ambassador to the Soviet Union, W. Averell Harriman,[40] issued the government with a warning regarding its attitude towards the Communists: 'Underlying both our current defence policies and our diplomacy has been a preoccupation with the idea of strength through our possession of nuclear weapons'.[41] He envisaged that the Communist bloc would achieve

---

[31] Sukarno, Speech at the Constituent Assembly, 22 April 1959.

[32] Independent and active foreign policy stemmed from the need of domestic politics so that Indonesia could begin its nation-building within national unity. Mohammad Hatta, the Vice President of Indonesia, said, 'A foreign policy that aligned the country with either bloc of the Great Powers would render this internal task [nation-building] infinitely more difficult'.(Mohammad Hatta, 'Indonesia's Foreign Policy', p. 449.)

[33] Mohammad Hatta, 'Indonesia's Foreign Policy', pp. 443-444.

[34] Evelyn Colbert, *Southeast Asia in International Politics*, p. 177.

[35] Nikita S. Khrushchev, 'On Peaceful Coexistence', *Foreign Affairs*, 38/1 (October 1959), p. 4.

[36] Douglas Dillon, Address made before the Virginia State Chamber of Commerce at Roanoke, Va.: 'Some Economic Aspects of U.S. Foreign Policy', on 15 April 1960.

[37] Ragna Boden, 'Cold War Economics: Soviet Aid to Indonesia', *Journal of Cold War Studies*, 10/3 (Summer 2008), p. 114. Although Indonesia was not recognised as a socialist country by the Soviet Union, its policy fighting against colonialism was seen as worth praising. (Ibid.) The Soviet Union announced that it would give Indonesia 'extraordinarily large share of Soviet aid', more than $400 million, since1956 (Ibid., p. 116) whereas American aid to Indonesia was $662 million in total in 15 years. (*Far Eastern Economic Review*, 27 July 1961, p. 183.) In 1956, when Indonesia received credits of $100 million, Sukarno visited Khrushchev. Sukarno's visit was done just after American President Eisenhower refused Sukarno's request for a loan.

[38] Nikita S. Khrushchev, 'On Peaceful Coexistence', p. 8.

[39] The Communist world reduced its power because of the Sino-Soviet ideological conflict over Khrushchev's proposal of peaceful coexistence, which also helped reduce the threat perception in the West.

[40] His tenure in Moscow was in 1943-46.

[41] W. Averell Harriman, 'Leadership in World Affairs', *Foreign Affairs*, 32/4 (July 1954), p. 528.

economic growth and the free world's margin of economic superiority would narrow. He then claimed,

> We can frustrate this Soviet design by using our energy and great resources not only to strengthen military defences throughout the free world, but to root freedom more firmly in economic development, rising standards of living, national dignity and the political and social conditions in which democracy flourishes.[42]

This view was shared broadly towards the end of 1950s. As Douglas MacArthur II put it,[43]

> The chief and present threat to independence in Asia is not an external military threat. It is the danger of unrest and subversion, directed from without, in countries where free governments seem unable to raise the material standards of living of their peoples. That is why Asian economic progress is so important for the peoples of free Asia.[44]

However, Dwight David Eisenhower, the President of the United States, was not able to tear himself away from his obsession with the possibility of a major war breaking out in Southeast Asia:

> The principal and continuing factor is the persistently aggressive design of Moscow and Peiping, which shows no evidence of genuine change despite their professed desire to relax tensions and to preserve peace. ….The major new factor in the world today, beside the absence of fighting, is the rapid development in military weapons – weapons that in total war would threaten catastrophe.[45]

The US was more actively engaged in South Vietnam after the Geneva Conference in 1954, in place of the French colonial government. It supported the new leadership of Ngo Dinh Diem and helped him purge Communist elements from South Vietnam. The State of Vietnam was taken over by the Republic of Vietnam in 1955 and Ngo Dinh Diem became its first President.

In early 1957, SEATO still held a militant perspective:[46] '[W]hile the immediate military threat to peace in Southeast Asia has diminished, the forces of international Communism is still working for the ultimate objective of world domination'.[47] It saw that the military strength in China and North Vietnam had not been reduced, and therefore 'SEATO could not relax its vigilance and must maintain its capacity to deter and repel aggression'.[48] Countries in Southeast Asia feared the recurrence of war in Indochina, which might give rise to an unstable situation in their countries. They recognised the fact that nation-building in such circumstances is impossible.

---

[42] Ibid., p. 540.
[43] Douglas MacArthur II, the former American Ambassador to Japan, was a nephew of General Douglas MacArthur.
[44] Douglas MacArthur II, Address before the Naigai Josei Chosakai (Research Institute of Japan) of 26 February 1959.
[45] Dwight David Eisenhower, Speech: 'Peace in Freedom' at the American Jewish Tercentenary Dinner at New York, 20 October 1954. The suspicious view to the Communist's propaganda, 'peaceful coexistence', was deep-rooted. See, for example, George F. Kennan, ''Peaceful Coexistence: A Western View', *Foreign Affairs*, 38/2 (January 1960), pp. 171-190.
[46] John Foster Dulles was the main organiser of SEATO; therefore, it was difficult to degrade its importance in the military sphere as long as he was in office. Frank C. Darling pointed out that the major turning point of the US's security policy was Douglas Dillon's replacing Dulles in April 1959. See his work, *Thailand and the United States* (Washington D. C.: Public Affairs Press, 1965), p.174.
[47] Final Communiqué of Third Meeting of the Council of the SEATO, 13 March 1957.
[48] Ibid.

However, a review of these perspectives was finally commenced in May 1957. Douglas Dillon, the Deputy Under-Secretary for Economic Affairs of the US, announced a new approach to security in Southeast Asia: 'During the past year our programs of mutual security have been going through a period of critical re-examination'.[49] He suggested that military-oriented aid since the Mutual Security Act of 1951 would be partially allocated to national development programmes in the region. John Foster Dulles, the Secretary of State, stated in June 1957, 'The President [Eisenhower] now recommends the establishment of a development loan fund as the most economical and effective way to stimulate the needed economic growth'.[50] Dillon made Dulles's statement clear: the US would accept the request from Southeast Asian countries, such as the Philippines and Thailand, because they 'can only survive as free governments if they can respond in some way to the demands of their peoples for economic growth. ... [T]he US must act if we wish to help these countries to remain free'.[51]

Towards self-reliance

However, as the British government saw it, '[t]he conduct of American foreign policy towards Asia…has left the United States with few friends, many enemies and almost universal critics amongst Asian Governments and peoples' during this period.[52] While the US was engaged in South Vietnam after the Geneva Conference in July 1954, disagreement over the American security policy arose among the countries of Southeast Asia. The Americans were seen as the 'real "war-mongers" in the world'.[53] In particular, the Philippines and Thailand, the members of SEATO, sought to distance their security policy from the American Cold War strategy. This is because they came to realise that they wanted to fight for their own interests, not 'for the vague concept of a free world'.[54] What the US was, in effect, doing in Vietnam was not in the interests of Southeast Asia, but in support of the Western bloc.[55] The Philippines and Thailand started to consider the way in which they should maintain their countries by themselves rather than relying heavily on the American security policy. Thanat Khoman, the Thai Foreign Minister, later referred to the imperative situation of small states: '[T]he Cold War…came into being without…the advice and consent of the smaller powers…. In the last resort, small nations may find that it is in their own interest to limit the degree of their involvement in the light of their assessment of the situation'.[56] Countries in Southeast Asia hoped for a situation in which it 'can freely determine its own destiny in accordance with the principle of self-determination'.[57]

Another background factor of influence to the process of gaining self-reliance was the end of the First Indochina War, in which both the Philippines and Thailand participated by sending troops. They believed that peace would allow them to concentrate their efforts on economic development. By doing so, they could eradicate poverty, which would give Communists an opportunity to infiltrate their societies. In this context, economic well-being was considered to

---

[49] Douglas Dillon, Address made before the American Assembly, at Harriman, N. Y., on 2 May 1957: 'A New Approach to Mutual Security'.

[50] John Foster Dulles, Address made before the House Foreign Affairs Committee: 'Major Purposes of the Mutual Security Programs (Press release on 10 June 1957)'.

[51] Douglas Dillon, Address made before the Advertising club of New Jersey at Newark, N. J.: 'Encouraging Economic Growth in Less Developed Countries of the Free World', on 4 June 1957. Indeed, economic aid to Thailand increased after this year. See, 'Foreign Aid – Too Little or Too Much?', *Far Eastern Economic Review*, 31 August 1961, pp. 389-390.

[52] FO 371/111852, no5, 8 August 1954 (Note by M J MacDonald (Singapore)).

[53] Ibid.

[54] Carlos P. Romuro, Address at University of Seattle, on June 1954.

[55] Ibid.

[56] Thanat Khoman, Address: 'Prospects of a New Pax Asiana', at the East-West Centre in Hawaii, 9 October 1969.

[57] Ferdinand Marcos, Address in the 1411th Plenary Meeting of the United Nations General Assembly, 21 September 1966.

be the most effective way to protect the country from Communism.[58] Carlos P. Romuro, the Philippine Foreign Secretary, pointed out in 1954 that:

> Military measures are best a short-term for staving off an immediate threat of Communist aggression. The long-term struggle against communism, however, requires economic and financial assistance that will enable the Asian peoples to raise their standards of living.[59]

Tunku Abdul Rahman later spoke about his idea of non-military national security against Communists: 'I am not referring to our armed strength because we are not strong but rather to the way we have run our country which has made the people of Malaysia happy and contented'.[60]

Both the Philippines and Thailand began to put a serious effort into tackling national development. Indeed, they had not been able to do this previously as they had been engaged in preventing the proliferation of communism in Asia by sending their people to the battlefield. King Bhumidol Adulyadej of Thailand visited Washington and gave a speech on 28 June 1960. He emphasised the importance of economic development, rather than military defence, by saying, 'When a country feels reasonably confident of its own security, it can devote more attention to economic development. ... You will understand what great urgent need there [in Thailand] is to increase the income and raise the living standard of my people'.[61]

In mid-May 1958, Carlos P. Garcia, the Philippine President, visited Eisenhower in Washington, and recommended that:

> we start a new chapter in the unending work of Nation building we face another great challenge, namely, the building of a national economy capable of affording down to the humblest citizen of a democratic Philippines economic well-being, social security, and stability.[62]

The Philippines and Thailand became aware of the advantages of 'standing on their own feet', and that they should 'rely more on neighbourly mutual support than on stronger states that serve their own national interests rather than those of smaller partners'.[63] In Thailand, the US government had praised the military regime as an ardent supporter of freedom. America's support provided legitimacy with the ruling Thai government and reduced the people's criticism against nepotism, corruption and suppression. However, by mid-1950s, the people's dissatisfaction was transferred to the development of an anti-American sentiment.[64] The people required the Thai government to cut its close ties with the US, to leave SEATO and to adopt an independent foreign policy. Eventually, a more 'neutral' policy direction was favoured[65] although the Thai government denied its adherence to neutralism because, ostensibly, it was 'not a solution'.[66]

---

[58] This idea stemmed from some Americans' view (not a unified view) on the Communist infiltration into Asia. The then Deputy Under Secretary of State, Robert Murphy, for example, stated, 'Communists seek to exploit these economic difficulties and gain converts by propaganda which paints a glowing picture of economic achievement in China and the U.S.S.R'. See Robert Murphy, Address: 'The Defence of Asia' before the National Foreign Trade Council at New York, on 16 November 1954.

[59] Carlos P. Romuro, Address at University of Seattle, on June 1954.

[60] Tunku Abdul Rahman, Speech at the Malaysian Alliance Convention, 17th April 1965.

[61] King Bhumidol Adulyadej, Address to the Congress, on 29 June 1960.

[62] Carlos P. Garcia, Address before the American Congress, on 18 June 1958.

[63] Thanat Khoman, 'ASEAN Conception and Evolution', 1 September 1992.

[64] Frank C. Darling, *Thailand and the United States*, p. 163.

[65] As Peter Lyon puts it, 'Ideological neutralism is overtly or covertly present in all countries.... Some obvious motives are: dislike of the dominant influence of great powers in world politics, ... dislike of economic dependence'. (Peter Lyon, *War and Peace in South-East Asia* (London: Oxford University Press, 1969), p. 162.) Indeed, all of ASEAN countries later embraced the idea of neutrality and declared the

In the Philippines, 'U.S. influence was predominant in almost every sphere' before Ramon Magsaysay came into office in 1953.[67] The US government said, 'We consider that we have a vital interest in the Philippines and that we must do everything necessary to insure its safety and reasonable stability'.[68] The Philippines were at odds with the US over a number of bilateral issues, such as the extraterritorial rights for US troops in the Philippines and the US's unilateral policy-making of national security in the Philippines. However, in this case, strong antagonism against the Americans did not emerge, as it did in Thailand. Instead, anti-American sentiment in the Philippines took pragmatic forms. The Philippine government sought to form a genuinely sovereign state, but doing so without sharply antagonising the US. This is the so-called new 'Philippine-American solidarity on the basis of equality'.[69] Indeed, when Eisenhower was invited to Manila in June 1960, Garcia told him that any anti-American sentiment would not harm the close bilateral ties.[70]

When Malaya became independent in 1957, it developed an independent and non-aligned foreign policy, although this new state did rely on the bilateral defence agreement with Britain (Anglo-Malayan Defence Agreement: AMDA) for its national security. In the agreement,

> In the event of a threat of armed attack against any of the territories or forces of the Federation of Malaya or any of the territories or protectorates of the United Kingdom in the Far East...the Governments of the Federation of Malaya and of the United Kingdom will consult together on the measures to be taken jointly or separately to enlist the fullest co-operation between them for the purpose of meeting the situation effectively.[71]

Eventually, Malaya did not join SEATO as it was 'quite satisfied with' AMDA.[72] However, it is often said that Malaya was linked with SEATO (or the US) indirectly via Britain.[73] Malayan leaders 'ritually scoffed at SEATO from time to time and they took care not to be too closely identified with American policies on Cold War issues'.[74] Tunku Abdul Rahman said about SEATO:

Zone of Peace, Freedom and Neutrality in 1971. See Zone of Peace, Freedom and Neutrality Declaration, 27 November 1971.

[66] Thanat Khoman, 'Which Road For Southeast Asia?', *Foreign Affairs*, 42/4 (July 1964), p. 639.

[67] George E. Taylor, *The Philippines and the United States: Problems of Partnership* (New York and London: Frederick A. Praeger, 1964), p. 197.

[68] Livingston T. Merchant, 'Notes on the Wake Conference', on 18 October 1950, Department of State, the United States of America, pp. 1-4. Livingston T. Merchant was the Deputy Assistant Secretary of State of the US (for Far Eastern Affairs).

[69] Carlos P. Garcia, Address before the American Congress, on 18 June 1958.

[70] Claude A. Buss, *The United States and the Philippines: Background for Policy* (AEI-Hoover policy Studies 23/ Hoover Institute Studies 59, Washington D.C.: American Enterprise Institute for Public Policy Research and Stanford: Hoover Institution on War, Revolution and Peace, Stanford University, 1977), p. 39.

[71] Agreement between the Government of the Untied Kingdom of Great Britain and Northern Ireland and the Government of the Federation of Malaya on External Defence and Mutual Assistance, 12 October 1957. Italics added.

[72] *Far Eastern Economic Review*, 28 July 1960, p. 163. Malaya was important for the British because of 'the first line of defence for Australia and New Zealand'. See CAB 131/14, D(54)41, 3 December 1954 (Defence in South-East Asia: memorandum by COS for Cabinet Defence Committee).

[73] A British Chief of Staff said, 'The United Kingdom...should be capable of jointly providing sufficient forces for the defence of Malaya against all but a full scale Communist attack, and in such an event we could almost certainly count on American assistance on the sea and in the air'. CAB 131/14, D(54)41, 3 December 1954 (Defence in South-East Asia: memorandum by COS for Cabinet Defence Committee).

[74] J. A. C. Mackie, *Konfrontasi*, p. 32.

Although it is agreed that Malaysia has both a military agreement and foreign bases, this arrangement is significantly different from such multilateral military alliances as SEATO, NATO... Malaysia's agreement with Britain is bilateral and for mutual defence and not concluded in the context of any East-West conflict.[75]

In Malaya, the awareness of self-reliance developed without particular anti-British sentiment.[76] The Tunku used a press conference in the early 1957 to state that he appreciated the excellent Government machinery that Malaya had inherited from the British, and it could successfully embark upon nation-building with this.[77] He saw that Malaya was able to achieve socio-economic progress quicker than any other country in the region. The Tunku added that the defence agreement with Britain 'has enabled us [the Malayan people] to make far more rapid progress in every field of development because we have not had to spend vast sums on our armed forces'.[78] Indeed, in the early 1960s, Malaya was praised by the World Bank as a model of a developing country.[79]

The birth of regional consciousness
The policy change in both the Philippines and Thailand – two countries which would prove to be devoted to the pursuit of economic development – allowed them to turn their attention towards neighbouring countries. They sought self-reliance through regional cooperation because they were too small and underdeveloped to achieve self-reliance alone. The awakening to neighbourliness made up the stepping-stones leading to the first regional organisation. In his letter to Garcia, the Tunku described their previous aloof relations.

> For historical reasons, the cultural and economic development of most countries of South East Asia has been principally influenced in the present century by the relations which they have had with other countries outside South East Asia. As a consequence, the growth of any sense of South East Asian consciousness, or of a common heritage in the great cultural achievements and possibilities of this part of Asia has been arrested. Through force of habit and historical circumstances, we have too often looked for help and inspiration outwards – instead of inwards depending on our own resources and effort.[80]

Two leaders of Malaya and the Philippines initiated this plan.[81] In February 1958, only half a year after Malaya's independence, the Tunku revealed the first initiative to create regional co-

---

[75] Tunku Abdul Rahman, Press Statement, 25 September 1964.
[76] Robert Elson, 'Reinventing a Region: Southeast Asia and the Colonial Experience', in Mark Beeson (ed.), *Contemporary Southeast Asia: Regional Dynamics, National Differences* (Basingstoke; NY: Palgrave Macmillan, 2004), p. 25.
[77] Harry Miller, *Prince and Premier: A Biography of Tunku Abdul Rahman Putre Ali-Haj, First Prime Minister of the Federation of Malaya* (London: George G. Harrap, 1959), p. 207.
[78] Tunku Abdul Rahman, 'Malaysia', p. 668.
[79] At the beginning, the standard of living in Malaya was only slightly higher than that of neighbouring countries when the Colombo Plan was launched although there was 'very little industry...apart from the tin mines'. (*New Horizons in the East: The Colombo Plan for Co-operative Economic Development in South and South-East Asia* (London: His Majesty's Stationery Office, 1950), p. 29.)
[80] Tunku Abdul Rahman, Letter from Tunku Abdul Rahman to President Garcia of the Philippines (Malayan Proposal for Regional Co-operation), 28 October 1959.
[81] It seems that the Tunku brought the idea to the Philippines because the latter was interested to take the initiative of regional cooperation organising the Asian Union (the Baguio Conference) in 1950. In addition to this, Malaya was indirectly linked with the Philippines via Britain as the Philippines and Britain were members of SEATO. Furthermore, it is possible to assume that the Tunku might have tried to establish amicable relations with the Philippines before the latter would pose a claim to Sabah. This is because the Philippine President Magsaysay 'promised to discuss the [Sabah] issue in cabinet' when he was in the

operation when he was in Colombo. In January 1959, he visited Garcia in Manila with his plan, the proposal for a Southeast Asian Friendship and Economic Treaty (SEAFET). His plan overtly aimed at broad economic and cultural cooperation, and covertly sought to establish the custom of consultation between neighbouring countries in the region. Although the Tunku expected to raise the standards of living through the treaty so that Malaya could forestall Communist infiltration, he tried not to emphasise the anti-Communist element to his proposal, so that the treaty could include non-aligned countries such as Indonesia and Burma.

Garcia, on the other hand, proposed the obvious pro-Western and anti-Communist security alliance.[82] Indeed, in December 1958, a month before the Tunku's visit, Garcia announced a new Philippine foreign policy, which aimed for 'fresh responsibilities on the international stage, and particularly in South-East Asia'.[83] Although the views on regional cooperation of the two leaders were different, they issued a Joint Statement, which stated that they sought regional co-operation based on racial kinship and friendship in order to raise the standards of living.

The Thai government showed its interest in regional cooperation in April 1959.[84] It circulated its own plan to countries in Southeast Asia in July of the same year. The Thai plan was broader in scope than the Malayan plan, including as it did an element of political cooperation too.[85] When the Malayan Premier sent a letter to countries in the region in October 1959, the objective of regional cooperation became clearer and the importance of 'consultation' between countries was emphasised. In his letter to Garcia, 'the countries of South East Asia should establish some organisation to facilitate *consultation* and closer collaboration between these countries'.[86] Indeed, they wanted to create neighbourliness, encourage frequent communication and foster a habit of cooperation. Except for these three countries, however, no other Southeast Asian State showed any interest in regional cooperation. Rather, Cambodia, Burma and Indonesia saw that the plans were pro-Western.[87]

The political situation in Indonesia

In Indonesia, an independent and active foreign policy could not successfully induce the sufficient amount of foreign aid and investment necessary for national development. Economic growth in Indonesia was less than that of its neighbouring countries in the mid-1950s. In the political sphere, many small parties competed with each other and each cabinet did not last long.[88] This led to a stalling of the nation-building process. Sukarno, the President of Indonesia, insisted that Indonesia's nation-building was at a standstill because it had employed a Western model of modernisation, and liberalism in politics and economy. He declared Guided Democracy in October 1956:

> I am suggesting that the leaders should hold a *musyawarah* and take a joint decision to bury the parties!' He continued, '...the democracy I crave for Indonesia is not a liberal democracy

---

office (1953-1957). See Michael Leifer, *The Philippine Claim to Sabah* (Hull Monographs on South-East Asia, No. 1, Centre for South-east Asian Studies, University of Hull, Zug, Switzerland: Inter Documentation, 1968), p. 9.

[82] Arnfinn Jorgensen-Dahl, *Regional Organization and Order on South-East Asia*, p. 16.

[83] J. L. Vellut, *The Asian Policy of the Philippines, 1954-1961* (Working Paper No. 6, Canberra: Department of International Relations, Research School of Pacific Studies, Institute of Advanced Studies, The Australian National University, 1965), p. 57.

[84] Arnfinn Jorgensen-Dahl, *Regional Organization and Order on South-East Asia*, p. 20.

[85] Gordon privately possesses the mimeo of the Thai proposal. See Bernard K. Gordon, *The Dimensions of Conflict in Southeast Asia*, pp. 167-168.

[86] Tunku Abdul Rahman, Letter from Tunku Abdul Rahman to President Garcia of the Philippines (Malayan Proposal for Regional Co-operation), 28 October 1959. Italics added.

[87] Nicholas Tarling, 'From SEAFET and ASA: Precursors of ASEAN', *International Journal of Asia-Pacific Studies*, 3/1 (May 2007), pp. 6-9.

[88] Lucian W. Pye, 'Southeast Asia', p. 338.

such as exists for Western Europe. No! What I want for Indonesia is a *guided democracy*, a democracy with leadership.[89]

In addition, the so-called PRRI rebellion let Indonesia remain largely aloof from its neighbouring countries.

Instability in domestic politics and the Indonesian economy finally led to an outbreak of political disturbances. On 15 February 1958, Central Sumatran commander Lieutenant Colonel Hussein declared the establishment of the Revolutionary Government of the Republic of Indonesia (PRRI) in Padan, Central Sumatra. It spread to the Celebes (Sulawesi) Island in June, but was suppressed by the end of July, although guerrilla activities by the defiant group continued until 1961. The rebellion originated in the power struggle between the two groups: one was composed of the Sukarno-phile and the Murba party;[90] the other group was made up of adherents to the Masyumi party.[91] The former advocated political centralisation and anti-Westernism, whereas the latter sought to pursue more liberal political lines and were anti-Communist. The latter occupied local councils in Central, North and South Sumatra from December 1956. The rebel leaders required Mohammad Hatta's return to Indonesian politics. They claimed that Hatta should be returned to the role of Prime Minister, and should form a duumvirate regime with Sukarno. Sukarno did not accept the demand and instead tabled a counter-proposal, according to which the political grouping should be composed of four parties: Communist, Masyumi, Nationalist and Nahdatul Ulama. The Army leader, Major General Abdul Haris Nasution, tried to act as a mediator. However, reconciliation was not brought. Hussein subsequently sent an ultimatum to the government.[92] Sukarno refused it, and then Hussein proclaimed the PRRI on 15 February.

The US covertly supported the rebellion, hoping that the Indonesian government could return to, at least, the neutral position, by putting Hatta in the leader's position.[93] The US government recognised that Indonesia leaned heavily towards the left, when the Russian President, Marshal Kliment Voroshilov, visited Sukarno in May 1957.[94] In addition, when the results of the local elections in mid-1957 favoured the Communists, the US became convinced that 'Indonesia was on the brink of falling into the Communist camp'.[95] It secretly delivered firearms through an air-drop over West Sumatra, and its officials gave statements in support of the rebellion.[96] However, eventually no country recognised the PRRI, because it failed to mobilise the people, and '[i]t quickly became obvious that the rebels would not succeed without overt American intervention'.[97]

---

[89] Sukarno, Speech at the Teachers' Union Congress, 30 October 1956.
[90] The Murba party was based on a Proletariat national-Communist.
[91] The Masyumi party was backed by Socialist.
[92] The seizure of property of the Dutch companies in December 1957 was also an issue for ringleaders of the PRRI. The seizure was retaliation by Indonesian labour groups for the rejection of the Indonesian resolution in the UN for recovery of West Irian in November.
[93] It is said that the US supplied military hardware to rebels from Singapore and Taiwan. See Herbert Feith and Daniel S. Lev, 'The End of the Indonesian Rebellion', *Pacific Affairs*, 36/1 (Spring 1963), p. 41.
[94] Karl Hack, *Defence and Decolonisation in Southeast Asia: Britain, Malaya and Singapore 1941-1968* (Richmond, VA: Curzon, 2001), p.274.
[95] Audrey R. and George McT. Kahin, *Subversion as Foreign Policy: The Secret Eisenhower and Dulles Debacle in Indonesia* (New York: The New Press, 1995), p. 69. The operation was done by Central Intelligence Agency of the United States. See Ibid, pp. 155-166.
[96] Herbert Feith and Daniel S. Lev, 'The End of the Indonesian Rebellion', pp. 35-36.
[97] John Subritzky, *Confronting Sukarno: British, American, Australian and New Zealand Diplomacy in the Malaysian-Indonesian Confrontation, 1961-5* (Basingstoke, Hampshire and London: Macmillan Press, 2000), p. 23.

The Indonesian government launched an offensive attack against the rebels and quickly suppressed them by the end of May.[98] Nevertheless, the PRRI rebellion was 'a turning point in Indonesian politics'.[99] After the rebellion, the regionalist groups, such as Masyumi, were excluded from the central government, and only the Sukarno group and the Army would remain in power.[100] Sukarno also completed the takeover of the Dutch companies by mid-1958 and launched the so-called 'Guided Economy', allowing the government to intervene more directly in the economy. Sukarno criticised the trade relationship between the Netherlands and Indonesia, in addition to his opposition to western-style democracy. After independence, Indonesian economy could not be completely independent from the Dutch because the exports in Indonesia relied on plantation products by Dutch-owned companies in Indonesia. Indonesian labourers were still exploited by the former colonial power; and the living standards in the country did not improve. Guided Economy was the tool of 'an attack on "economic liberalism"',[101] by saying that liberal economy failed to stimulate economic progress. Sukarno put Guided Democracy into practice in July 1959, and did so by Presidential decrees in order to focus political power on himself.[102]

Moreover, the domestic situation in Indonesia was not stable enough, and cooperation with the neighbouring countries was increasingly difficult because of the growing West Irian Campaign. Indonesia had been in negotiations with the Dutch for incorporating West Irian into the Indonesian territory since its independence in 1949. Indonesia successfully put the issue into the final communiqué of the Asian-African Conference in 1955: 'The Asian-African Conference, in the context of its expressed attitude on the abolition of colonialism, supported the position of Indonesia in the case of West Irian'.[103] However, it had not borne fruit. By the early 1960, the Indonesian navy and air force were greatly strengthened by the large support from both the Soviet Union and the US. In August 1960, Sukarno broke diplomatic relations with the Netherlands. Indonesia and the Netherlands debated the issue during the United Nations General Assembly in late 1961; however, both sides failed to secure sufficient support from the chamber. The United States gave a hand to Indonesia on the grounds that the latter, a major regional state in Southeast Asia in terms of its population and natural resources, was of 'strategic importance, together with the fact that its future political direction was still very much in doubt'.[104] The US was worried about the future of Indonesia, which, it thought, might fall into the power of Communist.

The United States 'was actively engaged in finding a solution on broadly pro-Indonesian terms'.[105] In February 1962, a US's investigating mission was involved in this issue.[106] In the following month, the US government organised negotiations between Indonesia and the Dutch in Washington. However, Indonesia abruptly withdrew from the negotiating table and resumed infiltration into West Irian.[107] It pressed the Dutch government to abandon West Irian, and did so by introducing sporadic military actions. On 15 August, Indonesia successfully made an agreement with the Dutch and took the territory over on 1 May 1963.

---

[98] After the suppression of the rebellion, the US and Britain resumed exporting weapons to Indonesia so that the Indonesian Army could keep attention to the free world. See Karl Hack, *Defence and Decolonisation in Southeast Asia*, p. 274.

[99] Herbert Feith and Daniel S. Lev, 'The End of the Indonesian Rebellion', p. 36.

[100] Ibid, pp. 36-37.

[101] Douglas S. Paauw, 'From Colonial to Guided Economy', in Ruth T. McVey (ed.), *Indonesia* (New Haven, CT: Human Relations Area Files, 1963), p. 155.

[102] See Sukarno, President's Independence Day Speech, 17 August 1959.

[103] Final Communiqué of the Asian-African Conference, 24 April 1955.

[104] John Subritzky, *Confronting Sukarno*, p. 24.

[105] Herbert Feith, 'Dynamics of Guided Democracy', in Ruth T. McVey (ed.), *Indonesia* (Southeast Asia Studies, Yale University, New Haven, CT: Hraf Press, 1963), p. 352.

[106] The American mission was headed by Robert Kennedy, the Attorney General.

[107] Herbert Feith, 'Indonesia', p. 269.

Through the West Irian Campaign, Indonesia eliminated the control of one of the former colonisers from Southeast Asia and successfully enhanced its reputation in the Afro-Asian World. In addition, it established 'the [use of] unconventional methods of diplomacy and low-level use of force' as a means to force the former coloniser out of the region.[108] Indeed, the success of the campaign heightened Sukarno's confidence in his political ideology (such as non-alignment and anti-colonialism) and its embodiment, the so-called Guided Democracy.

Indonesia 'was cool to say the least' about the regional cooperation plan.[109] It was not comfortable cooperating with the Philippines and Thailand because they were the members of SEATO, which Indonesia felt hostile to. In addition, tacit cross-strait tensions existed between Indonesia and Malaya: Malaya's suspicion of the expansionist policy of Indonesia, and Indonesia's doubt about Malaya's involvement in the PRRI rebellion. The Secretary-General of the Ministry of Foreign Affairs of Indonesia, Kusmowidadjo Suwito, explained Indonesia's view of the situation by saying that Indonesians tended to regard the regional cooperation plan 'as the SEATO countries' efforts to make a subtle link between SEATO and non-SEATO countries in Asia'.[110] As Hatta concluded:

> The memory of the colonial status that bound them [the newly independent states] for centuries makes them resist anything they consider an attempt to colonize them again, whether by economic or ideological domination. This psychological factor profoundly influences Indonesia in her insistence upon an independent policy.[111]

Three months after the Tunku-Garcia meeting on the regional cooperation scheme in January 1959, Malaya arrived at the Treaty of Friendship with Indonesia. In the Treaty, the two countries pledged '[to] strive through cooperation, collaboration and *consultation* to achieve the greatest possible uniformity in their use and development'.[112] Based on racial commonality, the two states were expected to hold consultations when issues arose between them. However, in the mid-1961, Suwito Kusumowidagdo expressed his objection to the Tunku's initiative of regional cooperation. In an interview in *Far Eastern Economic Review*, he said, 'I don't think there were any prior official consultations with us [about the regional cooperation plan]'.[113] While it is too simple to conclude that the entire reason of Indonesia's non-involvement in the first regional organisation scheme was due to the Tunku's mismanagement, it can be said that the Malaya's failure of consultation with Indonesia made Indonesia maintain its negative position towards regional cooperation.

---

[108] J. A. C. Mackie, *Konfrontasi*, pp. 98-99.

[109] Arnfinn Jorgensen-Dahl, *Regional Organization and Order on South-East Asia*, p. 17. Indeed, Indonesia did not need to cooperate with its neighbouring countries because it was large in size. It sought for self-reliance by itself rather than by creating regional cooperation. The idea of self-reliance in Indonesia was developed to 'national resilience' after the establishment of the Association of Southeast Asian Nations (ASEAN) in 1967.

[110] Kusmowidadjo Suwito, Interview by K. Krishna Moorthy, Kusmowidadjo Suwito was the Secretary-General of the Ministry of Foreign Affairs of Indonesia. Indeed, on various occasions, when discussing the new regional cooperation, the Tunku had expressed his anti-Communist stance. After having opposition to the ideological grouping from Indonesia and Burma, the ASA included the following statement in its foundation document: the ASA 'is in no way connected with any outside power bloc and is directed against no other country, but is essentially a free association of countries of Southeast Asia'. (Bangkok Declaration, 31 July 1961)

[111] Mohammad Hatta, 'Indonesia's Foreign Policy', p. 445.

[112] Treaty of Friendship between Malaya and Indonesia, 17 April 1959. Italics added.

[113] *Far Eastern Economic Review*, 13 July 1961, p. 55.

The development of the plan

In April 1960, the Malayan government decided to take the initiative in relation to the regional cooperation plan. The development of the plan proceeded with the help of the Philippines and Thailand. An envoy of the Malayan government, Mohamed Sopiee, was sent, to Manila and Bangkok. The talks in both countries were 'very encouraging indeed' and the three countries agreed to set up a Working Group to deal with the cooperation plan.[114] In July 1960, Malaya abandoned the treaty plan and proposed a more 'practical and informal' one.[115] The reason was that a formal organisation, based on the treaty, bound potential member countries to conform to the decisions of the organisation, whereas national policy varied among these countries.[116]

The new proposal was called the Association of South East Asian State (ASAS). It emphasised the importance of 'consultations'. The ASAS was to be a 'friendly association among South East Asian countries as a means of providing *consultation*, collaboration and mutual assistance in the economic, social, cultural and administrative fields'.[117] In a sense, the ASAS was expected to establish the practice of sitting down together and developing 'a new sense of community'.[118] In February 1961, the Foreign Ministers of the three countries met in Kuala Lumpur and agreed to set up a working group in each country in order to facilitate the establishment of the organisation.[119] The working group was first held in Bangkok in June. Although it was not able to include Indonesia, by far the largest country in the region, the first attempt at such a regional initiative bore fruit. On 31 July 1961, the first vehicle for regional cooperation, the Association of Southeast Asia (ASA), 'inspired and organised by Asians' was established.[120] In the initial Declaration, the ASA pledged to cooperate in 'the economic, social, cultural, scientific and administrative fields'.[121]

The second Foreign Ministerial Meeting was supposed to be held in late 1962 in Manila. However, it was postponed until April 1963 at Malaya's request. This is because since the mid-1962, bilateral tensions between Malaya and the Philippines over the Federation of Malaysia plan, which was announced by Malaya in May 1961, had intensified. The Philippines claimed its dominion over Sabah, one of the British colonies, which was to be incorporated into Malaysia.[122] In addition, Malaya accused the Philippine government of hiding Azahari bin Sheikh Mahmud, who raised the revolt in December 1962 against Brunei's joining Malaysia. Referring to the rebellion of Azahari, Indonesia posed a question to the Malaysia plan, because of lack of regional consensus. As political tensions between Malaya and Indonesia intensified, Indonesia declared its confrontation with Malaysia (known as *Konfrontasi*). Since 1963, skirmishes occurred along the Indonesian-British border in Borneo, and the region suffered from a pattern of disturbances. However, the ASA was not able to manage the three-sided issue including a non-

---

[114] *Far Eastern Economic Review*, 14 July 1960, p. 50.

[115] Tunku Abdul Rahman, Interview by Kayser Sung. Malaya envisaged several specific items for regional cooperation from the beginning of the plan, such as tourism, education, commodities, shipping and civil aviation, common market. See 'South East Asia at "Threes and Fives"', *Far Eastern Economic Review*, 14 July 1960, p. 51.

[116] Daniel Wolfstone, 'Manila's Image of ASAS', *Far Eastern Economic Review*, 15 September 1960, p. 596.

[117] *Far Eastern Economic Review*, 14 July 1960, p. 51. Italics added. By July 1960, Malaya had made up the detailed plan of ASAS. (Ibid.) The Tunku signed Treaty of Friendship with Indonesia on 17 April 1959. This treaty can be seen as a first step of Malaya to establish a friendly relationship with the neighbouring countries. The treaty included cooperation in 'cultural, intellectual, scientific and educational fields', which were later stipulated in the ASA in 1961. See Treaty of Friendship between Malaya and Indonesia, 17 April 1959.

[118] Daniel Wolfstone, 'Manila's Image of ASAS', p. 596.

[119] Nicholas Tarling, 'From SEAFET and ASA', p. 10.

[120] Bernard K. Gordon, *The Dimensions of Conflict in Southeast Asia*, p. 162.

[121] Bangkok Declaration, 31 July 1961.

[122] For the details of the Sabah issue, see Chapter 3.

member state, Indonesia. It was not able to manage even the bilateral issues between members, Malaya and the Philippines. '[T]he role of [the] ASA became limited' in the course of the development of disturbance among three countries.[123] The Ministerial Meeting of the ASA was suspended until 1966 when Indonesia, Malaysia and the Philippines resumed diplomatic relations.

The significance of the establishment of the ASA
It is said that Malayan Prime Minister Tunku Abdul Rahman, the proposer of regional cooperation in 1958, took the idea for regional cooperation in Southeast Asia from the European Economic Community.[124] However, as was described above, distrust of the US policy and disappointment in the inability of the SEATO to act effectively had grown among US allies in Southeast Asia, and notably in the Philippines and Thailand. Although they recognised the need of American military support, the Philippines and Thailand nonetheless tried to reduce their burden of military commitment to SEATO and turn their efforts to nation-building, which they had been neglecting since the end of World War II. This is because of the belief that socio-economic development was the most effective way to withstand Communist subversion. This belief prevailed among leaders in Southeast Asia. The Tunku picked up this movement and called for regional cooperation.

Therefore, the formation of the ASA can be said to be the first step of 'awakening to self-reliance' in Southeast Asia. In other words, the countries in the region realised that they should have responsibility for their own security by building up self-reliance, in particular, through the economic development. In doing so, they could stand on their own feet and then avoid extra-regional interference. At the same time, however, in this period they had no choice but to acknowledge that military presence of external power was essential in case of an emergency. Indeed, all three countries of the ASA were homes to foreign bases, and, more specifically, these were SEATO-related bases. This paradoxical reality created the specific view of national security in Malaya and of bilateral relations with external power. Namely, it was responsible for its national security only when it was peace time. When in emergency, Malaya was relying on external power, the British, to help it. As the Tunku said, British presence gave Malaya a free hand to focus on its national development, and doing so without spending their human resources to bolster defence security.[125] In the hope of having the same relations, both the Philippines and Thailand hoped the US would provide unilateral support without asking them to share military responsibility.[126]

Another factor for encouraging regional cooperation was the fact that all three countries were too small and too poor to achieve self-reliance separately. They realised that it was better to cooperate with each other in order to achieve self-reliance. As Thanat Khoman later said, 'What a rich nation can do single-handed, poor nations must accomplish in concert'.[127] This was echoed by Ahmad, who wrote that: '[F]ive is better than four than three...than one'.[128] Indeed, awareness of self-reliance stimulated the countries to look at their neighbours as their partners in national development. These two factors: awakening to self-reliance and a sense of neighbourliness, led the region into cooperation.

It is noteworthy that the importance of consultations had been continuously emphasised in the course of the formation of the ASA, and the term 'consultation' was stipulated in the Bang-

---

[123] Susumu Yamakage, *ASEAN*, p. 68. Author's translation.
[124] Arnfinn Jorgensen-Dahl, *Regional Organization and Order on South-East Asia*, p. 70.
[125] Tunku Abdul Rahman, 'Malaysia: Key Area in Southeast Asia', p. 668.
[126] Indonesia, which advocated non-alignment in foreign policy, could not accept their idea and did not join the ASA.
[127] Thanat Khoman, 'Reconstruction of Asia', *Foreign Affairs Bulletin*, 9/1 (August-September 1969), p. 12.
[128] Zakaria Haji Ahmad, 'The World of ASEAN Decision-makers', p. 205.

kok Declaration, the foundation document of the ASA. Indeed, it was the first step to the emergence of a sense of neighbourliness and mutual understanding. The orientation towards regional cooperation gained momentum when the Philippines and Thailand turned their policies to national development, leaving behind the commitment to the bipolar military rivalry. In other words, regional cooperation became a reality when these countries recognised that nation-building was far more important in insuring their countries against external interference.

There were two types of external interference, as recognised by the countries in question. The first one was Communists' externally-aided attempts to subvert their governments (aid was provided by China and North Vietnam). The second one they envisaged was a Western/American intervention provoked by Communist infiltration. They were witnesses of this during the conflict in Vietnam, and they did not want to see such tragedy at home. They realised that eradicating poverty was the most effective means to prevent the first step. Thus, it was most desirable to improve the socio-economic conditions at home.

The member states of the ASA determined to take responsibility for drawing the blueprint for national development. However, all of them were late starters of modernisation; therefore, there were a lot of obstacles in front of them. In addition, they had to rely on foreign aid and investment for national development. It was useful for exchanging views of nation-building, or for helping each other as neighbouring countries, which were experiencing similar problems. It can be said that first regional cooperation by the regional initiative was born as a result of the aspiration to attain self-reliance.

Concluding remarks

The sense of regionalism in Southeast Asia began to develop in the mid-1950s, which is earlier than is normally recognised by scholars. Regional consciousness in Southeast Asia was stimulated by the end of the First Indochina War and the formation of SEATO. Although not drastically so, SEATO member countries, the Philippines and Thailand, slightly shifted their regional policy from depending totally on the external power (the US) to taking the initiative for their own business. In the meantime, the Southeast Asian states recognised the imminent need for nation-building. As a result, countries in Southeast Asia began to look to their neighbours, and formed the first system of regional cooperation that had been led by the region. However, the regional organisation was destined to face difficulties as a result of the formation of Malaysia.

3 THE ATTEMPT TO FIND A REGIONAL SOLUTION TO A REGIONAL PROBLEM

Although the Association of Southeast Asia (ASA), the first locally made regional organisation, was successfully established in 1961, it became dysfunctional almost immediately. From the beginning of 1963 the region was plunged into a three-way dispute between Indonesia, Malaya and the Philippines over the formation of Malaysia. Since the ASA was not able to address the problem, the three countries were forced to look for an alternative. After reaching a series of agreements in Manila in mid-1963, they formed a new grouping, the so-called Maphilindo.[1] One of the major achievements of the agreements was that the three countries in this grouping agreed to work together and to hold frequent consultations. It is noteworthy that during this period these states began to recognise the region of Southeast Asia as their own. They formally acknowledged the need to assume primary responsibility in managing regional matters by strengthening ties between neighbouring countries and by breaking with their historical dependence on the West. This chapter elucidates these important changes of political perspectives in Maphilindo member states and identifies the key characteristic features of the organisation.

The declaration of the Malaysia plan

On 27 May 1961, at a press conference in Singapore,[2] Malayan Prime Minister Tunku Abdul Rahman announced his intention to explore the possibility of the formation of Malaysia. He stated:

> Malaya today as a nation realises that she cannot stand alone and in isolation. ... Sooner or later she should have an understanding with Britain and the peoples of the territories of Singapore, North Borneo [Sabah], Brunei and Sarawak. It is premature for me to say now how this closer understanding can be brought about, but it is inevitable that we should look ahead to this objective and think of a plan whereby these territories can be brought closer together in political and economic cooperation.[3]

The plan stemmed from Britain's long-cherished decolonisation scheme in the region,[4] which intended to incorporate the British Borneo territories and Singapore into the Federation of Malaya. Even when Singapore was administered separately from the Malay Union in 1949, the British government maintained its vision: Singapore would eventually be merged with Malaya. A major complication, however, was to calm down neighbouring states, which might fear the increasing scourge of Communism by redrawing of the regional map. On his way back to Jakarta from the Hague, Mohammad Hatta, the Vice-President of Indonesia, stopped over in Singapore in mid-November 1949 to talk with Malcom MacDonald, the British Commissioner-General in Southeast Asia.[5] At this time, MacDonald argued that the best plan to combat Communism in the region was to integrate the five British colonies in Southeast Asia – Malaya, Sin-

---

[1] The name Maphilindo is an acronym of its three members, *Ma*laya, the *Phi*lippines and *Indo*nesia.
[2] However, he did not disclose the details at that time.
[3] Tunku Abdul Rahman, Address Given to the Foreign Correspondents Association of Southeast Asia, 27 May 1961.
[4] The British officials had envisaged the plan since 1887 (Arnold Brackman, *Southeast Asia's Second Front: The Power Struggle in the Malay Archipelago* (London: Pall Mall Press, 1966), p. 42).
[5] He had just finished the conference for independence of Indonesia in The Hague.

gapore, Sabah, Sarawak and Brunei – into one federation under Malaya.[6] It was important for the British to avoid segmenting British Borneo territories – Sabah, Sarawak and Brunei – into three small countries, which were likely to provide fertile soil for subversive Communist activities. In addition, by including these three areas, the Chinese population would become a minority in the proposed Federation.[7]

Hatta had a feeling that the British 'had definitely decided to combine these three areas [Malaya, Singapore and North Borneo]' regardless of the wishes of local inhabitants.[8] Clearly, Indonesia did not want Malaya, and by extension Britain, to increase its influence in the region. This highlights the underlying hostility between the two countries.[9] Hatta said to MacDonald: 'This would not only be very dangerous for the Malays themselves, but also for us Indonesians'.[10] He did not welcome the creation of a pro-British country adjacent to Indonesia, and especially so if it included a shared land border on the island of Borneo. Instead, he proposed that the three North Borneo territories, Malaya and Singapore should each be granted independence to avoid uniting the Chinese in the five territories.

The Tunku's announcement of the Malaysia scheme[11] was grounded on his underlying fear of Indonesian expansionism, which had emerged since Indonesia's independence.[12] Apprehension about Indonesian expansionism stemmed from a speech given by Muhammad Yamin, an Indonesian leading parliamentarian and the former Chairman of the National Planning Council,[13] who held that Indonesia should incorporate Sabah as well as West Irian and East Timor into its territory. He made his address on 31 May 1945 at the meeting of the Investigating Committee for the Preparation of Indonesia's Independence, which was established during the wartime by the Japanese Military Administration:[14]

> As history shows, Papua and the islands adjacent to it have been inhabited by the Indonesian people since time immemorial…Before the war, the island of Papua was divided into two parts, one part being ruled by the Dutch and the other being part of Australian territory. What I mean by Papua in this context is that part which used to be ruled by the Dutch…Portuguese Timor and North Borneo, being outside the territory of former Dutch rule, constitute enclaves, and enclaves should not be allowed to exist in the territory of the State of Indonesia; so, these areas should come within the control and complete the unity of the State of Indonesia.[15]

---

[6] MacDonald was said to be 'a great enthusiast' for the five-in-one plan. See A. J. Stockwell, 'Britain and Brunei, 1945-1963: Imperial Retreat and Royal Ascendancy', *Modern Asian Studies*, 38/4 (2004), p. 789.

[7] Mohammad Hatta, 'One Indonesian View of the Malaysia Issue', *Asian Survey*, 5/3 (March 1965), p. 141.

[8] Ibid.

[9] The tacit antagonism originated in the different nature of their relations with the Western countries. Malaya kept close relations with Britain whereas Indonesia secured independence through bloody struggle against the Dutch.

[10] Mohammad Hatta, 'One Indonesian View of the Malaysia Issue', p. 140.

[11] It was on his mind 'for a considerable time'. See Tunku Abdul Rahman, Speech in the House of Representatives in Malaya, 16 October 1961.

[12] *Indonesian Intentions towards Malaysia* (Kuala Lumpur: The Federal Department of Information of Malaysia, 1964), p. 1. For the argument on Indonesian expansionism, see for example, Bernard K. Gordon, 'The Potential for Indonesian Expansionism', *Pacific Affairs*, 36/4 (Winter 1963-64), pp. 378-393; Donald Hindley, 'Indonesia's Confrontation with Malaysia: A Search for Motives', *Asian Survey*, 4/6 (June 1964), pp. 904-913; and Guy J. Pauker, 'Indonesia: Internal Development or External Expansion?', *Asian Survey*, 3/2 (February 1963), pp. 69-75. It is said that the Malaysia plan stemmed from Malayan anxiety for the future of Singapore being independent; however, Milne regards this explanation as 'too simple'. (R. S. Milne, 'Malaysia, Confrontation and Maphilindo', *Parliamentary Affairs*, 16/4 (May 1963), p. 405).

[13] He served as the Chairman between 1959 and 1962.

[14] It was established in March 1945.

[15] Muhammad Yamin, Address at the Investigating Committee for the Preparation of Indonesia's Independence, 31 May 1945. Sukarno expressed his complete agreement with Yamin's view on 11 July 1945

The matter of a federation plan was brought up for the first time by Tunku Abdul Rahman in a 'purely personal conversation' with Malcom MacDonald in December 1958.[16] Although his idea was rudimentary, it is said that the Tunku's promotion of the integration plan was also influenced by the British Ambassador in Manila.[17] In a communication between the two, the Ambassador said that the Philippines would possibly make a claim for dominion over Sabah.[18] The Tunku was apprehensive that the Philippines' claim on Sabah would foment Indonesia's claim over British Borneo territories. He imagined 'the possibility...of Sukarno mounting a claim to northern Borneo on the lines of his bid' for West Irian, in addition to the problem of Indonesian expansionism.[19] Therefore, he dreaded that 'the Indonesians might someday try to subvert Malay and other opinion in Sarawak and Brunei in order to create a local opinion in favour of joining Indonesia'.[20] After the talks with MacDonald, the Tunku was keen to instigate the scheme as quickly as possible, so that the British territories could be independent through incorporation into Malaya.[21]

However, the British government took a passive attitude towards quick independence of its colonies. Firstly, it was unconcerned about Indonesia's ambition and was certain that Indonesia would not claim its Borneo territories, and subsequently took the passive position of 'let sleeping dogs lie'.[22] Secondly, Britain argued that further national development, in particular, in the area of politics, was needed in Sabah and Sarawak before independence.[23] In addition, indigenous people, such as Dayaks and Susuns, still had a vivid memory of discriminative treatment from the Malays.[24] If these areas were to get incorporated in a Malay-dominant federation, such hostile attitudes against the Malay may become the seeds of discord.

The Tunku's lingering suspicion towards Indonesia was confirmed once again by the reinvigorated West Irian Campaign, when in the late 1950s, Indonesia entered the era of Guided Democracy. It was then that he started to prepare the blueprint for the establishment of Malaysia.[25] The Tunku thought that if Indonesia would successfully incorporate West Irian, then British Borneo territories would be its next ideological target.[26] He thought that the British 'must be ready for "an Indonesian move" against these territories [Sabah and Sarawak]'.[27] On 10 June 1960, during talks in London with Lord Perth, the British Minister of State in Colonial Office, Tunku Abdul Rahman proposed a federation plan incorporating all of the British Borneo territories into Malaya including Singapore.[28] According to Lord Perth's notes, Lord Selkirk, the British Commissioner for Singapore and Southeast Asia, showed strong support to the Tunku.[29]

---

in his speech. See Speech to the Investigating Committee for the Preparation of Indonesia's Independence, 11 July 1945.

[16] DC 35/10019, no 12, E/3, 22 December 1958 (Note by M MacDonald of his talks with Tunku Abdul Rahman on 20 December).

[17] Ibid.

[18] Ibid.

[19] A J Stockwell, 'Introduction' in A J Stockwell (ed.), *Malaysia* (British Documents on the End of Empire, Series B, Vol. 8, London: The Stationery Office, 2004), p. xl.

[20] DC 35/10019, no 12, E/3, 22 December 1958 (Note by M MacDonald of his talks with Tunku Abdul Rahman on 20 December).

[21] The Tunku did not consider incorporating Singapore into the federation at this stage.

[22] DC 35/10019, no 42, 9 June 1960 ('CO Memorandum for Lord Perth').

[23] CO 1030/982, no 498C, 24 August 1961 ('Crash programme for "Greater Malaysia"').

[24] DC 35/10019, no 42, 9 June 1960 ('CO Memorandum for Lord Perth').

[25] David Wurfel points out the Tunku's main threat was Indonesia. It pushed him through the establishment of Malaysia. See his article, 'A Changing Philippines', *Asian Survey*, 4/2 (February 1964), p. 704.

[26] Ibid.

[27] DC 35/10019, no 42, 9 June 1960 ('CO Memorandum for Lord Perth').

[28] CO 1030/1126, no 10, 10 June 1960 (Memorandum by Lord Perth Recording Tunku Abdul Rahman's Proposal for Closer Association of Independent Malaya and British Dependencies in SE Asia).

[29] He was appointed that position in January 1960, and his main concern was to protect the region from Communist.

Lord Selkirk recognised this as an opportunity for Singapore to join the federation: a matter that the Tunku had been reluctant to discuss, and he stressed that the Tunku's proposals should 'be examined very closely and urgently'.[30]

In Singapore, a possibility of a separate independence emerged because of the rapid growth of a new left-wing, *Barisan Socialis*, which was 'manipulated by the Communists'.[31] Although Lee Kuan Yew, who later became the first Singaporean Prime Minister, had been advocating Singapore's 'independence through merger' with Malaya since he took power in 1959, Malaya did not seem to consider it very thoroughly. This is because the 'differences in outlook' between the two countries were quite significant.[32] In addition, the incorporation of Singapore into Malaya would threaten to shift the ethnic balance to Chinese domination.[33] Furthermore, the Chinese in Singapore were more loyal to China than to Malaya. Therefore, a bilateral merger was of little benefit for Malaya; rather it was perceived as a threat to bring a recurrence of Communist-led disturbances, like the Malayan Emergency (1948-1960).

Lee Kuan Yew, on the other hand, saw it as an opportunity for merging Singapore with Malaya when Tunku Abdul Rahman was vigorously working on the federation plan. Lee held talks with the Tunku several times before sending the latter a proposal in May 1961. In that proposal, Lee expressed his apprehension regarding regional security if Singapore gained independence on its own and if the left-wing assumed government. In case of separate independence, the defence treaty with Britain would be 'replaced by ties with the Chinese mainland. This would ultimately lead to a Chinese Communist base right in the heart of South East Asia'.[34] The Tunku showed his apprehension: 'While Singapore [is] under the British there is no threat of open action by the Communists which might endanger the peace and security of the Federation, but with an independent Singapore anything could happen'.[35] Lee also suggested that the merger with Malaya would be the best, and indeed the only, way to avoid such a nightmare.[36] Furthermore, if the Federation incorporated the three British Borneo territories in addition to Singapore, 'the Malays would constitute the largest ethnic group' in Malaysia.[37] Indeed, the Tunku's first announcement of 27 May 1961 was encouraged by Lee's proposal.[38]

The regional situation in a broader context
If one took a broader perspective on the political map of Southeast Asia at this time, one would see that Prince Sihanouk was in power and embraced neutralism in Cambodia. Since the late 1950s, the government had been unstable because of recurrent abortive coups and assassina-

---

[30] PMO 11/3418, 17 June 1960 (Note by Lord Selkirk for Mr Selwyn Lloyd). Lord Selkirk thought it was time for all Borneo territories to be combined into one country, which would be a realisation of the British original blueprint.
[31] CO 1030/982, no 498C, 24 August 1961 (Letter from Lord Selkirk to Mr Macleod).
[32] Tunku Abdul Rahman, Speech in the House of Representatives in Malaya, 16 October 1961.
[33] DC 35/10019, no 12, E/3, 22 December 1958 (Note by M MacDonald of his talks with Tunku Abdul Rahman on 20 December).
[34] CO 1030/973, no E203, 9 May 1961 (Memorandum by Lee Kuan Yew for the Government of the Federation of Malaya).
[35] Tunku Abdul Rahman, Speech in the House of Representatives in Malaya, 16 October 1961.
[36] CO 1030/973, no E203, 9 May 1961 (Memorandum by Lee Kuan Yew for the Government of the Federation of Malaya).
[37] Ibid. The persuasion to the Tunku was also made by Tun Abdul Razak and the British government. For the detail, see CO 1030/986, no 959, 18 October 1961 (Letter from P B C Moore to W I J Wallace).
[38] 'Singapore could be more dangerous outside the Federation than in would be inside' (R. S. Milne, 'Malaysia, Confrontation and Maphilindo', p. 405). The abrupt unease drove Tunku Abdul Rahman to seek the possibility of merger with Singapore. The Tunku and the leaders of Singapore reached the agreement that 'merger with Singapore [was] an essential part of the Malaysia idea'. See Tunku Abdul Rahman, Speech in the House of Representatives in Malaya, 16 October 1961.

tions.³⁹ Prince Sihanouk strengthened the crackdown on rebels and the government became increasingly autocratic.⁴⁰ In Laos, a simmering civil war between three groups had been continuing since the Geneva Conference of 1954, which later on became 'an international hot war',⁴¹ adopting the bipolar structure of the international conflict between the Soviet Union and the United States, so foreign Communist elements remained present there.

In South Vietnam, the President of the Republic of Vietnam (South Vietnam), Ngo Dinh Diem, having full support from the US, was oppressing the remnants of the Communist groups.⁴² Since January 1959, the Diem regime, which did not have a strong political basis in South Vietnam, had suffered from anti-government riots at home. The rebels were supported by the Democratic Republic of Vietnam (North Vietnam), and successfully made bases in South Vietnam. The rebels then formed the National Liberation Front in December 1960, and its activities were expanded. The US interpreted the situation through a Cold War lens and viewed all anti-government activities as Communist plots.⁴³ Vice President Lyndon B. Johnson visited Saigon in May 1961 and decided to give military aid to the South Vietnamese government.⁴⁴ The precarious conditions in Indochina continued to be evident after the Geneva Conference in 1954. In addition, the penetration and expansion of Communist activities were 'very real and pressing'.⁴⁵ In particular, the situation in Indochina was influenced by external powers, such as the US, the Soviet Union and China. The unforeseeable circumstances in the neighbouring countries were also a factor prompting Malaya to proceed with the Malaysia plan in order to build up its national strength.⁴⁶

The reaction from potential claimants
In the period immediately after the Tunku's announcement of May 1961, neither Indonesia nor the Philippines raised any objections. Indonesia's reaction was 'not unfriendly'.⁴⁷ In August, Lord Selkirk visited Indonesia in order to exchange views on the Malaysia plan. Subandrio, the Indonesian Foreign Minister, purportedly said that Indonesia was 'agreeable to the plan'.⁴⁸ Lord Selkirk was an ardent advocate of the 'crash programme' of Malaysia for the sake of regional security.⁴⁹ However, the British government needed to consider two issues. Firstly, Sabah and Sarawak needed more time to develop sufficient internal political consciousness to decide their own future.⁵⁰ The second, and more pressing, issue was that of regional security. Given the un-

---

³⁹ Yumio Sakurai, 'Senjyou kara Shijyou he: Gekidou no Indoshina [From the Battle Field to the Market: Indochina in Turbulence]', in Yoneo Ishii and Yumio Sakurai (eds.), *Tounan Ajia Shi I [History of Southeast Asia I]* (Tokyo: Yamakawa Syuppan, 1999), p. 447.
⁴⁰ Ibid.
⁴¹ Ibid, p. 449. Author's translation.
⁴² Ibid, p. 453.
⁴³ Ibid.
⁴⁴ Milton C. Taylor, 'South Vietnam: Lavish Aid and Limited Progress', *Pacific Affairs*, 34/3 (Autumn, 1961), pp. 242-243.
⁴⁵ Emmanuel Pelaez, Speech in the 1134th Plenary Meeting of the United Nations General Assembly, 27 September 1962.
⁴⁶ Richard Butwell, 'Malaysia and Its Impact on the International Relations of Southeast Asia', *Asian Survey*, 4/7 (July 1964), pp. 940-941.
⁴⁷ *Malaya /Indonesia Relations: 31ˢᵗ August, 1957 to 15ᵗʰ September, 1963* (Kuala Lumpur: The government of Malaysia, 1963), p. 11.
⁴⁸ Howard Palfrey Jones, Howard Palfrey, *Indonesia: The Possible Dream* (New York: Harcourt Brace Jovanovich, 1971), p. 266.
⁴⁹ Especially, his view was based on Singapore's unpredictable political environment. See CO 1030/983, no 615, 16 September 1961 ('Crash programme for "Greater Malaysia"').
⁵⁰ An editorial in local newspapers, *North Borneo* and *Sabah Times*, on 11July 1961 showed the cold response. 'Whoever has been responsible for briefing the Tunku to the extent where he declared that "reaction among the people of Brunei and Sarawak – except the Party Rakyat – was quite favourable" to his idea that the Borneo territories should join the Federation of Malaysia as states and not as nations, should

stable conditions in Laos and Vietnam at that time, there was 'an absolute necessity for Britain to maintain confidence' in Southeast Asia as a vital member of the Southeast Asia Treaty Organisation (SEATO).[51] In communication with the British Prime Minister, Harold Macmillan, Malayan Prime Minister Tunku Abdul Rahman 'detected the note of anxiety over Singapore bases for he is a little hesitant on the idea of giving up their base for SEATO purposes'.[52] Britain assured member states that its bases in Singapore could continue to be used for SEATO. Malaya, however, was not a SEATO member, and seemed unlikely to become one in the future. Therefore, the future of the bases after Singapore's incorporation into Malaysia was uncertain at the time.[53]

The Malayan government needed to solve two issues in order to materialise the 'Grand Design' of the merger. Encouraged by Lord Selkirk's statement that 'the time has come',[54] the Malaya government held a series of meetings with London. Six months after the Tunku's first announcement, the two countries signed a basic agreement on the Malaysia scheme. They recognised that the Malaysia plan should be developed further because it was 'desirable and practicable'.[55] In the Joint Statement on 23 November 1961,

> Before coming to any final decision it is necessary to ascertain the views of the peoples of North Borneo [Sabah] and Sarawak. … At the same time the views of the Sultan of Brunei are being sought. … In regard to defence matters, it was decided that in the event of the formation of the proposed Federation of Malaysia the existing defence agreement between Britain and Malaya should be extended to embrace the other territories concerned. It was however agreed that the Government of the Federation of Malaysia will afford to the Government of the United Kingdom the right to continue to maintain bases at Singapore for the purpose of assisting in the defence of Malaysia and for Commonwealth defence and for the preservation of peace in South East Asia.[56]

The British role as a SEATO member was specified in the statement, so that Britain could continue to use the bases in Singapore to maintain security in Southeast Asia as a whole. Thus the British demand for a Southeast Asian bulwark against communism was integrated into the Malaysia plan.

Indonesian Foreign Minister Subandrio gave a speech at the United Nations General Assembly on 20 November 1961, and announced that Indonesia would not oppose the plan as long as the local people supported it:

> [W]hen Malaya told us of its intentions to merge with the three [sic] British Crown Colonies of Sarawak, Brunei and British North Borneo as one Federation, we told them that we had no objections and that we wished them success with this merger so that everyone might live in

---

be given the sack. Such a declaration is naïve in the extreme, for whom did the Tunku meet while he was in Brunei and Sarawak?'. (Peter Boyce (ed.), *Malaysia and Singapore in International Diplomacy*, pp. 8-9.)

[51] Tunku Abdul Rahman, Speech in the House of Representatives in Malaya, 16 October 1961.

[52] Ibid.

[53] The British thought that their major commitment to SEATO was an 'essential' for the regional defence in Southeast Asia. (CAB 128/35/2, CC 63(61)6, 16 November 1961 (Cabinet Conclusions on Discussions of the Project).) However, Malaya influenced by Indonesia preferred neutrality (Peter G. Edwards, *Crises and Commitments: The Politics and Diplomacy of Australia's Involvement in Southeast Asian Conflicts 1948-1965* (North Sydney: Allen and Unwin, 1992), pp. 188-189). As the Tunku said, 'we are not in SEATO'. See Tunku Abdul Rahman, Statement in Malayan Legislative Council, 11 December 1958.

[54] CO 1030/982, no 498C, 24 August 1961 (Letter from Lord Selkirk to Mr Macleod).

[55] Ibid.

[56] Joint Statement by the Governments of the United Kingdom and the Federation of Malaya, 23 November 1961.

peace and freedom. ...[W]e had no objection to such a merger, based upon the will for freedom of the peoples concerned.[57]

In early December 1961, the Indonesian Prime Minister, Raden Djuanda Kartawidjaja, said to the American Ambassador to Indonesia, Howard Palfrey Jones,[58] that Indonesia would be happy to have an independent neighbouring country instead of a British-influenced country.[59]

One month after the Joint Statement between Britain and Malaya was issued, the Indonesian Communist Party (PKI) showed its disapproval. The PKI resolutions of 1961 were 'one of the key factors in any assessment of the motivations of Indonesian policy towards Malaysia'.[60] The resolution indirectly criticised that Joint Statement because of the threat of external intervention in regional security. The PKI also pointed out that Malaysia 'will grant the United Kingdom the right to continue to use its war bases in Singapore' and consequently help 'SEATO activities which are also aimed against Indonesia, a country that does not like SEATO'.[61] However, Sukarno did not react to the PKI's statement at this stage.[62]

Britain appointed Lord Cobbold as a head of the Commission of Enquiry, and his team completed the fact-finding visit in Sabah and Sarawak between February and April 1962.[63] The result was not strongly supportive of Malaysia:[64] One-third of respondents were strongly in favour of joining the Federation of Malaysia and another one-third was supportive of doing so only under certain conditions. However, up to 20 % of those polled advocated independence and self-government.[65] These results nevertheless formed the basis of a Joint Statement delivered by the British and Malayan Ministers on 1 August 1962, following a series of meetings in London. The statement concluded that 'the Commission were [sic] unanimously agreed that a Federation of Malaysia is in the best interests of North Borneo and Sarawak'.[66] It was decided that the date of the establishment would be 31 August 1963.

At that time, after a long campaign against the Netherlands, Indonesia had already successfully incorporated the territory of West Irian. Just after the end of the campaign, in September 1962, Indonesian Foreign Minister Subandrio voiced his country's negative attitude towards Malaysia for the first time. He expressed his apprehension about foreign bases on Borneo Island: 'If Malaysia should permit a military base to be established there [British Northern Bor-

---

[57] Subandrio, Speech in the United Nations General Assembly on 20 November 1961. It has been argued by scholars that this speech was the evidence that Indonesia was not negative towards the Malaysia plan; however, his last sentence, 'we had no objection to such a merger, based upon the will for freedom of the peoples concerned', seems to express a passive attitude towards the plan.

[58] He is regarded by Sukarno as 'one of the few Westerners who really understood him and Indonesia' (Roger Hilsman, *To Move A Nation: The Politics of Foreign Policy in the Administration of John F. Kennedy* (Garden City, NY: Doubleday, 1967), p. 372).

[59] Howard Palfrey Jones, *Indonesia*, p. 266.

[60] *Malaya /Indonesia Relations*, p. 12.

[61] Resolutions of the Indonesian Communist Party, December 1961, in Peter Boyce (ed.), *Malaysia and Singapore in International Diplomacy*, pp. 68-69.

[62] This is because Indonesia was completely engaged in the final stages of its West Irian Campaign.

[63] The team was known as the Cobbold Commission. The Commission was formed on the agreement between Britain and Malaya on 23 November 1961. Both governments sent two representatives respectively as members of staff to Cobbold.

[64] Incomplete support from the inhabitants later became the cause of Britain's irritation with the UN's enquiry there in August 1963. See DC 169/216, no 176, 27 August 1963 (Inward Telegram SOSLON 62 from Mr Sandys to CRO), paragraph 7.

[65] For the detail of the report, see, The British Government, Report of the Commission of Enquiry, North Borneo and Sarawak, August 1962, in Department of Foreign Affairs, Australia (ed.), *Malaysia*, pp. 61-102.

[66] Joint Public Statement Issued by the British and Malayan Governments, 1 August 1962, in Department of Foreign Affairs, Australia (ed.), *Malaysia*, pp. 104-105.

neo territories] we are certain to take counter-action'.[67] He also indicated his concern about self-determination of the area: 'The Malaysia scheme is not the business of the Indonesian Government as long as 'everything goes on smoothly'.[68] He continued, '[b]ut if things go wrong then we must take notice to protect our own interests'.[69] However, the reluctant warning from Indonesia was issued only once. In November 1962, Mr Ruslan Abdul Gani, the Vice Chairman of the Indonesian Supreme Advisory Council, purportedly said that he saw both 'positive and negative points' in the Malaysia plan.[70] However, he said, 'Personally, I welcome any new country around us that wants to get rid of colonial chains'.[71]

It should be noted that, initially, an official opposition to the plan did not come from Indonesia, but from the Philippines. The Philippine president, Diosdado Macapagal,[72] initiated a claim to dominion over Sabah just after he took over the office from Carlos P. Garcia in January 1962.[73] During his successful presidential campaign, Macapagal criticised the Garcia administration for not taking an independent foreign policy. In addition, ever since the Garcia era, the Philippines had sought to change its identity from an appendage of the US to a genuinely independent Asian country.[74] Macapagal utilised the Sabah issue for highlighting the fact that his foreign policy is significantly different from his predecessor's, although the claim was lodged 'without adequate research or consideration of consequences'.[75]

In addition, as Gordon argues, the Sabah claim was also 'a catalyst in Manila's turn' towards Jakarta so that the Philippines could secure amicable diplomatic relations with Indonesia. He continues:

[N]ot only did it provide a reason for closer association with Indonesia, but it also helped to revive certain latent political currents in the Philippines. In the broadest sense, these currents

---

[67] *The Straits Times*, 27 September 1962.

[68] Ibid.

[69] Ibid.

[70] *Malaya /Indonesia Relations*, p. 13.

[71] Ibid.

[72] Macapagal had posed the question of the Sabah dominion while working as a government official in late 1940s. He consulted the American legal advisor and got the positive comment on it. Macapagal successfully passed a bill to the Philippine congress in 1950 when he became a member of the congress. For the detail, see Gerald Sussman, 'Macapagal, the Sabah Claim and Maphilindo: The Politics of Penetration', *Journal of Contemporary Asia*, 13/2 (1983), p. 212.

[73] The issue, on which the Sabah claim was based, initiated in January 1878 after the Sultan of Sulu sent the permission document to the British North Borneo Company, which exercised the administration power there until Sabah was taken over as a British Crown colony in 1946, for the use of the land. For the official view of the Philippine government, see *Philippine Claim to North Borneo (Sabah) Volume I*, (First reprint, Manila: Bureau of Printing, 1968). For the official view of the Malayan government, see *Malaya/Philippine Relations: 31st August, 1957 to 15th September, 1963* (The Government of Malaysia, 1963). Quite a few scholarly contributions to the issue of the dominion of Sabah have been published. See, for example, Lela Garner Noble, *Philippine Policy toward Sabah: A Claim to Independence* (Tucson, AZ: The University of Arizona Press, 1977); and Michael Leifer, *The Philippine Claim to Sabah*.

[74] Alejandro M. Fernandez, *The Philippines and The United States: The Forging of New Relations* (Quezon City: NSDB-UP Integrated Research Program, 1977), p. 247. However, the main focus of his foreign policy was still 'to enlarge economic relations with the United States'. (Gerald Sussman, 'Macapagal, the Sabah Claim and Maphilindo', p. 220.)

[75] Lela Garner Noble, 'The National Interest and the National Image: Philippine Policy in Asia', *Asian Survey*, 13/6 (June 1973), P. 565. The claim 'did not present a Philippine consensus'. (Ibid, p. 563.) Macapagal aimed to be re-elected for unprecedented second term as a Philippine president. In this context, he thought claiming Sabah was useful to forge the Philippine identity and reinforce his support among the people. See Gerald Sussman, 'Macapagal, the Sabah Claim and Maphilindo', p. 211.

represent the widespread desire among articulate and informed Filipinos to be accepted in Asia as Asians rather than as an "Asian branch" of the United States.[76]

On 5 April 1962, the Philippine Vice-President and Secretary of Foreign Affairs, Emmanuel Pelaez,[77] visited Kuala Lumpur to talk with Malayan Prime Minister Tunku Abdul Rahman to clarify the Malayan view on the issue of Sabah. The Tunku had taken a passive position at this time, saying that the Philippines' claim should be addressed to Britain, which had sovereignty over Sabah.[78] He also said that Malaya would incorporate Sabah only if the latter did not have any unsettle issues.[79] When the Filipino House of Representatives unanimously approved the bill for claiming dominion over Sabah on 24 April 1962, the British Ambassador in Manila handed a formal diplomatic note to the Philippine government. The note cautioned that the Philippines' claim would retard healthy development of politics in Sabah and that it might trigger off similar claims from other countries resulting in regional disturbances. The document further warned that such a claim would spoil the Malaysia plan. In addition, it would have ill-effects on the SEATO allies (Britain and the Philippines) and give rise to insecurity in Southeast Asia.[80]

Despite this warning, at a press conference on 22 June 1962, Macapagal formally stated that the Philippines did have a legal right to claim Sabah.[81] The Philippines claim was soon rejected by the representatives of the potential federation members of Malaysia,[82] which claimed it was baseless.[83] Macapagal's next strategy was, as announced in a press conference on 27 July, to propose 'a Greater Malayan Confederation', which would incorporate the Philippines into the proposed Malaysia federation.[84] However, both Malaya and Britain did not pay any attention to it.[85] Then the Philippine government sent a protest to the two governments on 2 August. Two months later, Malaya responded to the Philippines, saying that Malaya would proceed with developing the original Malaysia plan, and that it had received British confirmation that the Sabah issue was not negotiable.[86]

On 27 September 1962, Philippine Vice-President Emmanuel Pelaez gave a speech on the claim to Sabah at the United Nations General Assembly:

I have in mind particularly the claim of my Government to the territory of North Borneo [Sabah] which was annexed by the British Crown in 1946. This is neither the time nor the place to go into the details of this question, but we stand on what we consider to be valid le-

---

[76] Bernard K. Gordon, *The Dimensions of Conflict in Southeast Asia*, p. 21.
[77] Pelaez was 'not enthusiastic' about the claim. (Lela Garner Noble, 'The national Interest and the National Image', p. 563.)
[78] However, after the Philippines lodged the formal protest against Britain, Malaya notified the postponement of a meeting of the ASA in December 1962.
[79] Diosdado Macapagal, Statement of President Macapagal Proposing the Formation of a Malayan Confederation, 27 July 1962.
[80] H. B. Jacobini, 'Fundamentals of Philippine Policy towards Malaysia', *Asian Survey*, 4/11 (November, 1964), pp. 1144-1145.
[81] Susumu Yamakage, *ASEAN*, p. 59.
[82] The members were Malaya, Singapore, Sabah, Sarawak and Brunei.
[83] Susumu Yamakage, *ASEAN*, p. 60.
[84] Diosdado Macapagal, Statement of President Macapagal Proposing the Formation of a Malayan Confederation, 27 July 1962. Butwell points out that the Philippines' sentiment on pan-Malay federation was not first conceived by Macapagal. The late Philippine President, Manuel Quezon, had envisaged a federation with Indonesia and Malaya before the Second World War. (Richard Butwell, 'Malaysia and Its Impact on the International Relations of Southeast Asia', p. 943.)
[85] Susumu Yamakage, *ASEAN*, p. 62.
[86] For the correspondence between two countries, see Aide Me moiré Dated 2nd August 1962 Handed by Philippine Vice-President Emmanuel Pelaez to H. M. M. Ambassador in Malaya; and Aide Me moiré Dated 3rd October 1962 Handed by Permanent Secretary for External Affairs to Philippine Ambassador in Kuala Lumpur.

gal and historical grounds. Our claim has been put forward with sincere assurances of our desire that the issue should be settled by peaceful means, and without prejudice to the exercise of the right of self-determination by the inhabitants of North Borneo, preferably under United Nations auspices.[87]

However, he failed to secure support for it. Relations between the two countries worsened and the second Foreign Ministerial conference of the Association of Southeast Asia (ASA) of December was cancelled by Malaya.[88]

Starting the verbal war
The turning point in Indonesia's attitude towards the Malaysia plan was the Brunei rebellion of December 1962. Directed by A. M. Azahari bin Sheikh Mahmud,[89] the revolt itself was trivial.[90] Azahari, who was in Manila, directed the North Borneo National Army (TUNK) to rebel against its incorporation into Malaysia and declared itself the independent Unitary State of North Borneo (NKKU).[91] Rebellions occurred sporadically all over Brunei, including in the border regions of Sarawak; however, they were suppressed within a week by the British forces. On 9 December, the Indonesian Defence Minister, General Abdul Haris Nasution, alerted the people to the incident in Brunei.[92] In addition, on 11 December, an Indonesian political Party, Partindo, sent a supportive message to the Brunei Party Rakyat: 'We are at your side in the people's revolution you lead. Mobilise all your strength. Once revolution blasts, let it proceed till final victory'.[93] The Indonesian government, however, did not provide any official view on the rebellion.[94] Indonesian President Sukarno briefly referred to it, but in the context of the New Emerging Forces, in his speech at the State banquet in Jakarta for Yugoslav Vice President Edvard Karadelj: 'What is happening in Brunei has something to do with new emerging forces and the movement will come out as victor'.[95] He continued, 'This movement will change the world and make the people live in happiness'.[96]

Subsequently, Malaya instigated a verbal war with Indonesia. The statement by Malayan Premier Tunku Abdul Rahman on 11 December is said to have been the catalyst, even though it was 'extremely brief and oblique'.[97] While there was no clear evidence of Indonesia's involvement in the plot,[98] the Tunku was 'over-excited about Indonesian complicity',[99] and implied that

---

[87] Emmanuel Pelaez, Speech in the 1134th Plenary Meeting of the United Nations General Assembly, 27 September 1962.
[88] Both the Philippines and Malaya were the members of the ASA.
[89] He was a Brunei Malay and was born in a family having relationship with the Sultan of Brunei. He joined Indonesian revolution while he was a student of the Bogor veterinary school in Indonesia. He was 'considerably influenced by the radical and anti-colonialist political philosophies' there. See J. A. C. Mackie, *Konfrontasi*, p. 113. When he came back to Brunei in 1951, he was opposed to get in by the British because '[h]aving taken part in the Indonesian revolution, Azahari was regarded as a Sukarno-phile, an exponent of revolutionary ideology, and politically undesirable'. See Greg Poulgrain, *The Genesis of Konfrontasi: Malaysia, Brunei and Indonesia, 1945-1965* (Bathurst, NSW: Crawford House Publishing, 1998), p. 87.
[90] J. A. C. Mackie, *Konfrontasi*, p. 111.
[91] Jamie S. Davidson and Douglas Kammen, 'Indonesia's Unknown War and the Lineages of Violence in West Kalimantan', *Indonesia*, 73 (Apr., 2002), p. 55.
[92] *The Straits Times*, 11 December 1962.
[93] Ibid. *Partindo* is said to be an 'influential party' in Indonesian politics.
[94] J. A. C. Mackie, *Konfrontasi*, p. 122.
[95] *The Straits Times*, 12 December 1962.
[96] Ibid.
[97] J. A. C. Mackie, *Konfrontasi*, p.123.
[98] CO 1030/1466, ff103-105, 15 December 1962 (Memorandum on the Brunei Rising by Sir D White for Lord Selkirk).

the Indonesian government had sent aid to the revolt.[100] The leader of the Sabah Alliance Party, Donald Stephens, was certain of Indonesia's involvement in the revolt, and stated that the leaders of the rebellion had some connections with the PKI.[101] In addition, other 'indiscreet statements' about Indonesia's involvement, appeared in the Malayan press.[102]

In response to Malaya's accusations, on 14 December the Indonesian government officially denied its involvement in the Brunei revolt. Moreover, it began to rebut Malayan criticism: the Tunku's allegation was 'very provocative'.[103] Indonesian Foreign Minister Subandrio also reacted, 'If the Tunku is determined to use any occasion and any opportunity to be hostile towards Indonesia, for us there is no alternative other than to accept the challenge'.[104] Malaya lodged a formal protest with the Indonesian government over this statement. The Tunku, maintaining his position, commented, 'So long as words are used against us, we will return the compliments in full measure'.[105] The Indonesian government responded, 'We take side with the people who are struggling'.[106] In addition, President Sukarno offered Indonesian support to the Brunei rebels by saying that those who did not support the revolt were 'traitors to their own souls'.[107] In early January 1963, Indonesia requested that Britain should consider the Bruneian objection to the Malaysian plan. The Indonesian delegation visited the British Embassy in Jakarta and conveyed Indonesia's sympathy with the Brunei rebellion to the Ambassador, Sir Leslie Fry.[108] Furthermore, the Indonesian government showed its intention to send volunteers to Brunei to support its fight for independence.[109] This provoked the Tunku's underlying suspiciousness towards Indonesia, and he complained that Indonesia was 'trying to prevent the formation of Malay-

---

[99] TR 225/2551, 20 December 1962 (Letter from Lord Selkirk to Mr Macmillan). He is by nature 'extremely sensitive to personal criticism'. (Harry Miller, *Prince and Premier*, p. 211.) In the course of the verbal war, the Americans, Australians and New Zealanders pointed out his sensitivity in the quadripartite talks of February 1963 (among Britain, the US, Australia and New Zealand) that 'the Tunku must be asked to restrain his language during the present difficult period'. In addition, 'they would want him to make some statemanlike gesture such as resuming discussion' with the Philippines. (FO 371/169695, no 23, 12 February 1963 (Inward Telegram no 482 from Sir D Ormsby-Gore to Lord Home).) On the other hand, the Tunku pointed out Sukarno's oversensitivity: 'He [Sukarno] is very sensitive. It is hard for one to realise how sensitive he is. The slightest thing can make him very angry'. (*The Straits Times*, 6 June 1963.) The background of the Tunku's sensitivity towards Indonesia stems from antagonistic bilateral history and the size of Indonesia in addition to his personality. The Tunku later disclosed his fear for Indonesia's largeness in his speech. See Tunku Abdul Rahman, Speech at the Opening of the Commonwealth Prime Ministers' Conference, 6 September 1966.

[100] Roger Hilsman, for example, saw that Azahari 'had undoubtedly obtained some covert support from the Indonesians'. See Roger Hilsman, *To Move A Nation*, p. 386.

[101] *The Straits Times*, 12 December 1962. The similar view was thrown from Sir D White, the High Commissioner of Brunei in his communication with Duncan Sandys, the British Secretary of State for Commonwealth Relations. See CO 1030/1076, no 6, 20 December 1962 (Despatch from Sir D White to Mr Sandys), paragraph 28.

[102] Roger Hilsman, *To Move A Nation*, p. 387.

[103] *The Straits Times*, 15 December 1962.

[104] *The Straits Times*, 17 December 1962.

[105] *The Straits Times*, 2 January 1963.

[106] *The Straits Times*, 15 December 1962.

[107] *The Straits Times*, 20 December 1962. As Lord Selkirk said in his letter to Iain Norman Macleod, the British Secretary of State for colonies, in August 1961, three Borneo territories were 'quite unfitted as yet to enter an association of this sort on the basis of popular representation.' Lack of political awareness was making the inhabitants of Sabah and Sarawak particularly unequipped to express opinion on the Malaysia plan. Lord Selkirk said, 'I should give Sarawak about ten years and North Borneo at least twenty years before a clear-cut electoral opinion could be given on this subject'. See CO 1030/982, no 498C, 24 August 1961 (Letter from Lord Selkirk to Mr Macleod).

[108] *The Straits Times*, 5 January 1963.

[109] *The Straits Times*, 22 January 1963.

sia'.[110]

On 20 January 1963, the Indonesian Foreign Minister finally declared *Konfrontasi*: Indonesia's intention to confront Malaya:

> This time I will mention our neighbour, Malaya, against which, whether we like it or not, we have to pursue a policy of confrontation. I very much regret we have to adopt such a policy, because until now we have always considered Malaya as friends, as a brother. Because of this fact we have always taken a passive attitude against all agitations she has been inciting against us. But, of course, there is a limit.[111]

Indonesia also criticised Malaya by saying that the latter had become Britain's 'tools of colonialism'.[112] Subandrio later said, 'It is a great pity that the leaders in Malaya have not yet realised that they are being played with by foreign power and control'.[113]

From the Philippine side, the talks between the British Ambassador in Manila, John Pilcher, and Philippine Vice-President Emmanuel Pelaez were held in late December 1962 after the rebellion in Brunei, but '[n]o mention was made of the claim' there.[114] Subsequently, the British and Philippine governments agreed that they would exchange views on the matter of regional security in January 1963. On 28 January 1963, a week after Subandrio's declaration of *Konfrontasi*, Philippine President Macapagal gave a speech in the Philippine congress:

> Our claim to North Borneo [Sabah] cannot be less than the claim of Malaya to the territory not only on the basis of superior judicial and historic rights but in the vital interest of our national security. ... Malaya has no valid claim or right to take over North Borneo. ... It is vital to the security of the Philippines that North Borneo be not placed under the sovereignty and jurisdiction of another State [Malaya], ... [T]he people of North Borneo should be given an opportunity to determine whether they would wish to be independent or whether they would wish to be a part of the Philippines or be placed under another state.[115]

On the same day as Macapagal's speech, representatives of Britain and the Philippines met in London.[116] Following Macapagal's statement, the Philippine representatives raised objection to the Malaysia plan at the conference.[117] The British forced the Philippines to set aside its claim to Sabah for the sake of stability in Southeast Asia.[118] When the Malayan press accused

---

[110] *The Straits Times*, 4 January 1963.

[111] Subandrio, Speech to Mahakarta Regiment in Jogjyakarta, 20 January 1963.

[112] Ibid. In Western Europe, Charles de Gaulle, the French President, had a rift with the West and approached the Soviet Union. John F. Kennedy, the American President, appealed to de Galle: 'We can't possibly survive if Europe and the United States are isolated'. (*The Straits Times*, 26 January 1963.) Mackie points out that the international environment at that time gave a room for Sukarno to begin antagonism against Britain. Indonesia as well as France could 'thumb their noses at the super-powers to a quite unprecedented degree'. See J. A. C. Mackie, *Konfrontasi*, p. 334.

[113] Subandrio, *Indonesia's Foreign Policy* (Jakarta: The Government of the Republic of Indonesia, 1964?), p. 24. He said in the declaration of Indonesia's confrontation on 20 January 1963: 'What is to be regretted is that the confrontation policy has to be adopted against an Asian country, a neighbouring country'. See Subandrio, Speech to Mahakarta Regiment in Jogjyakarta, 20 January 1963.

[114] Michael Leifer, *The Philippine Claim to Sabah*, p. 40.

[115] Diosdado Macapagal, Address before the Joint Session of the Congress of the Philippines, 28 January 1963.

[116] Michael Leifer, *The Philippine Claim to Sabah*, p. 43

[117] The US gave 'little indication of support'. (Ibid, p. 43.)

[118] It is noteworthy that Macapagal proposed to hold the plebiscite under the UN, which would become one of main questions in the Manila conference in June 1963, for the first time in his speech on 28 January 1963: 'Such referendum, however, should be authentic and bona fide by holding it under conditions, preferably supervised by the United Nations, that would insure effective freedom to the people of North Bor-

the Philippine government of giving refuge to Azahari after the revolt, Macapagal reacted harshly, and called Malaysia 'the new colonial power'.[119] The Tunku expressed his resentment by cancelling his visit to Manila.[120] However, in March, the Philippines took a more balanced position and tried to ease the tension between Indonesia and Malaya, when relations between the two countries became particularly strained.[121] Although the Philippines did not want to be a mediator, it nonetheless opened the possibility of holding a tripartite conference.[122] Its position swung between a 'partisan and peacemaker' in the course of the three-sided dispute until 1966.[123]

Indonesian Foreign Minister Subandrio objected to the federation plan of Malaysia because Indonesia supported the revolt.[124] He said that Indonesia would give its 'full assistance' to the Brunei revolt to defeat the Malaysia plan.[125] On 13 February 1963, one day after Subandrio's statement, President Sukarno made a speech at the opening of the conference of National Front committees in Jakarta, saying:

> Malaysia is a manifestation of neo-colonialism. We do not want to have neo-colonialism in our vicinity. We consider Malaysia an encirclement of the Indonesian Republic. Malaysia is the product of the brain and efforts of neo-colonialism… For this reason, we are determinedly opposed, without any reservation, against Malaysia.[126]

Although several aggressive statements were issued by Indonesia,[127] its military activity was limited and no major actions were undertaken toward Malaya.[128] Malaya naturally reciprocated

---

neo to express their true and enlightened will'. (Diosdado Macapagal, Address before the Joint Session of the Congress of the Philippines, 28 January 1963.)

[119] *The Straits Times*, 29 January 1963.

[120] *The Straits Times*, 2 February 1963.

[121] It is pointed out that the personalities of the Tunku and Sukarno accelerated the verbal war between two countries. See, for example, Roger Hilsman, *To Move A Nation*, p. 391. The Earl of Home, the British Secretary of Foreign Affairs, also pointed out the problem of the blunt language they had in the early stage of *Konfrontasi*. See 'Ikeda Souri to Hyuumu Ei Gaisyou tono Kaidan Youshi [The proceedings of the talks of Prime Minister Ikeda with British Foreign Secretary, Earl of Hume]', Ou-A-kyoku, Eirenpou-ka [Department of the Commonwealth of Nations, Bureau of Eurasia, Ministry of Foreign Affairs of Japan], 2 April 1963, GSK File A'-411. The personality clash between Sukarno and the Tunku was studied by Gordon. See Bernard K. Gordon, *The Dimensions of Conflict in Southeast Asia*, pp. 129-132.

[122] Arnold C. Brackman, *Southeast Asia's Second Front*, p. 180.

[123] Lela Garner Noble, *Philippine Policy toward Sabah*, p. 119.

[124] At the end of January 1963, the United Nations Secretary-General, U Thant, said, '[T]he situation in South-east Asia, particularly in the area surrounding Brunei, has potentialities of becoming very serious'. He sent the UN Under-Secretary Chakravarthi V. Narashmhan to the three British Borneo territories on a fact-finding assignment. (*The Straits Times*, 31 January 1963.)

[125] *The Straits Times*, 14 February 1963.

[126] Sukarno, Speech at the Opening of the Conference of National Front Committees in Jakarta, 13 February 1963, in George Modelski (ed.), *The New Emerging Forces: Documents on the Ideology of Indonesian Foreign Policy* (Documents and Data Paper No. 2, Canberra: Department of International Relations, Research School of Pacific Studies, Institute of Advanced Studies, The Australian National University, 1963), pp. 74-77.

[127] For example, Major General Achmad Jani, the Army Chief of Staff, said that the Indonesian Army was 'awaiting the order' from the President to support Indonesia joining the Brunei rebellion. See *The Straits Times*, 2 February 1963. Subandrio also implied the possibility of armed conflicts if Sabah and Sarawak would be under the control of Malaya. (*The Straits Times*, 12 February 1963.)

[128] *The Straits Times*, 26 January and 12 February 1963. It is obvious that Indonesia tried to secure its regional leadership and to exclude the British influence by using the method of West Irian Campaign, the so-called 'coercive diplomacy'. See Michael Leifer, *Indonesia's Foreign Policy* (London, Boston and Sydney: George Allen and Unwin, 1983), p. 61. Brackman gives the same argument that Sukarno was tempted

Indonesia's aggressive statements. In February, Tun Abdul Razak, the Malayan Deputy Prime Minister, said that Malaya was 'determined to defend the nation at whatever cost'.[129]

Tunku Abdul Rahman tried to justify Malaya's struggle against Indonesia. He asserted that Malaysia would surely 'safeguard the territories concerned from Communist domination', and he accused Indonesia of attempting to defeat this plan.[130] He emphasised that the Malaysia plan was welcomed by Western countries: 'The British and Australian governments have pledged to support us in the event of war resulting from Indonesia's confrontation policy towards Malaya'.[131] Tun Abdul Razak flew over to Washington to ask for support from President John F. Kennedy. The Tunku stated, '[T]he aspirations of the people of Malaysia are well supported and backed by our friends in the Commonwealth and the free world'.[132]

In Washington, quadripartite talks between Ambassadors were held in February 1963 in order to enhance western support for Malaysia. While Western powers agreed with the formation of Malaysia, they, with the exception of Britain, did not fully support the antagonistic attitude adopted by Malaya towards Indonesia.[133] The American, Australian and New Zealand governments indicated that they 'could not contemplate any military commitment' in the event of Indonesian infiltration.[134] These three countries told the British that they wished the British government to talk 'in the first place bilaterally with the Indonesians'.[135] The US, Australia and New Zealand also shared the view that Indonesia 'must not be pushed towards the Soviet Union'.[136] They were concerned about the chaotic situation emerging in Indochina[137] and tried not to complicate the Southeast Asian political climate by further pushing the Malaysia issue. In addition, in order to prevent Russian or Chinese intervention in the region, the US insisted that the West should 'leave Asia to the Asians'.[138] Indeed, the United States had maintained a position of 'non-involved cordiality' with regard to the Malaysia issue.[139]

Malaya sought to reduce tension with the Philippines by saying, 'The Philippines and Malaya are friends and brothers and are partners in the ASA'.[140] When Tun Abdul Razak came to Manila in March 1963 to attend the meeting of the United Nations Economic Commission for Asia and the Far East (ECAFE), he discussed matters of common interest with the Philippine leaders, although he reiterated that the territorial issue should be solved between the British and the Philippine governments. He said after the talks, 'I was very happy. I was received with friendship and goodwill'.[141] On the other hand, Malaya did not attempt to ease tension with its

---

to use the original methods again in the Malaysia issue. See Arnold C. Brackman, *Southeast Asia's Second Front*, p. 151.

[129] *The Straits Times*, 14 February 1963.
[130] *The Straits Times*, 12 March 1963.
[131] *The Straits Times*, 11 March 1963.
[132] *The Straits Times*, 12 March 1963.
[133] Sir D Ormsby-Gore, the British Ambassador to Washington, concluded in his memorandum to Lord Home by saying, '[W]e were not entirely successful in obtaining assurances' from the US, Australia and New Zealand in the quadripartite talks. See FO 371/169908, no 18, 15 February 1963 (Despatch from Sir D Ormsby-Gore to Lord Home).
[134] FO 371/169695, no 21, 11 February 1963 (Inward Telegram no 471 from Sir D Ormsby-Gore to Lord Home).
[135] FO 371/169695, no 23, 12 February 1963 (Inward Telegram no 482 from Sir D Ormsby-Gore to Lord Home).
[136] Peter G. Edwards, *Crises and Commitments*, p. 259.
[137] Communist power was growing in South Vietnam and disturbances were ongoing in Laos.
[138] George Modelski, 'Indonesia and the Malaysia Issue', *The Year Book of World Affairs*, 1964, p. 144.
[139] Committee on Foreign Relations, United States Senate 88th Congress, 1st Session, *Vietnam and Southeast Asia*, Report of Senators Mike Mansfield, J. Caleb Beggs, Claiborne Pell, Benjamin A. Smith in Peter Boyce (ed.), *Malaysia and Singapore in International Diplomacy*, p. 159. Actually, the US was happy for Indonesia to dominate the region. See George Modelski, *The Year Book of World Affairs*, p. 144.
[140] *The Straits Times*, 6 March 1963.
[141] *The Straits Times*, 11 March 1963.

relations with Indonesia. Tun Razak said, 'Why should I talk to him [Subandrio]? I have nothing to tell him. If he wants to talk to me, that's a different matter. After all, they started … [*Konfrontasi*]'.[142]

While Malaya attempted to secure support from Western countries, Indonesia kept 'an active and independent policy between the two blocs in the Cold War'.[143] Actually, it pretended to turn its support to the Communist side demonstrating intention to go to the Communist camp. This was intended to secure American support to Indonesia over the Malaysia issue.[144] In late March 1963, Subandrio invited the Russian Defence Minister, Marshal Rodion Malinovsky, and talked with him about 'the development of Indonesian armed forces and the present situation in Southeast Asia'.[145] In June of the same year, the Soviet Union offered Indonesia $US330 million worth of modern military equipment.[146] In addition, the Indonesian delegation talked on economic matters with the Soviet representatives in the Kremlin on 3 June 1963.[147] Although bilateral relations apparently became closer, the Soviet backing was moderate because of the détente in Europe.[148] Sukarno seemed to be closer to China in the ideological sphere. China praised Indonesia for opposing the 'neo-colonialist scheme of Malaysia and supporting the revolutionary struggle of the people of North Borneo'.[149] When the Chairman of China, Liu Shaoqi, was invited to Jakarta in April 1963, it was reported that Sukarno was seeking a new world order with China.[150] Liu said, 'China and Indonesia always help each other in the struggle for freedom and world peace and we will keep doing so'.[151]

Seeking peaceful coexistence

In Malaya, Tunku Abdul Rahman reportedly made a plan for talking with Philippine President Macapagal in late February 1963.[152] In Indonesia, on the other hand, Suwito Kusumowidagdo, the Indonesian Deputy Foreign Minister, visited Manila on 1 March and spoke with Salvador P. Lopez,[153] the Philippine Under-Secretary for Foreign Affairs, to seek the possibility of tripartite Summit talks.[154] However, a friendly atmosphere among the three countries had yet to be created. Macapagal blamed the architects of the Malaysia plan for not having consulted with Indone-

---

[142] *The Straits Times*, 5 March 1963.
[143] Subandrio, *Indonesia's Foreign Policy*, p. 19.
[144] Indonesia said that it would not fully rely on the Communist backing as it understood that the Communist side did not unite firmly due to the Sino-Soviet rift. (Subandrio, *Indonesia's Foreign Policy*, p. 21.) Indonesia often used the Communist card as a negotiating chip towards the US. Indonesia mentioned that it might offer its bases to the Soviet Union if British troops were stationed in Malaysia for encircling Indonesia. See, for example, *The Straits Times*, 27 September 1962; and 'Sukaruno Daitouryou no Tai Maleishia Kan ni Kansuru Ken [The report of President Sukarno's view on Malaysia]', Zai Indoneshia Taishi kara Gaimu Daijin he [From the Ambassador to Indonesia to Foreign Minister], Ministry of Foreign Affairs of Japan, 1 October 1963, GSK File A'-432.
[145] *The Straits Times*, 29 March 1963.
[146] *South China Morning Post*, 4 June 1963.
[147] *South China Morning Post*, 4 June 1963.
[148] George McT. Kahin, 'Malaysia and Indonesia', *Pacific Affairs*, 37/3 (Autumn 1964), p. 267.
[149] *The Straits Times*, 15 April 1963.
[150] When Sukarno called for the Third World to hold the international games, an alternative to the Olympic Games, China showed its support for joining. Sukarno later said, 'We are grateful for the fact that the People's Republic of China was the first country…to respond to our call'. See Sukarno, Speech at the State Banquet in Jakarta, 13 April 1963, in George Modelski (ed.), *The New Emerging Forces*, pp. 69-72.
[151] *The Straits Times*, 20 April 1963.
[152] *The Straits Times*, 25 February 1963.
[153] He was 'ideologically sympathetic to Indonesia and hostile to Britain and, by extension, Malaya'. (Lela Garner Noble, 'The national Interest and the National Image', p. 565.)
[154] *The Straits Times*, 2 March 1963. The proposal for the tripartite talks was first given by the Philippine Vice President, Emmanuel Pelaez, when he attended the conference with the British in January 1963 to talk over the regional security matter.

sia and the Philippines, and he said it would plant the 'seed of eternal discord'.[155] Tun Abdul Razak insisted that Indonesia should take the initiative for reconciliation, saying, 'I shall not meet him [Subandrio]. I have nothing to say' to him.[156] Subandrio, on the other hand, showed a conciliatory attitude: 'I hope we can settle this by peaceful means'.[157]

On 11 March, Macapagal formally announced that the Philippines would organise the tripartite exploratory conference. Macapagal's proposal was approved by Tun Razak and Subandrio respectively on 9 March while they were staying in Manila for the Economic Commission for Asia and the Far East (ECAFE).[158] The agenda of the proposed conference was:

1. Problems arising from the proposal to establish the Federation of Malaysia.
2. The promotion of fraternal and neighbourly relations among the Philippines, Indonesia and Malaya.
3. The maintenance of enduring peace and stability of South East Asia.[159]

On 13 March 1963, Subandrio presented two conditions for the tripartite talks: Malaya should clarify its relations with Indonesia (hostile or friendly), and it should guarantee that Malaysia would not intend to subvert Indonesia.[160] The Tunku quickly returned a positive reply to Indonesia: 'This suits us fine…With the establishment of Malaysia we hope we will be closer neighbours'.[161]

The exploratory conference at the undersecretary level was supposed to be followed by a Ministerial conference in early April, at the same time that the ASA Meeting would be held in Manila. It was Indonesia that showed its desire for quick reconciliation with Malaya at that time. Indonesian Deputy Foreign Minister Suwito Kusumowidagdo had continued to stay in Manila in anticipation of the meeting of undersecretaries since the time when Tun Abdul Razak and Subandrio agreed to hold it on 9 March. Although Suwito Kusumowidagdo had stayed in Manila for more than 10 days waiting for the Malayan delegation to arrive, the meeting could not take place because Malaya was still suspicious about the aim of the talks.[162] Eventually, Tunku Abdul Rahman came to Manila and exchanged views with Macapagal, when the ASA Meeting was held. The bilateral talks produced 'a number of salutary results', one of which was the Tunku's consent to participate in the tripartite conference.[163] An announcement from the Ministry of Foreign Affairs of the Philippines on 5 April said, 'As a first step towards this end, the President and the Tunku confirmed a previous agreement to hold a meeting between the three countries at undersecretary level in Manila tomorrow'.[164] However, the conference was not held until 9 April because the Indonesian delegation was delayed.[165]

After the second session of the conference on 10 April 1963, Suwito said: 'Prospects are brighter'.[166] The meeting was closed on 17 April, in an atmosphere of 'friendship and cordiali-

---

[155] *The Straits Times*, 11 March 1963.
[156] *The Straits Times*, 5 March 1963.
[157] *The Straits Times*, 9 March 1963.
[158] ECAFE was the regional development arm of the United Nations. It was established in 1947 in order to 'assist in post-war economic reconstruction'. In 1974, the name was changed to the Economic and Social Commission for Asia and the Pacific (ESCAP) in order to expand its role and coverage. Currently, the member countries are 62.
[159] Diosdado Macapagal, Statement at the Veterans' Memorial Hospital, 11 March 1963.
[160] *The Straits Times*, 15 March 1963.
[161] Ibid.
[162] FCO 51/154, no 15, 10 July 1970 (FCO Research Department Memorandum), paragraph 239.
[163] *The Straits Times*, 11 April 1963.
[164] *The Straits Times*, 5 April 1963.
[165] *The Straits Times*, 6 April 1963.
[166] *The Straits Times*, 11 April 1963.

ty'.[167] At the conference, they mainly focused on developing a fraternal relationship with a spirit of mutual respect and tolerance rather than highlighting the difference of views on Malaysia.[168] In conference's final communiqué, 'the representatives [were] aware that on them rested the responsibility of paving the way for closer fraternal relations among their common task in *a spirit of humility*'.[169] All sides behaved with restraint, created a friendly atmosphere and contributed to the advancement of the ministerial talks. The three countries agreed to hold a ministerial conference, to be followed by a Summit meeting.[170]

However, the sincere desire for a peaceful settlement was not firm at this stage. There were ongoing sporadic skirmishes between Indonesian and British forces along the borders of Sabah and Sarawak, and the British military was reinforced.[171] The Malayan government also took a provocative position by saying that the Americans would provide military assistance to the British-Malayan side.[172] Indonesian President Sukarno warned, 'If Malaya refuses to negotiate with Indonesia and the Philippines over the proposed merger, I will lead a struggle by the Indonesian people until the Malaysian plan fails to materialise'.[173] Malayan Premier Tunku Abdul Rahman reacted against this in the following way: 'This is… strange behaviour of a man who with one breath is purportedly trying to make peace through a get-together in Manila at a summit talk and with the other breath is threatening war'.[174] Indeed, '[s]uch talk is not conductive to peace in this region of Asia'.[175] The Tunku remained focused on compromising with the Philippines, rather than with Indonesia, and on 26 April stated that Malaya and the Philippines should work together for a peace plan in the region.[176] He continued to provoke Indonesia with abusive rhetoric, saying in early May: 'Those who hurl threats of war are tyrants and agents and tools of the devil and as sure as there is a God, they will go the way of all devils'.[177]

While bilateral relations worsened and the ministerial talks were unpredictable, Sukarno invited the Tunku to Tokyo for discussions on reconciliation.[178] On his way to Tokyo, Sukarno showed his willingness to make peace with Malaya by saying: 'If the [tripartite Summit] meeting is held, I will certainly go'.[179] However, his underlying unpleasantness still remained: 'But, if they [Malaya] are going to be nasty about things, then we have got to be nasty, too'.[180] On 25 May 1963, and before the high level talks took place, Subandrio met with the Malayan Ambas-

---

[167] Joint Communiqué between Indonesia, Malaya and the Philippines, 17 April 1963.
[168] *The Straits Times*, 18 April 1963.
[169] Ibid. Italics added.
[170] *The Straits Times*, 19 April 1963.
[171] Ibid.
[172] It was said to be based on the defence agreement between the US and Britain. See *The Straits Times*, 19 April 1963.
[173] *The Straits Times*, 20 April 1963. At the same time, he showed his conciliatory attitude: 'Indonesia wants to a peaceful solution through negotiation'. (Ibid.)
[174] Ibid.
[175] Ibid.
[176] *The Straits Times*, 27 April 1963.
[177] *South China Morning Post*, 6 May 1963.
[178] The real intention why both Sukarno and the Tunku agreed to meet in deteriorated bilateral relations was unclear (J. A. C. Mackie, *Konfrontasi*, p. 233). Sukarno was said to hand his invitation to the Malayan Ambassador in Tokyo. (*The Straits Times*, 29 May 1963.) Although Mackie mentions that the talks happened 'unexpectedly and at very short notice' (J. A. C. Mackie, *Konfrontasi*, p. 148), Subandrio revealed to the Japanese Foreign Minister, Masayoshi Ohira, a week before the talks that Indonesia had secretly negotiated with Malaya to hold the talks between Sukarno and the Tunku. See 'Ohira Gaimu Daijin to Subandorio Indoneshia Gaimu Daijin no Kaidan ni Kansuru Ken [The Proceedings of the talks between Mr. Ohira, Foreign Minister of Japan and Dr. Subandrio, Foreign Minister of Indonesia]', Ajia-kyoku, Nantou Ajia-ka [Department of Southeast Asia, Bureau of Asia, Ministry of Foreign Affairs of Japan]', 24 May 1963, GSK File A'-423. Therefore, the talks in Tokyo were not arranged 'suddenly'.
[179] *The Straits Times*, 24 May 1963.
[180] Ibid.

sador in Tokyo, Dato Syed Sheh bin Syed Abdullah, and explained Indonesia's 'desirability of smoothing differences'.[181] Indonesia showed a more positive attitude towards reconciliation than Malaya at this stage.

On 31 May, Tokyo talks began in a cordial atmosphere and both Sukarno and Tunku Abdul Rahman recognised the importance of working towards peaceful co-existence. On the first day of the talks, the Tunku said, 'Obviously President Sukarno wants normal relations to be re-established between our two countries, and I will do everything possible to achieve this'.[182] The two leaders had an 'amicable and frank exchange of views' and the high level talks 'cleared the way' for ministerial talks to be held from 7 June.[183] In the Joint Communiqué issued after the talks, they agreed that:

1. The two countries should seek to settle outstanding differences with a spirit of neighbourliness and goodwill.
2. Their respective Governments would take every possible measure to refrain from making acrimonious attacks on and disparaging references to each other.
3. They would strive to achieve a closer understanding between the three countries in matters of common concern and mutual interest.[184]

As the Tokyo talks were concluded successfully, the Malaysia question was expected to be resolved quite soon. According to Subandrio's report to the Japanese Foreign Minister, Masayoshi Ohira, made just after the talks between Sukarno and the Tunku, the two leaders had already reached a verbal agreement:

1. They would find a mutually agreeable solution to the overseas Chinese issue in the region.
2. They would not take any further steps in the Malaysia issue before the Summit talks.
3. The Tunku would accept the change of the date of the Malaysia formation if the heads of the three countries agreed at the tripartite Summit meeting.[185]

At the conclusion of the meetings, the Tunku said, 'I am confident that a heart to heart talk, in plain language, in a sincere atmosphere will clear the path for successful talks in Manila'.[186] When Sukarno was leaving Tokyo in the early morning on 2 June, the Tunku went to Haneda airport to see the Indonesian president off.[187] It was 'further proof that the talks between the two statesmen, aimed at reducing tension between the two countries, had definitely been cordial and friendly'.[188]

---

[181] *The Straits Times*, 29 May 1963.

[182] *The Straits Times*, 31 May 1963.

[183] Joint Statement after the Tokyo talks between Sukarno and Tunku Abdul Rahman, 1 June 1963, in *Malaya /Indonesia Relations*, p. 44.

[184] Ibid.

[185] 'Ohira, Subandorio Kaidan (Dai Ni-kai) Youshi [The Proceedings of the Foreign Ministerial Talks between Ohira and Subandrio, The Second Session], Nantou Ajia-ka [Department of Southeast Asia, Ministry of Foreign Affairs of Japan], 1 June 1963, GSK File A'-423. Author's translation. However, the verbal agreement turned out to be ambiguous. According to Subandrio's report to Ohira, the date of the establishment of Malaysia was subject to change (Ibid.), whereas just after he returned to Malaya, the Tunku stated that it was not. (*The Straits Times*, 6 June 1963.)

[186] *The Straits Times*, 1 June 1963.

[187] Haneda airport is located at the South-western end of Tokyo and is 25 km from the heart of Tokyo, where the Tunku was supposed to stay.

[188] *South China Morning Post*, 3 June 1963. After going back to Jakarta, Sukarno was purportedly going to change his aggressive attitude towards the formation of Malaysia. However, he failed to do so. (Ibid.)

Direct talks between the two leaders facilitated an improvement in bilateral relations and the end of the verbal war. As a result, the ministerial conference in Manila (7-11 June) started amicably. The conference produced the Manila Accord, which included the following points:

1. Malaya agreed to invite the Secretary-General of the United Nations or his representative in order to ascertain the wishes of the inhabitants of the British North Borneo territories (Sabah and Sarawak).
2. Indonesia and the Philippines would accept the formation of Malaysia only if the result of the UN investigation showed that the people of the British territories support the Malaysia plan.
3. The three countries share a primary responsibility for the maintenance of the stability and security of the area from subversion in any form of manifestation in order to preserve their respective national identities, and to ensure the peaceful development of their respective countries and of their region.
4. The three countries agreed to attempt to form a regional cooperation organisation (based on Malay origin) to address common problems with the spirit of 'working together in closest harmony'.
5. The three countries will hold regular consultation at all levels to deal with matters of mutual interest and concern.[189]

After the Manila Conference, Malaya's attitude towards the Malaysian Plan also changed. As opposed to its previous stance on the issue, namely: 'We only come in after Malaysia is formed' (meaning that it should be exclusively a matter of Britain's concern), Malaya was now willing to become a player, rather than a mere observer.[190]

Malaya accepted the demand from Indonesia and the Philippines that the people of Sabah and Sarawak should exercise their right to self-determination through an enquiry under the auspices of the UN, and that Malaysia would be realised only if the people supported it.[191] In relation to this, the three countries agreed that their chief responsibility was to address regional problems, which further locked the Malaysia issue into the scope of regional affairs. It was at this point that Macapagal's proposal to establish a regional cooperation organisation, Maphilindo, was introduced.[192] Maphilindo had two aspects. Namely, on the one hand, it can be said to have been a form of short-lived diplomatic 'machinery'. On the other hand, it can be said to have been a prototype for a regional cooperation organisation, facilitating communication, and shelving problems arising between the three countries concerned.[193]

Ever since the Magsaysay administration, the Philippines had sought the opportunity to become a truly 'Asian' state, rather than a US satellite state. President Macapagal raised the claim over Sabah with this objective in mind. His aim was to evoke feelings of national unity by fos-

---

[189] The Manila Accord, 11 June 1963.
[190] *The Straits Times*, 6 March 1963.
[191] The Manila Accord, 11 June 1963.
[192] It is said that Maphilindo was 'implicitly anti-Chinese'. See Peter Lyon, *War and Peace in South-East Asia*, p. 157. Indeed, Subandrio said to the Japanese Foreign Minister in May 1963, 'If the Federation of Malaysia is formed, Communist elements in Malaya and Singapore come to Borneo (Sabah and Sarawak), which will influence the Indonesian territory of Kalimantan. Therefore, Indonesia cannot turn blind eye to it because of national security'. See 'Ohira Gaimu Daijin to Subandorio Indoneshia Gaimu Daijin no Kaidan ni Kansuru Ken [The Proceedings of the talks between Mr. Ohira, Foreign Minister of Japan and Dr. Subandrio, Foreign Minister of Indonesia]', Ajia-kyoku, Nantou Ajia-ka [Department of Southeast Asia, Bureau of Asia, Ministry of Foreign Affairs of Japan]', 24 May 1963, GSK File A'-423. Author's translation.
[193] George McT. Kahin, 'Malaysia and Indonesia', pp. 266-267.

tering Asian identity.[194] He also followed the Philippine foreign policy tradition, to take the initiative in matters of regional cooperation, started during the Quirino and the Garcia administrations.[195] The focus of Macapagal's regional policy was Malay identity.[196] As Emmanuel Pelaez put it, 'The Arabs and the Hindus, the Chinese and the Japanese, the Spaniards and the Americans have each left their mark upon us. But whatever foreign influences we may have absorbed over the centuries, ours is essentially and basically a Malay nation'.[197]

According to the Manila Accord, Macapagal's approach to the regional problem was based on frequent consultations and directed towards 'lasting peace, progress and prosperity for themselves and for their neighbours'.[198] This style of discussion was named *Musyawarah* Maphilindo.[199] Macapagal's approach aimed to reach consensus by holding *musyawarah* (consultations) in a friendly atmosphere to reduce tensions.[200] The reconciliatory attitude of Indonesia and the Philippines towards Malaya can be seen in the Manila agreements: the two countries agreed to support the formation of Malaysia if the UN's investigation in Sabah and Sarawak was positive. Indonesia and the Philippines also agreed to respect the outcome of the UN's investigation, effectively allowing the UN to make the final decision.[201]

However, the harmonious relations between the three countries were fragile. In early July, Britain, Malaya and other potential members of Malaysia (Singapore, Sarawak and Sabah) held a conference in London for the establishment of the Federation of Malaysia. They finally signed an agreement (the Malaysia Agreement) on 9 July.[202] It referred to the date of the establishment of Malaysia:

The government of the Federation of Malaya will take such steps as may be appropriate and available to them to secure the enactment by the Parliament of the Federation of Malaya of an Act in the form set out in Annex A to this Agreement and that it is brought into operation on 31st August, 1963.[203]

The agreement also stipulated that '[t]he Colonies of North Borneo [Sabah] and Sarawak and the State of Singapore shall be federated with the existing States of the Federation of Malaya as

---

[194] The pro-Asian policy was going to be boosted in mid-1963. Salvador P. Lopez said, 'The orientation of our diplomatic activities towards Asia might be likened to a 90 degree turn in the direction of a moving ship', and 'the powerful affinities of race, culture and geography and the imperatives of regional security and common destiny will inevitably push us towards our racial kin and next-door neighbours in Southeast Asia'. (*South China Morning Post*, 30 August 1963.) However, this policy was only a rallying cry as the Philippine economy continued to depend on the US market.

[195] Elpidio Quirino hosted the Asian Union (the Baguio Conference) in 1950, and Carlos P. Garcia established the ASA with Malaya and Thailand in 1961. Onofre D. Corpuz, the high official in the Garcia administration, said, the Philippines 'pursued a new and leading role in Southeast Asian diplomacy....our effort to serve as an honest broker in resolving the difficulties between our Maphilindo partners, promised to continue and argument the auspicious beginnings of Philippine leadership in regional affairs'. See Onofre D. Corpuz, 'Realities of Philippine Foreign Policy', in Frank H. Golay (ed.), *The United States and the Philippines* (Englewood Cliffs, NJ: Prentice-Hall, 1966), p. 54. Corpuz was the Under Secretary of Education in the Garcia administration and the Professor of the University of the Philippines.

[196] The Manila Accord, 11 June 1963.

[197] Emmanuel Pelaez, *Government by the People*, Quezon City: published privately by the author, 1964.

[198] The Manila Accord, 11 June 1963.

[199] Manila Declaration, 5 August 1963; and Manila Joint Statement, 5 August 1963.

[200] *Musyawarah* composed the decision-making process together with *mufakat* (consensus). This style of decision-making can be seen in the village politics in Indonesia, and to some extent, in Malaysia and the Philippines. For more detail, see Chapter 6.

[201] The Manila Accord, 11 June 1963.

[202] Brunei decided not to join Malaysia just before the conference.

[203] See, The Agreement Relating to Malaysia in London, 9 July 1963.

the States of Sabah, Sarawak and Singapore'.[204] Furthermore, the agreement expanded the defence coverage, based on the Anglo-Malaysian Defence Agreement in 1957. The latter was now applied to the whole Malaysian Federation. As such, it redefined its purpose: it was to provide security in Southeast Asia. The article six of the Malaysia Agreement says:

> The Agreement on External Defence and Mutual Assistance between the government of the United Kingdom and the government of the Federation of Malaya of 12th October, 1957, and its annexes shall apply to all territories of Malaysia, and any reference in that Agreement to the Federation of Malaya shall be deemed to apply to Malaysia, subject to the proviso that the government of Malaysia will afford to the government of the United Kingdom the right to continue to maintain the bases and other facilities at present occupied by their Service authorities within the State of Singapore and will permit the government of the United Kingdom to make such use of these bases and facilities as that government may consider necessary for the purpose of assisting in the defence of Malaysia and for Commonwealth defence and for the preservation of peace in Southeast Asia.[205]

Sukarno was offended by the Tunku's participating in the conference. He said that Tunku Abdul Rahman 'failed to keep [the] promise'[206] he made in Tokyo. As mentioned above, according to Subandrio's report just after the Tokyo talks, the two leaders agreed that they would not take any further action relating to Malaysia before the Summit.

In fact, Sukarno was 'infuriated' by the Tunku's signing the Malaysia Agreement without any consultation with Indonesia and the Philippines. He argued that the Tunku's unilateral action violated the agreement reached at the ministerial conference in Manila. While Sukarno had previously expressed his willingness to attend the Summit meeting,[207] the day after the Malaysia Agreement in London he said, 'With the action of the Tunku, we Indonesians are doubtful about the summit conference'.[208] Subandrio also criticised the Tunku's actions:

> It has been the basic understanding among the Philippines, Malaya and Indonesia as agreed in the Manila foreign ministers meeting, that we can support Malaysia only after self-determination of the people has been implemented under an independent authority like the United Nations Secretary-General or his deputy.[209]

Sukarno tried to exert pressure on Malaya. He held a special meeting at home with Ministers and defence chiefs. It was unanimously decided that the Malaysia plan should be attacked.[210] Subandrio threatened Malaya by saying, Malaya 'needs to be friends with Indonesia for their own sake, for their own security'; however, if Malaya disregarded Indonesia's opinion, then 'Indonesia c[ould] live without Malaya'.[211] Subandrio also implicitly showed Indonesia's intention to resume active military campaign if Malaya unilaterally continued with the Malaysia plan and ignored the right of self-determination in Sabah and Sarawak.[212] The possibility of military action was suggested on various occasions. The Indonesian Navy announced that it had formed an attack fleet of light, fast crafts for its anti-Malaysia policy. It also announced that it had suc-

---

[204] Ibid.
[205] Ibid.
[206] *The Straits Times*, 11 July 1963.
[207] *The Straits Times*, 9 July 1963.
[208] *The Straits Times*, 11 July 1963.
[209] Ibid.
[210] However, Indonesia was not really going to take military action. Subandrio said, '[W]e want to settle the Malaysia question peacefully on the basis of the Tokyo and Manila agreement'. See *South China Morning Post*, 16 July 1963.
[211] *South China Morning Post*, 10 July 1963.
[212] Ibid.

cessfully launched a surface-to-surface guided missile.[213] Indonesia was reportedly preparing for combined naval and air force exercises.[214]

Malaya responded defensively. It took the position that the London agreement did not spoil the harmonious mood from Tokyo and Manila.[215] Tunku Abdul Rahman said, 'I have done nothing to the best of my knowledge to break any word or promise I have given to President Sukarno [in Tokyo] in connection with Malaysia'.[216] According to an official publication issued by the Malaysian government in late 1963, Sukarno 'did not express an objection after that and appeared to have appreciated the Malayan view point' when the Tunku explained to him in Tokyo in late May 1963 that he would go to London to sign an Agreement to fix the date for the establishment of Malaysia on 31st August, 1963.[217] Tun Abdul Razak explained the need of the agreement for Malaysia: 'The Malaysia agreement that the Tunku signed in London was another step in a series of legal and constitutional procedures in preparation for the establishment of Malaysia and does not in any way conflict with the understanding reached by the foreign ministers in Manila'.[218] Malaya, according to him, did not break the Manila agreements. The Tunku reacted against Indonesia's provocation, saying that the new Malaysia would use arms to defend itself if Indonesia violated its sovereignty.[219]

Towards the start of the summit meeting, Malaya softened its attitude and the Malayan Ambassador to Jakarta, Dato Haji Kamaruddin, indicated that Malaya wanted to restore friendly relations with Indonesia.[220] The Tunku expressed his willingness to compromise at the coming Summit meeting: 'I am prepared to beg for peace'.[221] In addition, he specifically showed Malaya's concession on a central issue: 'It is up to the United Nations Secretary-General, U Thant, to decide on this [whether he will recommend a plebiscite to ascertain the wishes of the inhabitants in Sabah and Sarawak]'.[222] In return, when he was asked by the press whether there was room for concession, Subandrio showed Indonesia's restrained attitude: 'We believe in the spirit of friendly discussion'.[223] It seemed that both sides had realised the necessity of restoring the friendly atmosphere of the ministerial talks.

On 31 July 1963, Tunku Abdul Rahman visited Sukarno at his hotel.[224] The two conversed for half an hour before the commencement of the formal talks. The conversation was marked by its friendly tone, which 'certainly broke the ice' between the two countries.[225] The two leaders apparently enjoyed a very amicable conversation, because when the Tunku was about to leave the room, Sukarno purportedly said, 'What's the hurry?'[226] Just after this, the Tunku told the press that he went to see Sukarno '[a]ccording to the Malay *adat* [custom]'. With this, younger

---

[213] *South China Morning Post*, 24 July 1963.
[214] *The Straits Times*, 23 July 1963.
[215] *The Straits Times*, 16 July 1963.
[216] *South China Morning Post*, 13 July 1963.
[217] *Malaya /Indonesia Relations*, p. 16.
[218] *The Straits Times*, 16 July 1963.
[219] *The Straits Times*, 23 July 1963.
[220] *South China Morning Post*, 20 July 1963.
[221] *South China Morning Post*, 26 July 1963. He added that he would not totally yield to Sukarno by saying, 'I must uphold the honour and prestige of my country'. (Ibid.)
[222] *The Straits Times*, 30 July 1963. Britain opposed the plebiscite hating 'pandering to Sukarno'. (Howard Palfrey Jones, *Indonesia*, p. 282.)
[223] *The Straits Times*, 30 July 1963.
[224] *The Straits Times*, 1 August 1963.
[225] Ibid.
[226] Ibid.

people should express respect toward older ones.[227] The Tunku's visit proved to be an important stepping-stone to the success of the Summit.[228]

The mood of the Summit was 'exuberant and expansive'[229] and concessions from both sides created a 'formula capable of saving the face'.[230] The three countries concerned produced various concessive agreements, which displayed a spirit of regional initiative for regional matters.[231] Most notably, they agreed that there would be an investigation into the wishes of the people in Sabah and Sarawak by the UN before the establishment of Malaysia.[232] Indonesia and the Philippines were to accept the establishment of Malaysia if the UN investigation supported it. Concessive Malaya, on the other hand, was to postpone the establishment of Malaysia if the UN investigation was not completed before 31 August, the date which Britain and Malaya had already set.[233] Malaya also allowed Indonesia and the Philippines to send officials to observe the UN's activities. Furthermore, Malaya agreed to obtain the cooperation from the governments concerned when the UN performed its task.[234]

The next concession was between Indonesia and the two other countries over foreign bases. In the Joint Statement, 'the three countries will abstain from the use of arrangements of collective defence to serve the particular interests of any of the big powers'.[235] The British intervention in the Malaysia issue reminded the Indonesians of the alleged British involvement in the PRRI (Revolutionary Government of the Republic of Indonesia) rebellion in 1958.[236] Sukarno referred to the revolt in his Indonesian Independence Day address of 17 August 1963:

> Still fresh in our minds are the subversions from outside at the time of the P.R.R.I. and PERMESTA rebellions. They operated from bases abroad, around us! Some operated from Malaya, some operated from Singapore, ...all the foreign bases around Indonesia were used as bases of subversion against Indonesia.[237]

Subandrio expressed his displeasure by saying that 'the British influences [will] have a land border with Indonesia' when Malaysia is established.[238] Indonesia's fear of subversion was heightened by article 6 of the Malaysia Agreement, the so-called Anglo-Malaysian Defence Agreement.[239] Indonesia suspected that foreign bases might be used for subversive activities towards Indonesia. Malaya and the Philippines, both of which had defence cooperation agree-

---

[227] *The Straits Times*, 1 August 1963. The Tunku was two years younger than Sukarno.

[228] It was reported that the Tunku visited Sukarno to explain the reason of Tun Razak's absence from the Summit meeting, because Sukarno held some suspicion about his absence. (*The Straits Times*, 1 August 1963.) It can be inferred that his absence was decided by the Tunku and the British because Tun Razak was 'a bit more enthusiastic about forging close links with Indonesia' rather than respecting the colonial tie with Britain. (Marvin C. Ott, 'Foreign Policy Formation in Malaysia', *Asian Survey*, 12/3 (March 1972), p. 228.) It was assumed that he could sabotage Malaya's pro- British position at the Summit.

[229] George Modelski (ed.), *The New Emerging Forces*, p. 96. Yamakage, however, points out that the agreement made in Manila was 'simply the one that induced the concession from the counter party and was based on mutual misunderstanding'; therefore, it was not made on firm trust. See Susumu Yamakage *ASEAN*, p. 76. Author's translation.

[230] George McT. Kahin, 'Malaysia and Indonesia', p. 268.

[231] Ibid, pp. 226-227.

[232] The Manila Joint Statement, 5 August 1963.

[233] *The Straits Times*, 5 August 1963.

[234] The Manila Joint Statement, 5 August 1963.

[235] Ibid. In addition to the written agreement, Indonesia purportedly made the verbal agreement with Malaya that no further British bases would be built in Malaysia. (*The Straits Times*, 5 August 1963.)

[236] For the detail of the PRRI rebellion, see Chapter 2.

[237] Sukarno, President's Independence Day Speech, 17 August 1963.

[238] Subandrio, *Indonesia's Foreign Policy*, p. 23.

[239] The defence agreement of London on 9 July 1963 was the one that simply followed the agreement between Britain and Malaya of 23 November 1961.

ments with the West, accepted that foreign bases were 'temporary in nature'.[240] Indonesia, in return, did not insist on the immediate withdrawal of British bases in new Malaysia.

The beginnings of discord
While during this period the three countries successfully made agreements matching their own interests, Indonesia's hostility towards Britain significantly intensified.[241] This is because the British exerted pressure on Tunku Abdul Rahman, trying to keep him under British influence.[242] On 1 August 1963, The British Cabinet decided that they should 'impress on the Prime Minister of Malaya the importance of adhering to 31 August as the date for the formation of Malaysia and warn him of the dangers implicit in any further delay'.[243] On 2 August, Duncan Sandys, the British Secretary of State for Commonwealth Relations, and Lord Home, the British Secretary of Foreign Affairs, gave their messages to Tunku Abdul Rahman in Manila.[244] The messages stressed that the British government was worried about the postponement of Malaysia Day.[245] The British thought that the delay could 'create doubts and uncertainty throughout the area'.[246] The messages also conveyed that the result of the UN investigation would not change Sukarno's opposition to the Malaysia plan.[247] Furthermore, Sandys' message asserted that, with British backing, the Tunku could resist Indonesia in the Summit talks: 'If as a result of your stand, your relations with Indonesia become more difficult you know you can count on us to back you'.[248] The Tunku sent a reply to Sandys the next day. However, what should have been a decisive reply turned out to be a relatively weak one: 'I am just trying to manoeuvre in the hope of reaching a compromise....You can rest assured that Malaysia will be announced on the 31st of August as scheduled'.[249]

Ganis Harsono, a senior official in the Indonesian Ministry of Foreign Affairs, said that the agreement about the self-determination of the Borneo regions was ruined by the two notes Sandys and Lord Home sent to the Summit.[250] He continued that Britain had attempted to disrupt the meeting by sticking to the Malaysia Day of 31 August as 'an unalterable date for the formation of Malaysia', whereas the Malayan government had agreed to a postponement.[251]

---

[240] The Manila Joint Statement, 5 August 1963.

[241] An Indonesian senior official said that Indonesian hostility against the British was deep-rooted. See 'Ikeda Souri no Hou-"I" oyobi Maleishia Mondai ni Tsuite no "I"-Seifu Jyouhousuji no Kenkai Houkoku no Ken [The view of Indonesian government sources for the trip to Indonesia of the Japanese Prime Minister, Mr. Ikeda and the Malaysia issue]', Zai Indoneshia Fujiyama Rinji Dairi Taishi yori Gaisyou he [From Mr. Fujiyama, the special acting Ambassador to Indonesia to the Foreign Minister], Ministry of Foreign Affairs of Japan, 14 October 1963, GSK File A'-432.

[242] '[T]he British were a key factor in determining the Tunku's position' (Howard Palfrey Jones, *Indonesia*, p. 282).

[243] CAB 128/37, CC51(63)4, 1 August 1963 (Cabinet Conclusions)..

[244] Two messages from Duncan Sandys and Lord Home were delivered to the Tunku on 2 August in the Manila Hotel. *The Straits Times*, 3 August 1963.

[245] FO 371/169724, no 26, 2 August 1963 (Outward Telegram OCULAR 1003 from Lord Home to T Peters).

[246] Ibid.

[247] Ibid. On 2 August, the Malayan Ambassador in Manila, Zaidin said to Kahin that the British would not accept 'any testing of opinion' before the establishment of the Federation of Malaysia on 31 August 1963. See George McT. Kahin, *Southeast Asia: A Testament* (London: Routledge Curzon, 2003), p. 170.

[248] FO 371/169724, no 26, 2 August 1963 (Outward Telegram OCULAR 1003 from Lord Home to T Peters).

[249] FO 371/169724, no 26, 3 August 1963 (Inward Telegram OCULAR 593 from T Peters to Lord Home).

[250] *The Straits Times*, 3 August 1963.

[251] *The Straits Times*, 3 August 1963.

Sukarno, at the closing ceremony of the Summit, implicitly accused the British of interfering with the conference.[252]

On the other hand, the British were obviously unhappy with a series of Manila agreements,[253] and Sandys himself was described as being 'furious'.[254] They viewed the agreements as 'most unsatisfactory' because Tunku Abdul Rahman did not protect the Malaysia Agreement made in London.[255] In addition, '[i]n Britain's absence, the conferences had...discussed the disposition of British territories'.[256] Britain complained that there was no stipulation in the Manila agreements that Indonesia would abandon its confrontation policy towards Malaya, and there was no mention of the date of establishing Malaysia in the agreement. Furthermore, the British government strongly opposed an eventual re-investigation of its Borneo territories because such a process might nullify Britain's decision to establish Malaysia.[257] Britain also refused to change the date of the establishment of Malaysia. American President John F. Kennedy sent a message to British Prime Minister Harold Macmillan on 4 August. Kennedy was 'quite concerned that hopefully successful Manila summit will be torpedoed unless 31 August date for Malaysia can be postponed briefly to give Sukarno a fig leaf. If in fact the Tunku is willing..., we would urge you give this an urgent look. I well realise that kowtowing to Sukarno is a risky enterprise, but a little give now may be worth the risk'.[258] However, Macmillan sent a negative reply, saying 'what is postponed is lost'.[259]

Sir G. Tory, the British High Commissioner in Malaya, met Tunku Abdul Rahman after the Manila Summit on the morning of 9 August, and accused him of not producing desirable results in Manila. The Tunku was forced to affirm to Sir G. Tory that he would 'go ahead with Malaysia on whatever later date may now be agreed between the signatories.... [H]e would [he added] like this date to be 16th September irrespective of nature of the Secretary-General report'.[260] The Tunku was also compelled to accept his responsibility if the UN report was unfavourable: 'any further ascertainment of Bornean wishes would then be his responsibility and would not take place until after establishment of Malaysia'.[261] To prevent the Tunku's deviation from the terms of the verbal contract, Sandys sent him a letter of confirmation, stating that the British government would give him its 'full support in the implementation of this policy' if Malaya would act in accordance with British interests.[262] The Tunku became nervous. On 24 August, Sandys came to Kuala Lumpur and met the Tunku. Sandys protested that the British government 'had not been properly consulted' over the Manila agreements, and that 'this was the cause of most of the subsequent difficulties'.[263] The Tunku stated that although it was no question that he wanted to establish Malaysia on 31 August 1963 as scheduled, it was more important that Malaysia could coexist peacefully with neighbouring countries by saying: 'I, too, want it [the declaration of the creation of Malaysia] to be [on] August 31, but for the sake of

---

[252] Sukarno, Speech at the Closing Ceremonies of the Conference of Heads of Government of the Federation of Malaya, Republic of Indonesia and the Republic of the Philippines, in Manila, 5 August 1963. The same description can be seen in Subandrio's book. See Subandrio, *Indonesia's Foreign Policy*, p. 23.

[253] They were the Manila Accord, the Manila Declaration and the Manila Joint Statement.

[254] Roger Hilsman, *To Move a Nation*, p. 399.

[255] *South China Morning Post*, 7 August 1963.

[256] Arnold C. Blackman, *Southeast Asia's Second Front*, p. 186.

[257] 'Outward Telegram OCULAR 1003 from Lord Home to T Peters', 2 August 1963, FO 371/169724, no 26.

[258] PMO 11/4349, T430/63, 4 August 1963 (Outward Telegram No 7462 from the FO to Washington Embassy).

[259] PMO 11/4349, T434/63, 4 August 1963 (Outward Telegram No 2459 from the FO to Lord Home).

[260] PMO 11/4349, 9 August 1963 (Inward Telegram No 1503 from Sir G Tory to Mr Sandys).

[261] Ibid.

[262] PMO 11/4349, 10 August 1963 (Outward Telegram No 1946 from Mr Sandys to Sir G Tory).

[263] DC 169/216, no 176, 27 August 1963 (Inward Telegram SOSLON 62 from Mr Sandys to CRO).

peace and for the well-being of the nation and for the good of Malaysia, let us see what the United Nations has to say'.[264]

Nine UN officials, headed by Laurence Michaelmore, the UN Deputy Director of Personnel, flew to Singapore on 15 August, at which point a conflict blew up. At first, the British government permitted four observers to each territory.[265] However, Indonesia demanded 30 observers for each.[266] The British government disapproved of this and said: 'This could create the absurd situation in which ninety persons would be engaged in watching the work of nine representatives of the United Nations Secretary General'.[267] It continued, 'This was obviously absurd'.[268] Subandrio protested the British refusal on the grounds that it was against the spirit of the Manila conference.[269] He said that Indonesia was not able to accept the result of the UN investigation if Indonesia's request was not accommodated.[270] Although the UN team was going to begin its investigation from 22 August, Indonesia and the Philippines asked U Thant, the United Nations Secretary General, to postpone it until their demand was accepted in accordance to the Manila agreement.[271] U Thant eventually mediated, proposing the despatch of four assistants in addition to four observers.[272] Both sides accepted this, with Indonesia reluctantly acquiescing.[273] The UN team began its work on 26 August.[274]

Indonesian observers in the British Borneo territories were surely 'vexatious' for the British, in addition to the UN's investigation itself.[275] Britain's displeasure was revealed by its reluctance to issue visas for the Indonesians. The British Embassy officials in Jakarta said they were not able to issue visas because they had not received a request from Indonesia.[276] Subandrio said in this connection that '[i]t is regrettable that up to today [27 August] Britain had not issued the visas or a landing permit for our plane. This certainly cannot go on unresolved. I shall have to take action some time'.[277] Subandrio concluded in this regard that, '[w]e regret this British attitude because in the long run… it will not be beneficial for the British themselves'.[278] He continued, 'If the British intend to leave this area as a good coloniser they should undertake to create a harmonious atmosphere among the people here, and not leave behind explosive tensions'.[279] The antagonism between Britain and Indonesia became stronger.

U Thant later criticised the British government for its insincere treatment of Indonesia and the Philippines:

> It is a matter for regret that this understanding could not have been reached earlier, so that all observers could have been present in the territories for the entire period of the inquiries and that questions of detail pertaining to the status of the observers unnecessarily delayed even

---

[264] *The Straits Times*, 24 August 1963.
[265] Namely, two observers for each territory.
[266] *South China Morning Post*, 19 August 1963.
[267] Ibid.
[268] Ibid.
[269] *South China Morning Post*, 20 August 1963.
[270] Ibid.
[271] *The Straits Times*, 22 August 1963. However, U Thant was not formally responsible for the number of observers.
[272] Ibid.
[273] *South China Morning Post*, 24 August 1963.
[274] *South China Morning Post*, 27 August 1963.
[275] PMO 11/4349, T443B/63, 5 August 1963 (Outward Telegram No 2488 from Mr Macmillan to Lord Home).
[276] *The Straits Times*, 27 August 1963.
[277] *South China Morning Post*, 28 August 1963.
[278] *The Straits Times*, 28 August 1963.
[279] Ibid.

further their arrival. A more congenial atmosphere would have been achieved if the necessary facilities had been granted more promptly by the Administering Authority.[280]

Indonesian and Philippine observers and assistants finally arrived at Kuching in Sarawak on 1 September. They were able to attend the investigation for only three days out of six.[281]

There was an additional source of outrage for the Indonesians. On 29 August 1963, Tunku Abdul Rahman declared that Malaysia would be established on 16 September. His announcement destroyed the cooperative attitude created during the Manila agreements because the announcement was made unilaterally. When Sandys came to Kuala Lumpur on 24 August, the Tunku was compelled by his 'heavy pressure'[282] to change the Malaysia day to 16 September without consulting Indonesia or the Philippines, or even waiting for the result of the UN investigation.[283] The new date was approved by Britain and the Federation members of Malaysia (Duncan Sandys, Tunku Abdul Rahman, Donald Stephens, Lee Kuan Yew and Ningkan) on 26 August, although the Tunku wanted to keep harmony with Indonesia and the Philippines.

Subandrio was invited to Singapore for talks with Tun Abdul Razak over 'any misunderstanding that may have arisen over the question of observers and Malaya's stand in connection with this matter'.[284] The invitation was sent with a time limit of no later than 28 August, so that Subandrio could get to know the new Malaysia date, before its official proclamation. However, Subandrio declined the invitation because of 'a slight indisposition', but he said that he would 'welcome very much' seeing Tun Abdul Razak in Jakarta.[285] The Tunku replied that Ghazali Shafie, the Malayan Permanent Secretary of Foreign Affairs, would visit Jakarta.[286] Ghazali Shafie arrived at Jakarta on the very day the new federation date was proclaimed. He quickly informed Subandrio of Malaya's intention. It was 8 am on 29 August, a couple of hours before the proclamation. Subandrio said to him that the Indonesian government would reserve 'its position until after the announcement of the United Nations Secretary-General's findings in the Borneo territories'.[287] Then, the King of Malaysia, Yang di-Pertuan Agong, signed the proclamation: 'Malaysia shall come into being' on 16 September.[288]

Malaya's unilateral declaration of the new date for the establishment of Malaysia initiated the deterioration of relations among Maphilindo member states. The new date was announced without consulting Indonesia or the Philippines. On 4 September, the Indonesian Ambassador in Kuala Lumpur, Lt-Gen. Gusti Djatikusumo, formally sent a strong protest to the Malayan government against the latter's unilateral declaration of the new date which, as he pointed out, violated the Manila agreement.[289] The Philippine Foreign Secretary, Salvador Lopez, said: 'Our

---

[280] Final Conclusions of the Secretary-General Regarding Malaysia, 13 September 1963. The US Assistant Secretary of State for Far Eastern affairs, Roger Hilsman, stresses U Thant's accusation saying, '[I]t was more than a matter for regret'. See his book, *To Move a Nation*, p. 403. Howard Palfrey Jones, the American Ambassador to Indonesia, also criticises such British misconduct to the observer issue: The British government, especially Duncan Sandys, clearly made 'it as difficult as possible for the Indonesians to observe anything'. (Howard Palfrey Jones, *Indonesia*, p. 287.)
[281] *The Straits Times*, 2 September 1963.
[282] Roger Hilsman, *To Move a Nation*, p. 403.
[283] DC 169/216, no 176, 27 August 1963 (Inward Telegram SOSLON 62 from Mr Sandys to CRO).
[284] *The Straits Times*, 27 August 1963.
[285] *The Straits Times*, 28 August 1963. *The Straits Times* published on 27 August reported that Malaya was supposedly preparing for the proclamation of the new date by Yang di-Pertuan Agong, the King of Malaya, before 31 August (the original Malaysia day). Subandrio perhaps became aware of the Tunku's real intension and declined his offer.
[286] Tun Abdul Razak was not able to go overseas because of his busy schedule.
[287] *The Straits Times*, 30 August 1963.
[288] *The Straits Times*, 30 August 1963. Indonesia and the Philippines were advised it in advance through their Ambassadors before the proclamation was made. See *South China Morning Post*, 30 August 1963.
[289] *The Straits Times*, 6 September 1963.

position is that it does not appear to be in conformity with the spirit of the Manila agreements to have set a new date for the establishment of Malaysia in advance of the completion of the United Nations survey'.[290] He added that '[in] accordance with this view, Malaya's notification which was sent to the Philippine Government must be considered as premature'.[291] The Malaysia government later tried to justify its one-way decision in an official statement:

> It was pointed out to the Indonesian government that in view of the Federation's constitutional obligations and the United Nations Secretary-General's indication to the three parties that the task of ascertainment was expected to be completed and the findings made known by the 14th September, 1963 the Federation government's decision to announce 16th September as the new date for Malaysia was fully consistent with both the spirit and the letter of the Manila Accord.[292]

Tunku Abdul Rahman also explained the reason why Malaya unilaterally set and announced a new date by saying, 'We had to fix a date. You cannot make up your mind one day and celebrate the next. So long as we are confident over the results, things will go on all right'.[293] However, Malaya's action was surely against the spirit of the Manila agreements, which required that the three governments 'hold regular consultations...to deal with matters of mutual interest and concern'.[294] As Lopez later protested, 'setting a definite date presupposes an affirmative finding and we presume nobody knows at this time that the United Nations finding will be favourable'.[295]

To make matters worse, on 29 August, Donald Stephens, the Chief Minister-designate of Sarawak, gave a defiant statement in Jesselton[296] that disregarded the Manila agreements. When he came back from Kuala Lumpur, he said, 'If the United Nations report confirms the wishes of the peoples for Malaysia, then we will have Malaysia with the blessings of Indonesia and the Philippines'.[297] He continued, 'If, in the unlikely event the report says the majority don't want Malaysia, we will still go ahead with Malaysia, but without the blessings of Indonesia and the Philippines'.[298] His statement further insulted Sukarno and Macapagal, who by endorsing the Manila agreements were trying to 'climb down gracefully from their extreme positions' over Malaysia.[299]

U Thant's reaction was to accuse Malaya of dissonant behaviour towards the proclamation of the new Malaysia day. His final report expressed sorrow at the unilateral action of the British and Malayan governments:

> During the course of the inquiry, the date of 16 September 1963 was announced by the government of the Federation of Malaya with the concurrence of the British government, the Singapore government and the government of Sabah and Sarawak, for the establishment of the Federation of Malaysia. This has led to misunderstanding, confusion, and even resent-

---

[290] *The Straits Times*, 5 September 1963.

[291] Ibid.

[292] *Malaya /Indonesia Relations*, p. 20.

[293] *The Straits Times*, 7 September 1963. The US Ambassador to Indonesia, Howard P. Jones, gives another insight: Britain and Malaya hastened to establish Malaysia before 30 September because '[p]olitical prisoners in the territories would be released and have the right to be enrolled as electors' after that. See Howard Palfrey Jones, *Indonesia*, p. 282.

[294] The Manila Accord, 11 June 1963.

[295] *The Straits Times*, 5 September 1963.

[296] Jesselton is currently Kota Kinabalu in Sabah.

[297] *The Straits Times*, 30 August 1963.

[298] Ibid.

[299] George McT. Kahin, 'Malaysia and Indonesia', pp. 268-269. The same view can be seen in *Asahi Shimbun*, 2 June 1963.

ment among other parties to the Manila Agreement, which could have been avoided if the date could have been fixed after my conclusions had been reached and made known.[300]

The result of the United Nations investigation was that:

> [T]he majority of the peoples of the two territories, having taken them into account, wish to engage, with the peoples of the Federation of Malaya and Singapore, in an enlarged Federation of Malaysia through which they can strive together to realise the fulfilment of their destiny.[301]

With U Thant's report, Indonesia and the Philippines announced that they did not recognise Malaysia; and in response to this Tunku Abdul Rahman recalled all staff members from the Malayan Embassy in Indonesia.[302] He said, 'We asked Indonesia to think twice before taking any drastic action. They should consider the matter in the spirit of Maphilindo so that we can be as we once were'.[303] When Malaysia was finally born on 16 September, thousands of anti-Malaysia demonstrators gathered outside the Malaysian and British Embassies in Jakarta.[304] In Kuala Lumpur, more than a thousand Malaysian demonstrators threw stones at the Indonesian Embassy. The Malaysian government asked both Indonesia and the Philippines to clarify the reason for their reluctance to recognise Malaysia. The Tunku said, 'In view of the fact that the Indonesian government has broken off diplomatic relations with Malaysia without any apparent reason, we have no choice but to do likewise and to recall our Ambassador and the Embassy staff, and at the same time to close down our consulate in Medan'.[305]

After 16 September 1963 Indonesia's attitude towards Malaysia became increasingly militant.[306] Malaysia's defence committee decided to increase the strength of the armed forces, especially in Sabah and Sarawak.[307] The Tunku seriously considered the possibility of defending Malaysia by force from Indonesia's attack. He relied heavily on British military support. The friendly atmosphere and the cooperative spirit had completely vanished. Consequently, the Manila agreements collapsed.[308] 'The open breach between Indonesia and Malaysia ... constituted a major turning-point in the development of confrontation'[309] and led to the end of regional harmonisation. However, this episode provided some important glimmers of insight for future exploration of the matters of regional communication, cooperation, and accommodation.[310]

---

[300] The United Nations, Final Conclusions of the Secretary-General Regarding Malaysia, Doc. SG/1583, 13 September 1963.
[301] Ibid. On 12 September, one day before the formal issue of the result, U Thant called Ambassadors from Indonesia, Malaya and the Philippines. He gave them a copy of the result of the UN's investigation. (*South China Morning Post*, 13 September 1963.)
[302] *The Straits Times*, 16 September 1963.
[303] Ibid.
[304] *The Straits Times*, 17 September 1963.
[305] *The Straits Times*, 18 September 1963.
[306] Frederick P. Bunnell, 'Guided Democracy Foreign Policy: 1960-1965 President Sukarno Moves from Non-alignment to Confrontation', *Indonesia*, 2 (October 1964), p. 45.
[307] *The Straits Times*, 19 September 1963.
[308] Susumu Yamakage, *ASEAN*, p. 76. Modelski sees Maphilindo was 'weakened' not broken at that stage. See George Modelski, 'Indonesia and the Malaysia Issue', p. 134.
[309] J. A. C. Mackie, *Konfrontasi*, p. 200.
[310] The Manila conference was 'the historic significance of their coming together for the first time…after long struggles from colonial status to independence.' See The Manila Declaration, 5 August 1963, in Department of Foreign Affairs, Australia (ed.), *Malaysia*, pp. 195-196.

The significance of the Manila agreements and Maphilindo

The period between April and August 1963 was characterised by the creation of a 'mutually acceptable formula' through the series of Manila conferences, made possible with concessions from both sides.[311] An intention to harmonise their relations can be recognised since as early as the talks at under-secretary level in April 1963. The Manila conferences exemplified closer fraternal relations, mutual concessions, and the maintenance of moderate attitudes. In addition, throughout the Manila conferences they realised that the countries within the region ought to solve regional problems without external assistance. The desire to settle the dispute was most noticeable during the Tokyo talks (the end of May 1963) and the Manila Summit (early August 1963). Although it did not last, the emergence of a cooperative mood during this period was a notable staging post on the road towards cooperation for regional security in the form of the Association of Southeast Asian Nations (ASEAN). This is because the countries concerned held the talks by themselves when the tension developed. The examples here are the informal bilateral talks between Indonesian President Sukarno and Malayan Prime Minister Tunku Abdul Rahman in Tokyo on 31 May 1963, and at the hotel in Manila on 31 July 1963. It is noteworthy that Indonesia and Malaya preferred the informal negotiation style for their reconciliation, and did so over the more formal one dictated by international diplomacy. By using informal and frank conversation, they for a time successfully created regional harmony.

Although the Manila agreements (and Maphilindo) collapsed about one month after their signing, their influence on ASEAN, which was established in 1967, was considerable. The concept of 'regional primary responsibility', articulated in the Manila agreements (more specifically, the Manila Accord and the Manila Declaration), was brought into the ASEAN Declaration, which was the foundational document of ASEAN.[312] The idea of 'the temporality of foreign bases in the region' was also stipulated in the ASEAN Declaration.[313] In addition, the spirit of 'working together beyond difference' from the Manila Accord took firm root in ASEAN, and the promise of 'frequent consultation' from the Manila Joint Statement was established as a key practice in the Association.

The phrase 'working together' appeared in the Manila Accord for the first time in an official document in Southeast Asia. Malaya had previously ascribed responsibility for the Malaysia project to the British because the proposed federation involved some former British colonies. Therefore, Malaya did take a passive attitude towards objections from Indonesia and the Philippines until talks at the under-secretary level were held. Malaya was reluctant to take the initiative in settling the dispute, awaiting the Indonesians to take the first step.[314] As described above, although Indonesian Deputy Foreign Minister Suwito Kusumowidagdo had waited for Malaya's delegation for 10 days in Manila in March 1963, the tripartite talks were postponed and Suwito left Manila saying, 'I don't think Malaya is serious'.[315]

However, the series of tripartite talks clearly encouraged the three countries concerned (in particular Malaya) to realise that they should tackle the Malaysia question within their own circle.[316] Especially significant in this regard was Malaya's realisation that it should not leave the Malaysia issue as an exclusive British responsibility. The face-to-face talks with Sukarno in Tokyo were the starting point, after which Tunku Abdul Rahman recognised that he should address the Malaysia issue actively.[317] The Tunku softened his inflexible attitude towards Sukarno,

---

[311] George McT. Kahin, 'Malaysia and Indonesia', p. 268.
[312] See Manila Accord, 11 June 1963; Manila Declaration, 5 August 1963; and ASEAN Declaration, 8 August 1967.
[313] ASEAN Declaration, 8 August 1967.
[314] *The Straits Times*, 5 March 1963.
[315] *The Straits Times*, 30 March 1963.
[316] Richard Butwell, 'Malaysia and Its Impact on the International Relations of Southeast Asia', p. 941.
[317] The Tunku said in Tokyo, 'We are determined to discuss our problems in a brotherly way and find a solution to meet everyone's interests'. See *The Straits Times*, 6 June 1963.

when the latter showed his intention to peacefully settle the dispute in Tokyo.[318] After the first session of the talks, the Tunku felt Sukarno's humanity, saying Sukarno wanted to 'open his heart'.[319] Indeed, a consultation, and personal connection, between the two leaders was necessary. Just before the bilateral Summit meeting, at the talks with Japanese Foreign Minister Ohira, Subandrio expressed Indonesia's displeasure: 'Malaya should have consulted with Indonesia before it announced the Malaysia plan'.[320]

Face-to-face communication also occurred in the hotel where Sukarno stayed for the Manila Summit. He was impressed by the Tunku's courteous behaviour and they became friendly.[321] They met again two months after the Tokyo talks. The Tunku's courtesy visit was inspired by the sense of closeness towards Sukarno. This sense of closeness had emerged in Tokyo. These two episodes reveal the significance of informal and heart-to-heart talks between Sukarno and Tunku Abdul Rahman, especially after the long history of antagonism between the two countries since the end of the Second World War. In addition, their behaviour was one of the key elements of the Manila agreements: 'frequent consultations' to create regional cooperation. At the same time, Sukarno was able to nudge the Tunku to reach a compromise with Indonesia for the sake of regional peace. They successfully therefore achieved face-saving agreements in Manila.

The sense of 'regional responsibility' can be seen in the Tunku's attitude at the Summit. The British government was displeased to see that the Tunku respected regional relations more than colonial relations and it seemed to the British that the Malayan Prime Minister would concede too much in Manila.[322] During the summit, Duncan Sandys pushed him to follow the British policy of Malaysia. Although the Tunku appeared to acquiesce to Sandys' demands, his real intention was to pay more attention to the regional grouping for the future of Malaysia.[323] The frequent consultations in Maphilindo created a harmonious mood, which culminated in the Manila Summit. Even after verbal and written attempts from the British to intimidate Tunku Abdul Rahman, his desire for harmonisation of regional relations (and especially his sympathy with Sukarno) had not disappeared.

When Sandys came to Kuala Lumpur to remonstrate with the Malayan Premier about his actions during the Manila Summit, the Tunku simply replied that he wanted 'peace with his neighbours'.[324] Sandys forced the Tunku to ignore the Manila agreements and to announce the new date of the Malaysia formation without consulting Sukarno and Macapagal. The Tunku tried to consult with Subandrio about his decision before the public announcement, and to do so on the basis of the fraternal relationship established with Sukarno in Tokyo (as well as the Treaty of Friendship in 1959 between Indonesia and Malaya).[325] However, at this time his wish was not realised because of Sandys' strong objection.[326] Divided between Britain and Maphilindo, he came to say to Sandys: 'I have reached the end of my tether and I do not want to discuss anything further with anybody'.[327]

---

[318] *The Straits Times*, 31 May 1963.
[319] Ibid.
[320] 'Ohira Gaimu Daijin to Subandorio Indoneshia Gaimu Daijin no Kaidan ni Kansuru Ken [The Proceedings of the talks between Mr. Ohira, Foreign Minister of Japan and Dr. Subandrio, Foreign Minister of Indonesia]', Ajia-kyoku, Nantou Ajia-ka [Department of Southeast Asia, Bureau of Asia, Ministry of Foreign Affairs of Japan]', 24 May 1963, GSK File A'-423. Author's translation.
[321] *The Straits Times*, 1 August 1963.
[322] Roger Hilsman, *To Move a Nation*, p. 399.
[323] *The Straits Times*, 24 August 1963.
[324] DC 169/216, no 176, 27 August 1963 (Inward Telegram SOSLON 62 from Mr Sandys to CRO), paragraph 3.
[325] Ibid., paragraph 10.
[326] Ibid., paragraph 17.
[327] Ibid., paragraph 19.

The Tunku had become increasingly cooperative in the course of the frequent consultation at the Manila conference, in contrast to his initial position of non-involvement in the dispute over the formation of Malaysia (because he re-described it as a British matter). While the Tunku's sympathy for the regional bond resulted in failure, this episode reveals his underlying adherence to the objective of regional harmonisation. Indeed, he was the one who believed frequent consultation was most important between neighbouring countries in Southeast Asia when he took the initiative of the establishment of the ASA. This episode can be interpreted as the Tunku's desire for frequent consultations with Indonesia and the Philippines, with the aim of transcending their differences.

Indonesia's attitude towards regional cooperation resulted in the disintegration of cooperation. The harmonious atmosphere in the Manila agreements was a by-product of Sukarno's attempt to eliminate British (colonial) influence from the regional affair. Most countries in Southeast Asia felt a sense of inferiority to Western countries and were sensitive to political interference from them. Therefore, when Sukarno advocated anti-colonialism during a series of the Manila conferences, Malaya sympathised with him. This atmosphere fashioned a common, if fragile, bond among them. However, anti-colonial sentiment was a double-edged sword. Sukarno's overtly aggressive attitude towards the British also broke the harmonious and cooperative mood because his antagonism against Britain was also often directed to Malaya. Indeed, Subandrio said at the declaration of Confrontation on 20 January 1963: 'We have always been pursuing a confrontation policy against colonialism… It is unfortunate that Malaya, too, has lent itself to become tools of colonialism'.[328] In this way, Indonesia regarded confronting Malaya as being the equivalent of confronting Britain and, to some extent, fighting colonialism in general.[329]

In addition, the failure of the Manila agreements can be attributed to British pressure on the Tunku and his indecisive attitude towards the Malaysia issue.[330] Sukarno thought that he was able to turn the Tunku's allegiance to the region, away from its former coloniser through their talks in Tokyo. On the other hand, the British government resented the Tunku for giving way to the counter party in Manila and forced him to neglect the agreements. The Tunku was not able to reject British pressure completely and became torn between Britain and Maphilindo countries. He was not able to trust completely Sukarno's Indonesia as a partner in the region. Therefore, in the interests of Malayan security, he could not sever the colonial connection with Britain.[331] As a result, he could not act consistently and failed to consult the other Maphilindo members about the new matters relating to the Malaysia issue. Signing the Malaysia Agreement of 9 July 1963 was the Tunku's first blunder. The second was unilaterally announcing the new date for the federation of Malaysia upon the advice of Sandys. Neglecting the consultative process violated the fragile trust which was growing up among the three countries, and resulted in a setback to ongoing regional cooperation.

It should be noted that Indonesia significantly influenced the Manila conferences. It has been observed that the Manila agreements 'clearly represented a diplomatic victory for Sukarno',[332] as they were heavily influenced by Indonesian ideology. Modelski points out that external powers had 'exerted predominant influence in the making of regional decisions'[333] in the post-war

---

[328] Subandrio, Speech to Mahakarta Regiment in Jogjyakarta, 20 January 1963.
[329] Ibid.
[330] Ott points out that his background made him move 'easily between two cultures'. The Tunku came from aristocratic Malay and was Western-educated. He was an English gentleman, at the same time, 'the quintessential Malay'. (Marvin C. Ott, 'Foreign Policy Formation in Malaysia', p. 225.)
[331] 'Inward Telegram OCULAR 593 from T Peters to Lord Home', 3 August 1963, FO 371/169724, no 26.
[332] Howard Palfrey Jones, *Indonesia*, p. 284. The same view is seen in Gerald Sussman, 'Macapagal, the Sabah Claim and Maphilindo', p. 217.
[333] George Modelski, 'Indonesia and the Malaysia Issue', p. 129.

era of Southeast Asia; therefore, the formation of Malaysia was one of Indonesia's attempts 'to reduce the share of outside Powers'.[334]

As Indonesian Vice-President Mohammad Hatta explained in 1949, it seemed to Indonesia that the blueprint of Malaysia was a British-made plan rather than a Southeast Asian one. Indonesia had been sensitive to the use of terms such as sovereignty and self-determination, as it had itself secured its independence the hard way: through bloody struggle. For Indonesia, Malaysia did not appear to be built on the basis of the wishes of the inhabitants.[335] The formation of a seemingly British-influenced country was undesirable for Indonesia, as it would challenge Indonesian revolutionary ideology. In addition to this, Indonesia suspected that the PRRI rebellion in 1958 was supported, or even operated, through the use of British and American bases within Asia. With the formation of Malaysia, Indonesia would be adjacent to the land upon which British-controlled bases could be built. This would have the effect of intensifying domestic unrest and directly threaten national security.

Sukarno, together with Philippine President Macapagal, tried to bring together the three Maphilindo countries by invoking their racial and cultural affinity and their shared colonial experience. In other words, they attempted to forge a regional identity by making a distinction between Maphilindo countries (Asian countries) and former colonisers (Western countries). Invoking regional and national identity worked to unite the region and assist nation-building. Sukarno successfully united the people against the Dutch in the independence struggle and the West Irian campaign. He tried to apply this method to the international arena; namely, he tried to unite Malaya, Indonesia and the Philippines by making a clear distinction between them and the West. However, he ultimately failed to do so as he over-emphasised Indonesian antagonism against Western countries.

The cultural affinities between the three countries, all being of ethnic Malay origin, should also be noted.[336] These affinities were useful to strengthen the bond. Maphilindo emphasised the fraternity of ethnic Malays and employed the traditional conflict settlement process, *musyawarah*. Further traditional practice, that the younger people respects the older one, for example, can be seen between Tunku Abdul Rahman and Sukarno. In one such instance, the Tunku went to Haneda Tokyo airport to see Sukarno off after the Tokyo talks in June 1963. Another example is that the Tunku visited Sukarno's hotel room in Manila at the first day of the Summit in August. Sukarno welcomed the visit and they had an amicable conversation. After the conversation, the Tunku told the press that he went to see Sukarno '[a]ccording to the Malay *adat* (custom)' in which the younger people should respect the older one.[337] The Tunku's behaviour was accepted by Sukarno because of cultural affinity and it obviously relaxed tensions between the two leaders.

Concluding remarks

Relations between Indonesia, Malaya and the Philippines during this period displayed the impetus to see regional cooperation as a serious regional strategy. The three Maphilindo countries emphasised their own responsibility for regional matters, and for regional security in particular. In addition, they recognised the importance of 'working together' for the sake of the region. That is to say, this period reinforced their recognition of Southeast Asia as a region. Furthermore, three specific techniques to harmonise the Maphilindo countries were identified: 'consultations', 'face-saving' and 'informality'. Through the process of making the Manila agreements,

---

[334] Ibid, p. 130.

[335] Sukarno, Speech at the Opening of the Conference of National Front Committees in Jakarta, 13 February 1963.

[336] Thai Foreign Minister Thanat Khoman later stated that he opposed to Maphilindo because 'we are not interested in anything racial...we like practical cooperation not cooperation on a racial basis'. *Far Eastern Economic Review*, 16 June 1966, p. 511.

[337] *The Straits Times*, 1 August 1963. The Tunku was two years younger than Sukarno.

Indonesia, Malaya and the Philippines developed the idea of regional cooperation, which was originally initiated in the formation process of the ASA. Although Maphilindo collapsed one month after the Manila Summit meeting, the desire to create a successful regional organisation became stronger in this period.

4 THE SETTLEMENT OF THE REGIONAL PROBLEM AND THE FORMATION OF ASEAN

The three-way dispute over the formation of Malaysia continued for more than two years. Although Sukarno, Tunku Abdul Rahman and Macapagal made certain attempts to fix their deteriorated relations, these attempts were neither earnest, nor persevering. In line with the drastic changes in Indonesian politics from 1966,[1] the new Indonesian government quickly turned its policy direction towards a peaceful settlement with Malaysia.[2] In parallel with the political change in Indonesia, the Philippine government was also actively seeking normalisation of diplomatic relations with Malaysia.[3] By mid-1966, the three countries had resumed official relations.[4] With the new atmosphere of peace in the region, Indonesia, Malaysia, the Philippines and Thailand began to discuss new ways for regional cooperation.[5] After a year discussion, a new organisation, ASEAN, was launched in 1967.[6] This chapter identifies the specific elements for regional cooperation by describing a regional transition from 'antagonising each other' to 'working together.'

The Malaysia issue after the establishment of Malaysia

After the establishment of Malaysia, Indonesian mobs damaged the British and Malaysian embassies.[7] In Kuala Lumpur, Malaysians attacked the Indonesian Embassy. Indonesia banned trade with Malaysia and refused Colombo plan aid from Britain and Australia. Although they were still sporadic, Indonesian military threats against Malaysia had intensified. Indonesian Naval gunboats fired on Malaysian vessels and the Indonesian Army deployed guerrilla forces in Sabah and Sarawak.[8]

---

[1] The political change resulted from the abortive coup of 30 September 1966, the so-called Gestapu (*Gerakan September Tigahpuluh*). As a result of the coup, Sukarno was eventually forced to step down from Indonesian politics. For the details of the abortive coup, see, for example, Arnold C. Brackman, *Indonesia, the Gestapu affair* (New York: American-Asian Educational Exchange, 1969); Donald E. Weatherbee, *Approaches to the Interpretation of Gestapu: the Indonesian Coup Attempt of 1 October, 1965* (Columbia: University of South Carolina, 1968); and Harold Crouch, 'Another Look at the Indonesian "Coup"', *Indonesia*, 15 (April 1973), pp. 1-20.
[2] Adam Malik, 'Promise of Indonesia', *Foreign Affairs*, 46/2 (January 1968), p. 301.
[3] Lela Garner Noble, 'The National Interest and the National Image', p. 566.
[4] The diplomatic relations between Malaysia and the Philippines resumed on 3 June 1966 (Joint Statement between Malaysia and the Philippines on 3 June 1966), p. 128.), and between Indonesia and Malaysia on 11 August 1966 (The Agreement to Normalize Relations between the Republic of Indonesia and Malaysia, 11 August 1966.).
[5] Rudimentary discussions about a new form of regional cooperation, which was to include Indonesia, were held in early 1966. See Franklin B. Weinstein, *Indonesia Abandons Confrontation*, p. 88; and 'Tounan Ajia Syokoku Rengou (ASEAN) no Sousetsu ni Tsuite [The Establishment of the Association of Southeast Asian Nations, ASEAN]', Nansei Ajia-ka [Department of Southwest Asia, Ministry of Foreign Affairs of Japan], 18 August 1967, GSK File B'-200.
[6] Yoneji Kuroyanagi, *ASEAN 35 Nen no Kiseki*, pp. 25-27.
[7] *The Straits Times*, 17 September 1963.
[8] *The Straits Times*, 2 October 1963.

The Philippines attempted to resume the tripartite conference within Maphilindo.[9] Just after the establishment of Malaysia, the Philippine acting Foreign Secretary, Librado Cayco, said, 'I do not think Maphilindo is (*sic*) collapsed'.[10] The Philippine government stated that it would recognise Malaysia if recognition would suit its national interest.[11] Then, in late October, the Philippines proposed two conditions for its recognition of Malaysia: Malaysia should observe the Manila agreements[12] and agree with the peaceful settlement of the Sabah territorial dispute. However, these conditions were flatly rejected by Malaysia. As Indonesia's militant actions intensified, the Philippines stated that it would try to solve the Sabah issue and recognise Malaysia without Indonesia,[13] whereas Sukarno tried to persuade Macapagal to cooperate with him.[14]

While Indonesian President Sukarno strongly advocated crushing Malaysia, on 16 January 1964, he entered into discussions with US Attorney General Robert Kennedy in Tokyo.[15] Sukarno showed his willingness for Kennedy's proposition of a peaceful settlement of the conflict over Malaysia.[16] Although the tripartite ministerial conference between Indonesia, Malaysia and the Philippines was going to be held in Bangkok early in February, this meeting was postponed because Indonesia and Malaysia could not reach a cease-fire agreement regarding the battles on the Indonesian-Malaysian border in Sarawak.[17]

In March 1964, Philippine Foreign Secretary Salvador Lopez held several separate bilateral sessions with Malaysia and Indonesia in Bangkok, and he succeeded in organising foreign ministerial talks between the three countries concerned.[18] However, Indonesia and Malaysia once again failed to agree to a cease-fire. Lopez also played a mediator's role between Indonesia and Malaysia during the Tokyo tripartite Summit meeting on 20 June.[19] However, the negotiations were broken off on the same day.[20] The King of Malaysia, Sayyid Putra, was wary of the Tunku's inflexible attitude in the run-up to the latter's discussions with Sukarno in Tokyo in June 1964: 'I hope Malaysia can go along with Indonesia and other countries in the world peacefully'.[21]

After the Tokyo talks broke off, Indonesia resumed military activities. The Philippines no longer attempted to mediate the conflict after the Indonesian guerrillas landed in Johor state (Malaysia) on the Malay Peninsula in August 1964, and as a consequence the dispute became more focused on Indonesia and Malaysia.[22] Under the circumstances, Britain was going to resist

---

[9] Philippine President Diosdado Macapagal had proposed Maphilindo in 1963. See Chapter 3.

[10] *Asahi Shimbun*, 17 September 1963. Author's translation.

[11] *The Straits Times*, 25 September 1963.

[12] It had been reiterated until the end of the dispute in 1966 by Indonesia and the Philippines.

[13] *Asahi Shimbun*, 1 November 1963. The Philippine government resumed the consular relations in mid-1964.

[14] The Philippines did not oppose having Malaysia as a member of the Second Afro-Asia conference in Algiers to be held in the following year whereas Indonesia launched a negative campaign against Malaysia's participation. However, the conference was not materialised because of the coup happening in Algeria.

[15] *Asahi Shimbun*, 17 January 1964. Robert Kennedy had a favourable impression from the Indonesian government. See *Asahi Shimbun*, Evening Edition, 14 January 1964.

[16] Ibid.

[17] *Asahi Shimbun*, 27 February 1964.

[18] Susumu Yamakage, *ASEAN*, p. 78.

[19] In the course of the tripartite Ministerial talks in Tokyo in June 1964, Macapagal's new proposal of the Afro-Asian Conciliation Commission was accepted. The commission was supposed to be composed of three Afro-Asian countries which should be nominated by each country concerned and one country which should be nominated by consensus of the three. However, it was never materialised.

[20] *Asahi Shimbun*, 21 June 1964.

[21] *Asahi Shimbun*, Evening edition, 17 June 1964. Author's translation.

[22] Gerald Sussman, 'Macapagal, the Sabah Claim and Maphilindo', p. 219. The Japanese government continued to mediate Indonesia and Malaysia after the Philippines took the distance from the issue.

Indonesia's military action until Sukarno abandoned his aggressive policy.[23] The issue was debated in the United Nations Security Council in September although the Soviet Union vetoed the proposed resolution that condemned Indonesia's military action.

In October 1964, Sukarno secretly proposed a meeting with Tunku Abdul Rahman, but Malaysia declined this.[24] In the meantime, Indonesia, pursuing closer relations with China,[25] left the United Nations in January 1965.[26] By withdrawing from the UN and allying itself with China, Indonesia renounced '"peaceful coexistence" with the West' and began to call the US, the leader of imperialism.[27] The Japanese government had actively played the role of mediator, proposing and organising Tokyo talks between Sukarno and the Tunku for May 1965. However, these talks were cancelled because of opposition from the Indonesian Communist Party (PKI).[28] Indonesia's approach to China was also related to the PKI's growing influence on Indonesian politics.[29] Subandrio, the PKI-backed Indonesian Foreign Minister, who was an emerging power in Indonesian politics,[30] upset the balance between the Army and the PKI; a balance which had been maintained by Sukarno for some years,[31] thus intensifying the power struggle between the Army and the PKI. When Sukarno was hospitalised in August 1965, there was a rumour that he had retired. The rumour caused the abortive coup of 30 September 1965.

Just after the establishment of Malaysia in 1963, the issue of the government's disparate treatment of the ethnic Chinese emerged in the country.[32] The adoption of Malay as the official national language and government favouritism had led some to argue that ethnic Malays were

---

[23] 'Dai Sankai Nichi-Ei Teiki Kyougi, Shiina Daijin to Goodonwooka Gaisyo tono Kaidan Roku, Zai-Ei Taishi yori no Houkoku [The Proceedings of the Third Japan-Britain Regular Conference, the talks between Foreign Minister, Shiina and British Foreign Secretary, Gordon-Walker, The report by the Ambassador to Britain]', Oua-kyoku Eirenpou-ka [Department of Commonwealth of Nations, Bureau of Eurasia, Ministry of Foreign Affairs of Japan], 2 February 1965, GSK File A'-427.

[24] 'Sukaruno Daitouryou Hounichi no Sai no Cyoutei Kousaku ni Tsuite [The memorandum of the mediation for Presudent Sukarno]', Ministry of Foreign Affairs of Japan, 23 September 1964, GSK File A'-423.

[25] Sukarno had taken balance between the Soviet and China in Indonesia's diplomatic relations. However, he inclined to China more after the latter succeeded in the nuclear test in October 1964 so that Indonesia could increase its voice in the international community. Indeed, Sukarno praised China for its success of the nuclear test by saying, 'I am proud that the Asian country can have what the Westerners have monopolised'. See 'Kouda Jikan to Sukarno Daitouryou tono Kaidan Youshi [The Proceedings of the talks between the subordinate officer Kouda and President Sukarno]', Kouda Jikan [The Subordinate Officer Kouda, Ministry of Foreign Affairs of Japan], 29 October 1964, GSK File A'-423. Author's translation. China was keen to secure ideological support from Indonesia because of the severe Sino-Soviet ideological war. The Soviet Union, on the other hand, hesitated to support Indonesia and antagonise Britain because of the success of the detente in Europe.

[26] The real reason for this is unknown: Sukarno's protest against the UN where Malaysia was going to be a member of the Security Council in 1965; or the pressure from China. (J. A. C. Mackie, *Konfrontasi*, p. 282.)

[27] John O. Sutter, 'Two Faces of Konfrontasi: "Crush Malaysia" and the *GESTAPU*', *Asian Survey*, 6/10 (October 1966), p. 533.

[28] 'Shiina Gaisyou to Sir Paul Gore-Booth tono Kaidan ni Tsuite [The report of the talks between Foreign Minister, Shiina, and Sir Paul Gore-Booth], Ouei 246 Gou, Oua-kyoku, Eirennpou-ka [Department of the Commonwealth of Nations, Bureau of Eurasia, Ministry of Foreign Affairs of Japan], 18 March 1965, GSK File A'-410.

[29] John O. Sutter, 'Two Faces of Konfrontasi', pp. 531-532.

[30] *Asahi Shimbun*, 12 September 1964.

[31] Sultan Hamengku Buwono later said, 'Sukarno heavily depended on Subandrio in his foreign policy'. See 'Indonesia Hamenku Buono Fukusyusyou to Shiina Gaimu Daijin tono Kaidan Youroku [The Proceedings of the talks between Indonesian Deputy Prime Minister, Sultan Hamenengku Buwono and Foreign Minister Shina]', Nantou Ajia-ka [Department of Southeast Asia, Ministry of Foreign Affairs of Japan], 25 May 1966, GSK File A'-396. Author's translation.

[32] Yoneji Kuroyanagi, *ASEAN 35 Nen no Kiseki*, p. 20.

accorded a 'special position'.[33] In March 1965, Lee Kuan Yew, the Singaporean Prime Minister, warned that Malaysia could not survive an ethnic conflict:

> [L]et me admit that in this plural society of Malaysia also lies the danger of her own destruction. If under the external pressure of Indonesian confrontation, the leaders of the various communities in Malaysia respond not as Malaysians, but as so many Malays, Chinese, Indians and others, then the end must be disintegration.[34]

In reply, the Malaysian Prime Minister tersely rebuked Lee:

> The state of Singapore is under the control of another opposition group, the People's Action Party, led by its Premier, Mr Lee Kuan Yew. Singapore has had no previous experience of working in a federal nation, and due to the fact of being the "New York" of Malaysia it probably feels that its position is far more important than that of the rest of Malaysia.[35]

Singapore finally left Malaysia on 9 August 1965. After Singapore's secession, bilateral relations did not improve. Sukarno pointed to this in a speech he gave at the time:

> The weakness of the 'Malaysia' project has been obvious from the very beginning. I have said this hundreds of times! As the whole world knows, Brunei, which was where the North Kalimantan revolution first broke out under the leadership of Mahmud Azahari rejected 'Malaysia' and has never been federated in 'Malaysia'. ... [I]t is a fact that Singapore has separated itself from 'Malaysia'. Yes, 'Malaysia' is beginning to fall apart from the inside! And it will fall apart completely and go to pieces.[36]

Suharto's rise to power

In Indonesia, the abortive coup of 30 September ignited social unrest.[37] In addition, the economy was deteriorating. On 2 October, Sukarno announced that Major General Mohamed Suharto had 'responsibility for the restoration of security and order'.[38] Sukarno gave Suharto important posts, such as Minister of the Army. However, the former still had the strong support of the people and of one of the major political groupings in Indonesia.[39] Suharto ascribed the 9.30 coup to the PKI's plot to subvert the Sukarno government and said that his primary duty was 'to destroy the PKI'.[40] Sukarno, however, objected to a ban on the PKI.

The political disturbances had still not calmed down in early 1966. In fact, civil demonstrations were becoming prevalent. The demonstrators demanded the elimination of the communists

---

[33] N. Ganesan, *Bilateral Tensions in Post-Cold War ASEAN* (Singapore: Institute of Southeast Asian Studies, 1999), p. 36.

[34] Lee Kuan Yew, Speech to the National Press Club at Canberra, 16 March 1965.

[35] Tunku Abdul Rahman, 'Malaysia', p. 663.

[36] Sukarno, President's Independence Day Speech, 17 August 1965. *Asahi Shimbun* also reported that 'the independence of Singapore meant "the substantive collapse of Malaysia" because Singapore was the base for tin and rubber which were main items of Malaysian industry'. See *Asahi Shimbun*, 10 August 1965. Author's translation.

[37] It is known as *Gestapu*: *Gerakan September Tigahpuluh*.

[38] Suharto, *Soeharto: My Thoughts, Words and Deeds (An Autobiography)* (Jakarta: PT. Citra Lamtoro Gung Persada, 1991), p. 109.

[39] *The Straits Times*, 25 March 1966.

[40] Ibid., p. 113. Sukarno, on the other hand, 'had a different assessment' of the abortive coup. (Ibid., p. 116.)

and the restoration of the Indonesian economy.[41] In addition, the people began to criticise the Sukarno government.[42] By March 1966 the situation was out of control. In the so-called 'Letter of 11 March', General Suharto seized full power from Sukarno in order to take 'all necessary steps to guarantee security and calm and the stability of the running of the government'.[43]

Suharto proclaimed as his top priority the rebuilding of the Indonesian economy in order to secure domestic stability.[44] The day after he came into power, Suharto also dissolved Indonesian Communist Party (PKI) and banned communist activities throughout the country.[45] He also concluded that *Konfrontasi* 'had only been a PKI tactic to drag the country into as many confrontations as possible so that the communists could mobilise their forces and finally revolt and seize power'.[46] He arrested 15 members of the Cabinet (including the Foreign Minister, Subandrio) because of their suspected involvement with the PKI.[47]

Suharto declared that the new government would not indulge in 'right or left' rhetoric, but would instead maintain a balanced approach.[48] He also advocated social harmonisation[49] and appointed new ministers from various groups. Suharto nominated Adam Malik[50] as a Foreign Minister and Deputy Prime Minister, and Sultan Hamengku Buwono of Jogjakarta as the Minister of Economic Affairs. The three of them, in effect, formed a triumvirate. Malik, in line with Suharto, declared that he would keep a balance in foreign policy.[51] He announced that Indonesia would return to an 'independent and active foreign policy'.[52] In fact, Malik took a pragmatic line with 'the realities existing in the outside world'.[53] Indeed, the new Indonesian government 'leaned heavily towards the West'[54] because Suharto expected foreign aid mainly from the United States and Japan.

Indonesia's new foreign policy

Indonesia needed to coexist with the international community, especially the Western countries, in order to secure foreign aid for its economic recovery. Adam Malik spurned autarky, stating that, 'We believe that no nation in this age of rapid technological progress and scientific advances can live in isolated self-sufficiency'.[55] He also showed his intention to return to interna-

---

[41] KAMI (Indonesian Students' Action Committee) held large demonstrations in early 1966 demanding to dissolve the PKI, recover national economy and reshuffle the Cabinet. The inflation rate in Indonesia was about 600% at the end of Sukarno era.

[42] *Asahi Shimbun*, 10 January 1965.

[43] Sukarno, Executive Order of 11 March, 11 March 1966.

[44] *Far Eastern Economic Review*, 28 April 1966, p. 177. It was widely seen that economic difficulties would give fertile soil for communist to subvert the country. See, for example, 'Ikeda Souri, Nikuson Zen Beikoku Fuku Daitouryou Kaiken Roku [The Proceedings of the talks between the Japanese Prime Minister, Ikeda and the former US Vice-President, Nixon]', Amerika-kyoku, Hokubei-ka [Department of North America, Bureau of America, Ministry of Foreign Affairs of Japan], 10 April 1964, GSK File A'-401.

[45] Suharto later mentioned in his book that the ban was 'the people's demand'. (Suharto, *Soeharto*, p. 147.)

[46] Ibid., p. 153.

[47] The arrested ministers were seen as 'the followers of Subandrio'. (Harold Crouch, *The Army and Politics in Indonesia*, p. 200.) Subandrio was sentenced to death, later commuted to life imprisonment under Suharto's amnesty.

[48] *Asahi Shimbun*, 13 March 1966.

[49] Suharto advocated returning to the spirit of *Pancasila*. For the details of *Pancasila*, see Chapter 1.

[50] He was the former member of Murba party, Proletariat national-Communist in Indonesia.

[51] *South China Morning Post*, 5 April 1966.

[52] *The Straits Times*, 23 March 1966. The Indonesian government formed 'independent and active foreign policy' in 1948. In view of the unstable world circumstances at the beginning of the Cold War, Indonesia maintained that it would play 'no favourites between the two opposed blocs' and follow 'its own path' to relax tension 'generated by the two blocs'. (Mohammad Hatta, 'Indonesia's foreign policy', p. 444.)

[53] *The Straits Times*, 5 April 1966.

[54] Harold Crouch, *The Army and Politics in Indonesia*, p. 331.

[55] Adam Malik, 'Promise of Indonesia', p. 301.

tional organisations, such as the United Nations, as quickly as possible.[56] Malik suggested that he would also improve diplomatic relations with the US, the country's largest potential benefactor. At the same time, Indonesia distanced itself from China and other Sukarno-era communist allies in Asia.[57] The US was still apprehensive about communist infiltration into Southeast Asia at that time and hoped that Indonesia would not be driven to the communist side.[58] In addition, the tension between the US and China became stronger over the deepening of the Vietnam War.[59] Maintaining a political distance from China was therefore essential in securing financial aid from the US.[60]

Furthermore, Indonesia softened its aggressive policy towards Malaysia and was anxious to appear cooperative, and change its image of aggressor in the eyes of the international community.[61] *Konfrontasi* was also harmful to the Indonesian economy because it was consuming manpower and resources which should be allocated to economic recovery. The new government wanted to end *Konfrontasi* and 'concentrate more on Indonesia's economic ills'.[62]

As Weinstein puts it, this period was 'a time of the most significant change in the political climate in Indonesia'.[63] Particularly unclear was the direction of Indonesia's foreign policy.[64] Sukarno, who was still a very influential figure in Indonesian politics, continued to pay attention to Indonesia's prestige, especially its leading position in the Afro-Asian world.[65] He was confident that Indonesia had, during the Manila conference in 1963, maintained its reputation as a leader of the third world.[66] He insisted that Indonesia should continue *Konfrontasi* until Ma-

---

[56] *South China Morning Post*, 5 April 1966. Malik began its official procedure in June. Indonesia successfully became a member once again in September 1966. It also rejoined the International Labour Organization (ILO) and the International Monetary Fund (IMF) in July 1966.

[57] Other communist countries were North Vietnam, North Korea and Cambodia. Indonesia cut off its financial aid to Cambodia. (*The Manila Times*, 2 May 1966.)

[58] In this respect, Japan was strongly expected to take the steering of Southeast Asian politics through its financial aid as the US was not respected in the area because of its unfavourable engagement in the Vietnam War. See 'Ikeda Souri, Nikuson Zen Beikoku Fuku Daitouryou Kaiken Roku [The Proceedings of the talks between the Japanese Prime Minister, Ikeda and the former US Vice-President, Nixon]', Amerika-kyoku, Hokubei-ka [Department of North America, Bureau of America, Ministry of Foreign Affairs of Japan], 10 April 1964, GSK File A'-401; and 'Satou Souri, Nikuson Zen Bei Fuku Daitouryou Kaidan Youshi [The Proceedings of the talks between Prime Minister, Sato and the former American Vice President, Nixon]', America-kyoku, Hokubei-ka [Department of North America, Bureau of America, Ministry of Foreign Affairs of Japan], 27 August 1965, GSK File A'-401.

[59] *South China Morning Post*, 17 June 1966.

[60] Malik said, 'If Peking is not satisfied with our new policy, it is of course not our business', although he stated the government's attitude towards China would not change. (*The Straits Times*, 5 April 1966.)

[61] Franklin B. Weinstein, *Indonesia Abandons Confrontation: An Inquiry Into the Functions of Indonesian Foreign Policy* (Modern Indonesia Project, Interim Reports Series No.45, Ithaca, NY: Southeast Asia Program, Department of Asian Studies, Cornell University, 1969), p. 41. Indonesia secretly negotiated Malaysia before the abortive coup (since August 1965) to end *Konfrontasi*. It is said that *Opsus* (Special Operations, headed by Ali Murtopo) was established within *Kostrad* (Army Strategic Reserve Command) in 1964 and sought the possibility of the end of *Konfrontasi*. (David Jenkins, *Suharto and His Generals: Indonesian Military Politics 1975-1983* (Cornell Modern Indonesia Project No. 64, Ithaca, NY: Southeast Asia Program, Cornell University, 1984), p. 22.) Just after the abortive coup, Ali Murtopo and Benni Murdani informally started negotiation with Malaysia. (*The Straits Times*, 21 June 1966.)

[62] *The Manila Times*, 2 May 1966.

[63] Franklin B. Weinstein, *Indonesia Abandons Confrontation*, p. 40.

[64] The international community, and in particular, Malaysia, were sceptical about Indonesia's desire for ending *Konfrontasi* because Indonesian foreign policy was sometimes inconsistent, reflecting confused domestic situation. (Franklin B. Weinstein, *Indonesia Abandons Confrontation*, p. 34.)

[65] This is based on the victorious West Irian Campaign of 1962 against the Netherlands.

[66] George McT. Kahin, 'Malaysia and Indonesia', p. 269. In the course of the conference, he stuck to two issues (both stipulated in the Manila agreements) as the conditions for the recognition of Malaysia: self-determination in Sabah and Sarawak should be respected, and the British presence in Malaysia and Singa-

laysia conformed to the Manila agreements of 1963.[67] As British Foreign Secretary Michael Stewart pointed out, 'Sukarno had no choice but to depend on his past glory in order to maintain support from the people'.[68]

Adam Malik, on the other hand, took a pragmatic approach to Indonesia's future. As opposed to Sukarno, he considered food, clothing and shelter as more important for Indonesia than its international prestige. Rather, a belligerent attitude towards Malaysia would degrade Indonesia's reputation and jeopardise its foreign aid agreements. He insisted, instead, that foreign policy should be formed in accordance with the national interest and that economic recovery should be the new government's top priority.[69] In this context, Malik argued that Indonesia should take a flexible attitude towards the Malaysia issue so that it could be settled quickly. He implied that at this stage Indonesia should not argue strongly over the detailed positions in the Manila agreements of 1963.[70]

The Indonesian Army's position was more complicated. The Army was keen to restore the country's economy as quickly as possible, because many of its officials were involved in commerce.[71] However, it was reluctant to end *Konfrontasi* if Indonesia's concessions were not reciprocated by Malaysia.[72] In this regard, the position of Suharto, who was also the supreme leader of the Army, was rather ambiguous as he was trying to balance between different interest groups at home.[73] In order to bring peace and stability to the Indonesian politics, he had to create political consensus between three groups: Sukarno, who was the father of Indonesia and still an ideological leader of the people, Malik, who was the intellectual driving force behind the New Order government, and the Army, the most dominant political force in Indonesia. Therefore, Suharto took 'a more realistic and pragmatic way of thinking without sacrificing the ideals of the national struggle'.[74]

In an interview with *Asahi Shimbun* in April 1966, Suharto clarified the Army's two main objectives: the implementation of Indonesian revolution and the maintenance of national defence.[75] These two points were consistent with the two claims, which Sukarno had been insisting on: firstly, self-determination of the people in Sabah and Sarawak should be observed from the view point of Indonesian revolutionary ideology; and, secondly, foreign military bases in the region were perceived as threats to Indonesia's national security.[76] Suharto was reluctant to abandon the confrontation policy quickly without any concession from the Malaysian side whereas Malaysia expressed its desire to end the conflict with Indonesia by saying, 'We would like to have peace...with Indonesia'.[77]

---

pore should end. (*The Straits Times*, 2 August 1963) For the details of the Manila conference, see Chapter 3.

[67] However, he confessed in his book that he wanted to cease the militant confrontation policy by, at least, late 1965. (*Asahi Shimbun*, 10 November 1965.)

[68] 'Dai Yon-kai Nichi-Ei Teiki Kyougi, Shiina-Stuart Ryou Gaisyou Kaidan [The fourth Japan-Britain regular conference, Foreign ministerial talks between Shina and Stewart]', Ou-A-kyoku, Eirenpou-ka [Department of the Commonwealth of Nations, Bureau of Eurasia, Ministry of Foreign Affairs of Japan], 19 October 1965, GSK File A'-427. Author's translation.

[69] Nicholas Turner, 'Malik Manoeuvres', *Far Eastern Economic Review*, 28 April 1966, p. 177.

[70] *The Straits Times*, 4 May 1966.

[71] Harold Crouch, 'Generals and Business in Indonesia', *Pacific Affairs*, 48/4 (Winter, 1975-1976), pp. 519-520.

[72] *The Straits Times*, 2 May 1966.

[73] *Asahi Shimbun*, 13 March 1966.

[74] Suharto, *Soeharto*, p. 153.

[75] *Asahi Shimbun*, 20 April 1966.

[76] The US used bases in Singapore when the PRRI rebellion happened in Indonesia in late 1950s. See Herbert Feith and Daniel S. Lev, 'The End of the Indonesian Rebellion', p. 41. For the details of the PRRI rebellion, see Chapter 2.

[77] *The Straits Times*, 11 March 1966.

Furthermore, Suharto hoped that *Konfrontasi* would finish without loss of face for Sukarno, the Indonesian Army, or Indonesia as a whole.[78] He recognised that the revolutionary identity, which was formed through a dogged struggle for independence during the Sukarno era, was strong among the people in Indonesia.[79] Suharto paid regard to Sukarno because the latter was still 'the great leader of revolution' for many of Indonesians.[80] In addition, Suharto needed to be patient in order that the Army would adjust itself to the new political leadership in Indonesia.[81] Therefore, he initially repeated the views, already prevailing in Indonesia, by saying that the establishment of Malaysia posed a threat to Indonesian revolution and that it was a deviation from the Manila agreements.[82] The next step for Suharto was to reduce military confrontation to a political form instead.

In this regard, it was difficult to make a coherent foreign policy with such strongly competing political perspectives. In early April 1966, Adam Malik announced that Indonesia would soon recognise Singapore.[83] He had apparently realised that the recognition of Singapore was '"the first step" toward ending the policy of confrontation'.[84] Malik wanted to stimulate the Indonesian economy by resuming trade with Singapore, since Indonesia 'had been relying almost 100 per cent on Singapore' for its trade before entering *Konfrontasi*.[85] However, the importance of Malik's announcement was belittled by Sukarno's troublesome statement that Indonesia intended to intensify the Crush Malaysia Campaign by opening diplomatic relations with Singapore.[86] In addition, the *Indonesian Herald* reported that the government aimed to break the neo-colonialists' encirclement of Malaysia by giving recognition to Singapore.[87] Malik himself issued a statement, but it only provoked the Malaysian government and contradicted his previous statement:

> With regard to confrontation of Malaysia, it will continue. But I hope that our recognition of Singapore will contribute to show clearly that confrontation does not necessarily mean use of physical force. The recognition of Singapore could extend the opportunity to Malaysia to reconsider its policies towards Indonesia.[88]

The intricate political agenda towards Singapore irritated the Malaysian government.[89] Malaysia was particularly sensitive with regard to Singapore because its secession from the Federation was recognised as a severe vulnerability. Malaysian Prime Minister Tunku Abdul Rahman remained hostile and sharply criticised Indonesia's position: 'Offering to recognise Singapore, at the same time expressing determination to crush Malaysia, shows the belligerent and spiteful attitude of Indonesia towards us'.[90] His government also warned that Singapore must choose friendship with either Malaysia or Indonesia, not with both.

---

[78] Suharto, *Soeharto*, p. 153.
[79] *Asahi Shimbun*, 20 April 1966.
[80] Ibid. Author's translation.
[81] *South China Morning Post*, 10 June 1966.
[82] *The Straits Times*, 2 April 1966.
[83] *The Straits Times*, 11 April 1966.
[84] *The New York Times*, 12 April 1966.
[85] *The Straits Times*, 21 June 1966.
[86] The bilateral relations between two countries were not amicable.
[87] *South China Morning Post*, 13 April 1966.
[88] *The Straits Times*, 19 April 1966. This statement is understood as a face-saver for Sukarno because it contradicted his amicable foreign policies. Nicholas Turner, for example, described Malik's real intention when he had an interview with him: 'Malik let it be known privately that despite public statements about continuing and even intensifying the confrontation against Malaysia, his intention is to end it as quickly as possible'. (Nicholas Turner, 'Malik Manoeuvres', p. 178.)
[89] *The Straits Times*, 16 April 1966.
[90] Ibid.

In the Philippines, President Diosdado Macapagal could not break the jinx of being 'never re-elected'.[91] In the 1965 Presidential elections, he was beaten by Ferdinand Marcos. After the Philippines abandoned its mediator's role, when the Indonesian Army landed on the Malay Peninsula in August 1964, Macapagal's foreign policy became unpopular because many Filipinos had been 'proud of the country's role as peacemakers' in the Malaysia issue.[92] Ferdinand Marcos pledged himself to resume diplomatic relations with Malaysia during his election campaign in 1965.[93] The policy of the Marcos administration was more focused on economic development than on the creation of an Asian identity.[94] He began negotiations with Malaysia soon after he came into office. The two countries reached an agreement of normalisation in mid-February 1966 and resumed diplomatic relations.[95] Both countries agreed to the rapprochement in early February. Marcos said, 'I am certain that our recognition of Malaysia will be accepted by Indonesia in this light'.[96]

A month before the agreement, Marcos released a statement, emphasising the importance of economic development by saying, 'it is our solemn obligation to strive as best we can towards...economic wellbeing of the peoples within the region'.[97] He believed that peace and stability would be essential for economic development and rapprochement with Malaysia should be made in this context. However, Indonesia opposed his policy at that time. Indonesian Foreign Minister Subandrio said that the Philippines' recognition of Malaysia would not help the reconciliation between Indonesia and Malaysia.[98] He added that recognition of Malaysia would only exacerbate Southeast Asia's already volatile political climate.[99] Thus, the Philippines' initiative was quickly suspended at Indonesia's opposition.[100]

Towards reconciliation

Fresh progress in bilateral relations between Indonesia and Malaysia appeared in early April 1966, a month after Suharto came to office. Indonesia sent an observer to the first Ministerial Conference on Economic Development in Southeast Asia (MCEDSEA)[101] in Tokyo on 6 April, which was attended by Laos, Malaysia, the Philippines, Singapore, Thailand and South Vietnam. It was regarded as 'epoch-making' that the new Indonesian government showed its willingness to sit with the Malaysian government at the same table during the conference.[102] On the same day, when Indonesia showed its softened attitude, Malaysian Prime Minister Tunku Abdul Rahman put forward the following conditions for resuming peace talks with Sukarno: (1) Philippine President Marcos must talk with Sukarno and confirm his genuine desire for a peaceful settlement; (2) The Tunku would be willing to meet with Sukarno even before Indonesian hos-

---

[91] Richard Butwell, 'The Philippines: Changing of the Guard', *Asian Survey*, 6/1 (January 1966), p. 44.
[92] Lela Garner Noble, *Philippine Policy toward Sabah*, p. 156.
[93] Lela Garner Noble, 'The National Interest and the National Image', p. 566.
[94] Ibid.
[95] Bernard K. Gordon, 'Regionalism in Southeast Asia' in Robert O. Tilman (ed.), *Man, State, and Society in Contemporary Southeast Asia* (London: Pall Mall Press, 1969), p. 509. The full diplomatic relations between two countries resumed on 3 June 1966. See the Joint Statement between Malaysia and the Philippines on 3 June 1966.
[96] Ferdinand Marcos, Foreign Policy Statement, 7 February 1966.
[97] Ibid.
[98] *Asahi Shimbun*, 12 February 1966.
[99] Ibid.
[100] On 24 March, the Indonesian government called for the Philippine Ambassador, Narciso Reyes, and asked the Philippines to suspend the recognition of Malaysia for a while. (*The Straits Times*, 25 March 1966)
[101] MCEDSEA was established by the initiative of the Japanese government. The member countries were Laos, Malaysia, Singapore, the Philippines, Thailand and South Vietnam. Cambodia also sent an observer to the conference.
[102] *Asahi Shimbun*, 3 April 1966.

tilities ceased if his first condition were met.¹⁰³ On 12 April, in response to the Tunku's statement, the Philippine official, Consul Juan Dionisio, informed the Tunku of Indonesia's willingness to talk about bringing an end of *Konfrontasi*.¹⁰⁴ On the same day, Marcos called for a tripartite ministerial conference.¹⁰⁵ However, at this stage Malaysia still seemed to doubt Indonesia's willingness to resume diplomatic relations with Malaysia,¹⁰⁶ which probably stemmed from Indonesia's inconsistent statements about the recognition of Singapore. It was reported that Malaysia declined the Philippines' proposal at this stage.¹⁰⁷ A week after the Tunku issued his conditions for the bilateral talks with Sukarno, it was reported that Indonesia was going to drop its pre-condition for the talks with Malaysia.¹⁰⁸

The external powers, such as the United States and Britain, were indirectly helping the new Indonesia. They realised that this was a chance to encourage Indonesia to return to the international community. The two countries were quick in showing favourable attitudes and willingness to offer aid to the Indonesian government. On 18 April, the US government announced it would send emergency food supplies to the country.¹⁰⁹ On 25 April, British Foreign Secretary Michael Stewart expressed Britain's intention to end its antagonism towards Indonesia, and he said, '[W]e are in touch with the Indonesian government to that end'.¹¹⁰ The British government offered one million pounds in economic aid to Indonesia on the condition that Indonesia would cease military incursions into Malaysia.¹¹¹

The talks between Indonesian Foreign Minister Adam Malik and Philippine Secretary of Foreign Affairs Narciso Ramos were held in Bangkok between 30 April and 1 May 1966.¹¹² They seemed to be in accord with the Tunku's requirements of 6 April.¹¹³ In the Joint Statement after the talks, Malik expressed Indonesia's desire 'to find a peaceful solution' for the Malaysia issue.¹¹⁴ It should be noted that it was the first time that Indonesia officially expressed its intention to end *Konfrontasi*.¹¹⁵ Ramos said with confidence, 'I think I can say the differences between Indonesia and Malaysia will be solved by peaceful means'.¹¹⁶ He also disclosed to the press that the Indonesian government had ordered the troops, which had deployed to the Rhio

---

¹⁰³ *The Straits Times*, 7 April 1966.
¹⁰⁴ *The Straits Times*, 13 April 1966.
¹⁰⁵ Ibid.
¹⁰⁶ Ibid.
¹⁰⁷ *South China Morning Post*, 13 April 1966.
¹⁰⁸ *The Straits Times*, 15 April 1966.
¹⁰⁹ *South China Morning Post*, 19 April 1966.
¹¹⁰ *The Straits Times*, 26 April 1966.
¹¹¹ *South China Morning Post*, 28 April 1966. The amount of British aid was one million pounds. The British government said that the large amount of aid would be an 'absolute gamble'; however, it would be cheaper considering that it had spent 150,000 pounds every year for defending Malaysia against Indonesia. See 'Delama Eikoku Gaimu Jikanho (Kyokutou Tantou) tono Kaidan Kiroku [The Proceedings of the Talks with Delamere, The deputy of the Subordinate Officer of the Ministry of Foreign Affairs of the United Kingdom]', Ou-A-kyoku, Eirenpou-ka [Department of the Commonwealth of Nations, Bureau of Eurasia, Ministry of Foreign Affairs of Japan], 5 July 1966, GSK File A'-410.
¹¹² Thai Foreign Minister Thanat Khoman took the initiative of the talks.
¹¹³ The Malaysian Permanent Secretary of Ministry of External Affairs, Inche Ghazali bin Shafie, secretly attended the talks (Michael Leifer, *Indonesia's Foreign Policy*, p. 108). Yamakage sees differently: there was another secret meeting between Ghazali and Malik in Bangkok. (Susumu Yamakage, *ASEAN*, p. 90.)
¹¹⁴ The Joint Statement between Indonesia and the Philippines, 1 May 1966. (*The Bangkok Post*, 2 May 1966.)
¹¹⁵ The Tunku suggested that Indonesia should make a 'straightforward and forthright approach to us' if it seriously wanted to end *Konfrontasi*. (*The Straits Times*, 10 May 1966.)
¹¹⁶ *South China Morning Post*, 5 May 1966.

Islands near Singapore, to cease firing on Malaysian aircraft.[117] Malik seemed eager for a rapid settlement, saying that he wanted to 'find a short cut'.[118]

The Malaysian attitude towards Indonesia softened after the talks between Malik and Ramos. Malaysian Deputy Prime Minister Tun Abdul Razak said, 'I am happy to note from press reports that Dr Malik wishes a speedy settlement of his country's dispute with Malaysia by peaceful means and that chances for such a peaceful settlement are better now than they were before the September 30 coup attempt'.[119] He added the comment about the recognition of Singapore by saying, 'We are also relieved to note that the Indonesian decision to recognise Singapore is not with the intention of intensifying confrontation against Malaysia'.[120] Malaysia finally expressed its willingness to abandon the pre-conditions for the talks with Indonesia.[121]

However, Malik's intention to quickly end *Konfrontasi* was not shared by all the interest groups in Indonesia. Sukarno, for example, denounced Malik's approach to the Bangkok talks as cowardly due to the failure of the latter to properly address the Malaysian issue.[122] In addition, the Army was also not happy with Malik's policy on the Malaysia issue. The Indonesian military spokesman, Brigadier General Ibnu Subroto, argued that the campaign should be continued as long as British troops continued to be stationed in Malaysia.[123] General Abdul Haris Nasution, the Deputy Chief of Crush Malaysia Command (KOGAM),[124] said that *Konfrontasi* would end only when both countries strictly abided by the Manila agreements, and particularly the two conditions Indonesia had reiterated.[125] Sukarno brought up the Singapore issue again by saying that Indonesia regarded the recognition of Singapore as a confrontational political tactic against Malaysia.[126] A consensus about the end of *Konfrontasi* was yet to be formed. Suharto emphasised harmony in domestic politics and said, 'National unity is important'.[127] In an interview with the *Straits Times*, Suharto again underlined his support to the two oft-reiterated reasons for Indonesia's confrontation against Malaysia.[128]

Adam Malik was forced to tone down his vociferous support for a rapid settlement, so that Indonesians could reach a consensus. He said, 'It takes time for us to prepare them to accept the new situation', and he added that, '[t]here must be mental preparation of our people to accept the fact that we have settled our problems'.[129] This period was characterised by adjustments in domestic politics, and even Malik sometimes had to reverse statements made previously in support of the peace process. That, however, was merely 'a reflection of a still existing, though diminishing, need to protect themselves against allegations of rightism'.[130]

---

[117] Ibid.
[118] *The Straits Times*, 4 May 1966.
[119] *The Straits Times*, 2 May 1966.
[120] Ibid.
[121] *The Straits Times*, 5 May 1966.
[122] *The Straits Times*, 6 May 1966. Sultan Hamengku Buwono, the Minister of Economic Affairs of Indonesia, said that it was hard for Sukarno to change his views quickly, although '[he too] agreed with peaceful settlement of confrontation'. ('Indonesia Hamenku Buono Fukusyusyou to Shiina Gaimu Daijin tono Kaidan Youroku [The Proceedings of the talks between Indonesian Deputy Prime Minister, Sultan Hamenengku Buwono and Foreign Minister Shina]', Nantou Ajia-ka [Department of Southeast Asia, Ministry of Foreign Affairs of Japan], 25 May 1966, GSK File A'-396. Author's translation.)
[123] *The Bangkok Post*, 14 May 1966.
[124] KOGAM was the reorganised entity of KOTI (*Komando Tertinggi*, Supreme Operations Command) on 22 February 1966 which was a 'part of the effort to rally support for Sukarno'. (Franklin B. Weinstein, *Indonesia Abandons Confrontation*, p. 28.)
[125] *The Bangkok Post*, 16 May 1966.
[126] *The Straits Times*, 16 May 1966.
[127] *The Straits Times*, 6 May 1966.
[128] *The Straits Times*, 2 May 1966.
[129] *The Straits Times*, 1 June 1966.
[130] Franklin B. Weinstein, *Indonesia Abandons Confrontation*, p. 56.

Malik stated that Indonesia would be willing to meet Malaysia without any pre-conditions. On 18 May in an interview with the Australian Broadcasting Commission, he declared that Indonesia would not insist on another referendum in Sabah and Sarawak.[131] With this concession, Indonesia substantially dropped demands concerning its two oft-iterated issues[132] from the preconditions of the talks.[133] The Malaysian government recognised this opportunity as a significant one and asked Deputy Prime Minister Tun Abdul Razak to 'use the present favourable and hopeful atmosphere'.[134] Tun Razak offered to talk with Malik.[135] Malik mentioned the question of self-determination again by saying that Malaysia would not need to hold a new referendum in Sabah and Sarawak, but instead it had only to convince Indonesia that the UN investigation of 1963 had revealed the genuine will of the people there.[136] In addition, he stated that British troops would pull out from Southeast Asia if countries in the region could gain British confidence.[137] In reply to Malik's concession, Malaysia also showed the positive initiative by suggesting the possibility of reviewing the result of the UN investigation of 1963 in Sabah and Sarawak under the auspices of Thailand and Japan.[138] Meanwhile, Indonesia and Malaysia successfully opened up avenues for direct communication, aimed at securing a peaceful settlement, and began to prepare for bilateral talks.[139]

On 27 May 1966, just before the ministerial talks between Indonesia and Malaysia, Suharto sent eight heads of the Indonesian army in Crush Malaysia Command (KOGAM) to Kuala Lumpur.[140] Their visit was enthusiastically welcomed by the Malaysian government. Malaysian Deputy Prime Minister Tun Abdul Razak stated that KOGAM's visit showed 'the military government's desire to establish peace'.[141] He also compared their visit with the Malay traditional custom *kenduri*, which is a feast held before an important meeting aimed at wishing its success by overcoming differences.[142] Indeed, KOGAM's visit had, in effect, 'paved the way' for the bilateral talks.[143]

The ministerial talks between Malik and Tun Razak were held in Bangkok from 29 May to 1 June.[144] Indonesia and Malaysia agreed 'to restore friendly relations' and to maintain 'direct and continuous contact'.[145] After the talks, Malik emphasised Indonesia's desire for peaceful coexistence in the region: 'We want to make peace with all countries, especially our neighbours....We want peace, friendly relations and cooperation'.[146] Tun Razak underlined the importance of maintaining a peaceful and friendly atmosphere at the talks and said that the agreement in Bangkok was 'for the love of peace and in the spirit of coexistence'.[147] However, the

---

[131] *South China Morning Post*, 19 May 1966.

[132] Namely, British bases in Malaysia and referendum in Sabah and Sarawak.

[133] In early May 1966, Malik still emphasised the importance of the two reasons of *Konfrontasi* at the parliament in Indonesia. See *The Straits Times*, 7 May 1966.

[134] *The Straits Times*, 19 May 1966.

[135] *South China Morning Post*, 19 May 1966. Suharto later pointed out the important role of his assistants, Ali Murtopo, Benny Murdani and other military high-ranking officials. They secretly got in contact with Tun Abdul Razak and Ghazali Shafie. They 'agreed that confrontation should cease and reconciliation take place at once'. This secret agreement successfully led to the ministerial talks between Malik and Tun Razak in late May. See Suharto, *Soeharto*, p. 153.

[136] *The Straits Times*, 20 May 1966.

[137] Ibid.

[138] *The Bangkok Post*, 20 May 1966.

[139] *The Straits Times*, 20 May 1966.

[140] *The Straits Times*, 28 May 1966.

[141] Ibid.

[142] *Far Eastern Economic Review*, 9 June 1966, p. 471.

[143] Tun Abdul Razak, *Far Eastern Economic Review*, 9 June 1966, p. 471.

[144] It was held at the initiative of Thai Prime Minister Thanom Kittikachorn.

[145] The Joint Ministerial Statement between Indonesia and Malaysia, 1 June 1966.

[146] *The Bangkok Post*, 3 June 1966.

[147] *The Bangkok Post*, 10 July 1966. The agreement between Malik and Tun Razak was not disclosed at all.

ministerial talks were 'the beginning of the end of Confrontation [*Konfrontasi*] rather than the end itself'[148] as they did not find any solution to Indonesia's concerns over the self-determination in Sabah and Sarawak and the existence of British bases in Malaysia.

Immediately following the success of the Ministerial talks between Indonesia and Malaysia, the Philippine government recognised Malaysia and, on 3 June 1966, formally opened full diplomatic relations.[149] The Joint Statement of the two countries stated that: 'The strengthening of relations between the two countries will pave the way for closer cooperation between them, making it possible for both nations to pursue even greater regional collaboration through the reactivation of the Association of Southeast Asia'.[150]

Post-Bangkok talks

The Army, to say nothing of Sukarno, was not satisfied with the results of the Bangkok talks, because Adam Malik could not draw any concessions from Malaysia regarding the two issues reiterated by Indonesia.[151] On 8 June, Suharto made a statement after the meeting in Crush Malaysia Command (KOGAM), in which he suggested that the Bangkok talks were 'only the first stage' of the ending process of *Konfrontasi* and the results still included 'some problems needing clarification and solution'.[152] Indonesia's Provisional People's Consultative Assembly (MPRS)[153] was also dissatisfied with the outcome of the negotiations.[154] KOGAM required that the two countries should hold further talks in order to bridge their differences and continued to insist on adherence to the 1963 Manila agreements.[155] KOGAM also suggested that Suharto should replace Malik and take full responsibility for further negotiation with the Malaysian government.[156] The Indonesian government authorised Suharto to exercise power for the furtherance of the peace process, and announced that it should take more time to ensure that the people of Indonesia would approve of the result of the Bangkok talks.[157] Although the government did not clarify the exact nature of the issues, Malik, speaking to the press, said, '[these] may be military matters'.[158]

Soon after he was appointed, Suharto began negotiations with his counterpart in Kuala Lumpur, in order to bridge the gap between KOGAM and the Malaysian government. Inche Ghazali bin Shafie, the Malaysian permanent Secretary of the Ministry of External Affairs, visited Suharto and the Army leaders[159] about the treatment of 50,000 British troops in Malaysia, many of whom were stationed in Sabah and Sarawak.[160] When he returned to Kuala Lumpur on 14 June, Ghazali Shafie said, 'They all agree that confrontation should be settled peacefully and in a

---

[148] *Far Eastern Economic Review*, 16 June 1966, p. 510.

[149] The Philippines had suspended its recognition of Malaysia since February because of Indonesia's request.

[150] The Joint Statement between Malaysia and the Philippines on 3 June 1966. Malaysia and the Philippines recognised 'the need of sitting down together, as soon as possible, for the purpose of clarifying the claim and discussing means of settling it to the satisfaction of both parties' when they agreed with rapprochement in June 1966. (Ibid)

[151] *The Straits Times*, 1 June 1966.

[152] *The Straits Times*, 10 June 1966.

[153] It is known as MPRS, *Madjelis Permusjawaratan Rakjat Sementara*.

[154] Franklin B. Weinstein, *Indonesia Abandons Confrontation*, p. 66.

[155] *The Straits Times*, 10 June 1966.

[156] Ibid.

[157] Suharto replaced Malik as the negotiator with the Malaysian side because Malik could not cope with criticism from the government: he was 'clearly a weaker opponent than Suharto'. (Franklin B. Weinstein, *Indonesia Abandons Confrontation*, p. 62.)

[158] *South China Morning Post*, 10 June 1966.

[159] The Army leaders were from *Kostrad*, the Army Strategic Reserve Command.

[160] *The Bangkok Post*, 13 June 1966. On the question of self-determination in Sabah and Sarawak, Indonesia and Malaysia were still not able to reach an agreement at this stage. (*New York Times*, 14 June 1966.)

friendly fashion'.[161] He also implied that there would be room for compromise on the Malaysian side and said, 'I think we have found a formula to end confrontation'.[162]

Just after the talks between Suharto and Ghazali Shafie, Suharto directed his staff to set up a temporary office of the Indonesian government at a hotel in Kuala Lumpur, so that the two countries could accelerate the negotiation for a peaceful settlement.[163] Indonesian representatives had discussions with Tun Abdul Razak on 19 June and predicted that a rapprochement would not take long.[164] Tun Razak announced that the Malaysian government would, in the near future, discuss the withdrawal of the troops with the governments of Britain, Australia and New Zealand.[165] In reply to Tun Razak's request, the British Secretary of Defence, Denis Healey, said that the British military staff would arrive in Malaysia within a couple of months in order to negotiate the gradual withdrawal of British troops from Sabah and Sarawak.[166] Suharto was successful in achieving mutual compromise with Malaysia over the question of British bases, whereas Malik had attempted to make a one-sided concession, in order to achieve quick settlement.[167]

Malik implied that the issue of self-determination would also be resolved by saying, '[W]ith the holding of general elections in Sabah and Sarawak later, the Malaysian issue would be definitely settled'.[168] However, KOGAM had yet to find an entirely satisfactory agreement on this issue. In addition, Sukarno was still advocating confrontation with Malaysia: 'Yet Kuala Lumpur says confrontation has stopped. No, confrontation continues'.[169] After the high-level secret meeting, Suharto sent a special courier to Kuala Lumpur on 31 July together with a new formula.[170] Suharto 'proposed to postpone formal recognition until the General Elections were held in Sabah and Sarawak'.[171] His proposal was accepted by the Malaysian government.[172] In addition, it 'did help tone down criticism at home'.[173] Eventually, the question of self-determination was accommodated and stipulated in the final draft of the Peace Agreement between the two countries: Malaysia 'agrees to afford the people of Sabah and Sarawak…an opportunity to reaffirm…their previous decision about their status in Malaysia' by general elections.[174] On 11 Au-

---

[161] *The Straits Times*, 15 June 1966.

[162] Ibid. Malik also mentioned that the two countries found 'a method for conducting' the differences. See *South China Morning Post*, 16 June 1966.

[163] *The Straits Times*, 21 June 1966. This was headed by Lieutenant Colonel Benny Murdani and the four members of the Strategic Army Command.

[164] *South China Morning Post*, 20 June 1966.

[165] *The Bangkok Post*, 21 June 1966.

[166] *The Straits Times*, 8 July 1966. On 1 July, the British Foreign Secretary, Michael Stewart, visited Indonesia and talked with Malik about the withdrawal of British troops. See *South China Morning Post*, 23 June 1966. In the following week, Indonesian missions headed by the Deputy Foreign Minister, Umarjadi, visited London on 8 July. See *South China Morning Post*, 9 July 1966.

[167] It can be said that Malaysia's concession to Indonesia was related to the declining power of Sukarno. Sukarno considerably lost his power by this time because the MPRS deprived him of presidency for life. See *The Bangkok Post*, 6 July 1966.

[168] *The Straits Times*, 1 August 1966.

[169] *The Bangkok Post*, 29 July 1966.

[170] *The Straits Times*, 1 August 1966.

[171] Suharto, *Soeharto*, p. 153.

[172] Ibid. It is the so-called 'secret annex' which both countries denied its existence since the peace agreement had been signed. For details, see Franklin B. Weinstein, *Indonesia Abandons Confrontation*, pp. 82-88.

[173] Suharto, *Soeharto*, p. 153.

[174] The Agreement to Normalise Relations between the Republic of Indonesia and Malaysia, 11 August 1966.

gust 1966, Malik and Tun Razak signed the Peace Agreement in Jakarta and the longstanding antagonism between the two countries ended: 'It was a victory for both countries'.[175]

Towards regional cooperation

When the ministerial talks between Indonesia and the Philippines were held (30 April to 1 May 1966), Adam Malik and Narciso Ramos also discussed matters of regional cooperation with Thai Foreign Minister Thanat Khoman.[176] A month later, Thanat talked with Malik and Tun Abdul Razak about economic and cultural cooperation including Indonesia, Malaysia, the Philippines and Thailand during the bilateral ministerial talks between Malik and Tun Razak (29 May to 1 June 1966).[177] After the Peace Agreement between Indonesia and Malaysia was reached on 11 August 1966, the idea of new regional cooperation began to crystallise.[178]

There was rivalry between Indonesia and Malaysia over how to formalise cooperation. In Malaysia, Prime Minister Tunku Abdul Rahman maintained that no new organisation was needed because the Association of Southeast Asia (ASA), which was established by the initiative of Malaya, had already existed.[179] The Tunku said, 'I am confident that in time the membership of [the] ASA will grow and with it, its viability and its aims of promoting the economic and social well-being of the people of this region'.[180] Indeed, Malaysia recognised itself as taking a leading role in regional cooperation, because it had achieved high economic growth and earned a reputation from the World Bank and the latter's view of the value of its economic development model in the third world.[181] In this context, the Tunku encouraged Indonesia to join the ASA.[182]

---

[175] Tun Abdul Razak, Speech in the 1416th Plenary Meeting of the United Nations General Assembly, 26 September 1966.

[176] Franklin B. Weinstein, *Indonesia Abandons Confrontation*, p. 88.

[177] 'Tounan Ajia Syokoku Rengou (ASEAN) no Sousetsu ni Tsuite [The Establishment of the Association of Southeast Asian Nations, ASEAN]', Nansei Ajia-ka [Department of Southwest Asia, Ministry of Foreign Affairs of Japan], 18 August 1967, GSK File B'-200.

[178] Susumu Yamakage, *ASEAN*, p. 95.

[179] In Malaysia, there were two views on new regional cooperation at that time: one was the enlargement of the ASA, and the other was the formation of the new organisation so that Indonesia could easily join it. In late June 1966, the Malaysian Acting Minister for Foreign Affairs, Tun Ismail bin Dato Abdul Rahman, said, '[T]he stage is now set for the formation of a South-East Asian Association...It need not to be [the] ASA'. See Tun Ismail bin Dato Abdul Rahman, Address to the Foreign Correspondents Association, Johore Bahru, 23 June 1966.

[180] *The Straits Times*, 1 August 1966.

[181] *The Straits Times*, 24 March 1966. The Tunku adopted the British style of modernisation in his own nation-building policy when his country became independent. (Harry Miller, *Prince and Premier*, p. 207.) Indeed, the British government was proud that Malaya (Malaysia) was the second-most developed democratic country in Asia after Japan. ('Dai Sankai Nichi-Ei Teiki Kyougi, Shiina Daijin to Goodonwooka Gaisyo tono Kaidan Roku, Zai-Ei Taishi yori no Houkoku [The Proceedings of the Third Japan-Britain Regular Conference, the talks between Foreign Minister, Shiina and British Foreign Secretary, Gordon-Walker, The report by the Ambassador to Britain]', Oua-kyoku Eirenpou-ka [Department of Commonwealth of Nations, Bureau of Eurasia, Ministry of Foreign Affairs of Japan], 2 February 1965, GSK File A'-427.)

[182] *The Straits Times*, 1 August 1966. Malaysia also encouraged Australia and New Zealand to join the ASA. (*The Bangkok Post*, 25 February 1967.) In addition, the Tunku proposed an anti-Communist treaty, a friendship treaty including Thailand, Malaysia and other Southeast Asian countries to address the Communist menace. (*The Bangkok Post*, 12 June 1966.) However, an inconsistency within the Malaysian government can be seen at that time. A Malaysian Minister, Tun Ismail bin Dato Abdul Rahman suggested that the new regional grouping should not take a side in the Cold War antagonism: 'It [new regional cooperation] would not be an anti-communists alliance. Nor, for that matter, would it be an anti-western alliance'. (Tun Ismail bin Dato Abdul Rahman, Address to the Foreign Correspondents Association, Johore Bahru, 23 June 1966.)

Indonesia was willing to collaborate with the countries in the region. In this regard, Adam Malik observed that '[he] fully agree[d] with the idea of regional cooperation'.[183] However, at the same time, Indonesia expressed the opinion that the ASA could not deal with the interests of all the countries in Southeast Asia.[184] Indonesia's opposition to the expansion of the ASA stemmed from domestic need: 'The strongly pro-Western image of the ASA could not be reconciled with the ideas of an independent and neutral foreign policy' of Indonesia.[185] Therefore, Indonesia wanted to establish a new regional institution and sought to secure a leading role there: 'We intend to set up a Southeast Asia union for economic, cultural, and technical cooperation'.[186] Indeed, Indonesia was proud of its leadership role in the third world through the hosting of the Asian-African Conference (1955) and achieving a victory in the West Irian Campaign (1962). Therefore, it could not afford to appear as a late-comer in an already existing regional organisation. With these factors in the background, Indonesia began to develop a new scheme with Thailand.[187]

The Philippines had traditionally taken a leading role in regional cooperation. As Onofre D. Corpuz, the then Under Secretary of Education of the Philippines and Professor at the University of the Philippines, put it:

> Soon after independence, many of us [Filipinos] had hoped that the Philippines could make a constructive contribution toward understanding in a troubled world by undertaking the combined roles of representative of Asia to the West, and the interpreter of the West to Asia.[188]

Elpidio Quirino, the former Philippine President, had hosted the Baguio Conference in April 1950, which was the Philippines' initiative for Asian regional cooperation, composed of the Philippines, Thailand, Indonesia, India, Ceylon, Pakistan and Australia.[189] In addition, Philippine President Carlos P. Garcia had been actively involved in the process of forming the ASA in 1961 by working with Tunku Abdul Rahman.[190] Furthermore, his own successor, Diosdado Macapagal, had proposed Maphilindo in 1963.[191] These initiatives helped the Philippines to establish its place as a leading Asian country, and shake off the image of its being an American outpost in Asia.[192] Working towards creating regional cooperation was a significant element in

---

[183] *The Bangkok Post*, 3 June 1966.

[184] *The Straits Times*, 2 August 1966.

[185] Arnfinn Jorgensen-Dahl, *Regional Organization and Order on South-East Asia*, p. 35. Indonesia was considering inviting Burma and Cambodia to the new regional cooperation in addition to Malaysia, the Philippines and Thailand. (*The Straits Times*, 12 April 1967.)

[186] *The Bangkok Post*, 3 June 1966.

[187] In the ministerial talks with Indonesia and the Philippines in November 1963, Thailand proposed a regional association, expanding the ASA and Maphilindo, in order to solve the Malaysia issue. See *Asahi Shimbun*, 17 November 1963.

[188] Onofre D. Corpuz, 'Realities of Philippine Foreign Policy', p. 53. The Philippines traditionally had a sense of superiority and the consciousness of a leading power in the region. This is because they believed that they had acquired the most modernised way of thinking in the world during their colonial period by the Americans. Emmanuel Pelaez warned the people to become modest: 'Let us rid ourselves of such hackneyed notions as the Philippines serving as a bridge between East and West, the Philippines as the show-window of American democracy in Asia, the Philippines as a bastion of the free world in the Western Pacific, and so forth'. See Emmanuel Pelaez, *Government by the People*, p. 527.

[189] Roger M. Smith, *The Philippines and the Southeast Asia Treaty Organisation* (Data Paper No. 38, Ithaca, NY: Southeast Asia Program, Cornell University, 1959), pp. 2-3.

[190] Tunku Abdul Rahman, Letter from Tunku Abdul Rahman to President Garcia of the Philippines (Malayan Proposal for Regional Co-operation), 28 October 1959.

[191] The Manila Accord, 11 June 1963. For details of Maphilindo, see Chapter 3.

[192] Estrella D. Solidum, 'Philippine Perceptions of Crucial Issues Affecting Southeast Asia', *Asian Survey*, 22/6 (June 1982), p. 537.

Ferdinand Marcos's presidency as well, although he gave economic development a higher priority than fostering the creation of an Asian identity per se.[193]

In early 1966, the Philippines first propounded the importance of national development and peace and stability in the region.[194] In this context, the Philippines declared the possibility of reconciliation with Malaysia. President Marcos said, 'I am certain that our recognition of Malaysia will be accepted by Indonesia in this light'.[195] He also stressed the importance of regional harmonisation for the sake of regional prosperity: 'economic wellbeing of the people within the region' is vital; and to do so, we 'shall strive to bring together those at variance and reconcile their conflicting views in a spirit of mutual accommodation'.[196] Referring in late May 1966 to the devastating situation in Vietnam, the Philippine Ambassador to Kuala Lumpur, Narciso G. Reyes, stated that Southeast Asia should work through their differences together for the sake of regional peace and stability.[197] The idea of 'working together beyond difference' can be seen in these Philippine statements, and it came to provide the basis of the philosophy of ASEAN.

The Philippines encouraged Indonesia to join the ASA. In August 1966, Philippine Foreign Secretary Narciso Ramos expressed the hope that Burma, Laos, Cambodia and Singapore, in addition to Indonesia, would participate in the ASA.[198] However, after the Indonesian special envoy, Director-General for Political Affairs of Foreign Office, C. Anwar Sani, visited Manila in late March 1967, Ramos began to help to form new regional cooperation, so that Indonesia and Malaysia could coexist peacefully.[199] He suggested that Indonesia's participation was important to 'secure unity of action for regional economic growth and cooperation'.[200]

Thai Foreign Minister Thanat Khoman also recognised that regional peace was essential to promote socio-economic development.[201] He advocated regional solidarity in order to protect infiltration from neighbouring Communist countries, such as North Vietnam, Laos, Cambodia and China, saying, 'some enemy nations are afraid that if we can work together, schemes of aggression against us cannot be fulfilled'.[202] At the beginning of the discussions on regional cooperation, in May 1966, during the talks between Malik and Tun Razak, Thanat Khoman actually encouraged Malik to insist upon Indonesian membership in the association.[203] However, Malik declined his suggestion because Indonesia had opposed the ASA since its formation and, instead, wanted to establish a new organisation.[204] Thanat accepted Indonesia's position

---

[193] Ferdinand Marcos, Foreign Policy Statement, 7 February 1966.

[194] In July 1966, the Deputy of the subordinate officer of the British Ministry of Foreign Affairs (in charge of Far East), Delamere, said that countries in Southeast Asia gradually realised that they should take responsibility for their own countries. He pointed out that Narciso Ramos was an advocator of such way of thinking. See 'Delama Eikoku Gaimu Jikanho (Kyokutou Tantou) tono Kaidan Kiroku [The Proceedings of the Talks with Delamere, The deputy of the Subordinate Officer of the Ministry of Foreign Affairs of the United Kingdom]', Ou-A-kyoku, Eirenpou-ka [Department of the Commonwealth of Nations, Bureau of Eurasia, Ministry of Foreign Affairs of Japan], 5 July 1966, GSK File A'-410.

[195] Ferdinand Marcos, Foreign Policy Statement, 7 February 1966.

[196] Ibid.

[197] *The Bangkok Post*, 31 May 1966.

[198] *The Bangkok Post*, 8 August 1966.

[199] *The Bangkok Post*, 31 March 1967.

[200] Ibid.

[201] *The Bangkok Post*, 4 August 1966. The security issue for Thailand strongly focused on Communist infiltration from Indochina.

[202] *The Bangkok Post*, 22 July 1966.

[203] Susumu Yamakage, *ASEAN*, p. 94.

[204] 'Tounan Ajia Syokoku Rengou (ASEAN) no Sousetsu ni Tsuite [The Establishment of the Association of Southeast Asian Nations, ASEAN]', Nansei Ajia-ka [Department of Southwest Asia, Ministry of Foreign Affairs of Japan], 18 August 1967, GSK File B'-200. The ASA Declaration of 31 July 1961 stipulated, 'this Association is in no way connected with any outside power bloc'. See Bangkok Declaration, 31 July 1961. The revolutionary ideology was still the main tenet among the people in Suharto's Indonesia.

and started to work on forming a new organisation with Indonesia.²⁰⁵ Malik and Thanat met in Bangkok at the end of August 1966, and issued a Joint statement to this end. They agreed that,

> close and mutually beneficial cooperation amongst the countries of the region would be the best means to ensure the continued progress and prosperity of their peoples, and at the same time it would contribute significantly towards the effects to preserve peace and security in the area. They, therefore, agreed on the necessity of taking practical steps in order to provide an effective framework within which this cooperation could be further promoted.²⁰⁶

A draft of new regional cooperation was completed in late 1966. Its authors then sought consent to the plan from other countries in the region.

The movement towards regional cooperation was also facilitated in the context of external relations of Southeast Asia. The Vietnam War was intensified by US military action in the Gulf of Tonkin in 1964.²⁰⁷ The West, however, was not a homogenous force at the time; there was disagreement between the US and France over activities towards Vietnam in Southeast Asia Treaty Organisation (SEATO).²⁰⁸ Indeed, SEATO was required to reassess itself because members' interests increasingly diverged.²⁰⁹

Under these circumstances, Thailand, a member of SEATO, felt threatened by a possible Communist infiltration from neighbouring countries in Indochina.²¹⁰ Furthermore, Thailand was suspicious about SEATO's solidarity against the Communists, because of the Organisation's previous ineffectiveness in addressing Communist power in Laos and Vietnam.²¹¹ It advocated regional solidarity in Southeast Asia, rather than relying on external military power to prevent Communist infiltration. Thanat Khoman concluded in this respect that the Southeast Asian countries '…should get together and join hands because we cannot rely on outside help and the independence of Asia must be safeguarded by Asians'.²¹²

The Philippines also felt threatened by the Communists, but less so than Thailand.²¹³ The former's view on SEATO was an ambiguous one. On the one hand, Philippine Secretary of Foreign Affairs Narciso Ramos hoped that other countries in Southeast Asia would join SEATO.²¹⁴ On the other hand, he said that because of 'a grave danger to their security and independence' Asian countries should get together.²¹⁵ Ramos stated that the Vietnam War could

---

Although the country was implicitly a pro-Western, it would not state it overtly. Therefore, Indonesia was unable to join the ASA.

²⁰⁵ Arnfinn Jorgensen-Dahl, *Regional Organization and Order on South-East Asia*, p. 33.
²⁰⁶ The Joint Statement between Indonesia and Thailand, 31 August 1966, in *Foreign Affairs Bulletin*, 6/1 (August-September 1966), p. 22-23.
²⁰⁷ Yumio Sakurai, 'Senjyou kara Shijyou he: Gekidou no Indoshina [From the Battle Field to the Market: Indochina in Turbulence]', in Yoneo Ishii and Yumio Sakurai (eds.), *Tounan Ajia Shi I [History of Southeast Asia I]* (Tokyo: Yamakawa Syuppan, 1999), p. 455.
²⁰⁸ *South China Morning Post*, 2 July 1966. France sent only one observer to the SEATO annual meeting in Canberra in late June 1966. See *South China Morning Post*, 24 June 1966. The rift between the two countries in SEATO stemmed from their discord in North Atlantic Treaty Organisation (NATO) where France left on 1 July 1966.
²⁰⁹ *South China Morning Post*, 15 June 1966.
²¹⁰ *South China Morning Post*, 11 June 1966; and *The Bangkok Post*, 4 August 1966..
²¹¹ *South China Morning Post*, 6 August 1966.
²¹² *The Bangkok Post*, 22 July 1966.
²¹³ 'Ikeda Souri to Serukaaku Eikoku Tounan Ajia Sou-benmukan tono Kaidan Naiyou [The Proceedings of the talks between Prime Minister, Ikeda and British General Commissioner for Southeast Asia, Lord Selkirk]', Ou-A-kyoku, Eirenpou-ka [Department of the Commonwealth of Nations, Bureau of Eurasia, Ministry of Foreign Affairs of Japan], 18 October 1962, File GSK A'-411.
²¹⁴ *South China Morning Post*, 15 June 1966.
²¹⁵ *The Bangkok Post*, 31 May 1966.

be solved through the adoption of an Asian way of accommodation rather than external military intervention.[216]

China undertook a successful nuclear test in 1964, and it also developed the hydrogen bomb in May 1966.[217] A nuclear-armed China increased the possibility of a Third World War with the West, this potentially being triggered by contest over the region. As the Malaysian Premier said, 'China's emergence as a powerful military force, expressing the most militant form of Communism, has made the problem of survival for all the countries of Southeast Asia extremely acute'.[218] Speculation was rife among countries in the region that the deterioration of the Vietnam War would give rise to a World War III. This was vividly expressed by Tunku Abdul Rahman:

> If affairs continue to deteriorate as at present we face the spectre of another world war. ... We in Malaysia see our role as one of contributing to the stability of Southeast Asia through social and economic progress, by carrying out a policy of good will and cooperation and by firmly adhering to the free world and strongly supporting the United Nations.[219]

The British announcement of the withdrawal from the 'East of Suez' in July 1967 was also a large concern for countries in the region.[220]

Uncertainty about regional security in Southeast Asia became sharply heightened because, as Thai Foreign Minister Thanat Khoman said, countries in the region 'have relied on outside power to save us...and we seem to have abdicated our responsibility for peace keeping'.[221] The Philippines and Thailand advocated the idea that the region should work together for a peaceful settlement of the Vietnam War.[222] Philippine President Ferdinand Marcos struck a cooperative tone in arguing that Asians should work together 'as brothers, not at cross purposes but for each other's prosperity and happiness'.[223] In the course of the discussion on an Asian initiative for the Vietnam peace process, a desire for peace and harmony was spread among countries in the region. Thanat Khoman said that this desire for peace and freedom 'has driven us to exert efforts to seek a more harmonious relationship among our neighbours in Southeast Asia'.[224]

While jointly addressing the deteriorated situation in Indochina, the countries in Southeast Asia were also gradually recognising the importance of regional harmonisation.[225] In the course of developing the regional cooperation plan, which Indonesia and Thailand were dealing with,[226] Indonesia showed its restrained and amicable attitude in order to invite Malaysia to take part in the proposed plan. Suharto tried to ease the rivalry with Malaysia over the plan. He said on the radio at the end of 1966: 'We must get rid especially of arrogance...to make room for a more proper approach based on equality and mutual respect'.[227] Indonesia tried to bridge the gap between the proposed organisation and the existing ASA by stating that the proposed or-

---

[216] The Philippine government sought its new regional leadership in lieu of Maphilindo by advocating the Asian solution in the Vietnam War. *South China Morning Post*, 20 August 1966.

[217] *South China Morning Post*, 10 May 1966.

[218] Tunku Abdul Rahman, 'Malaysia', p. 670.

[219] Ibid.

[220] Yoneji Kuroyanagi, *ASEAN 35 Nen no Kiseki*, p. 41.

[221] *The Bangkok Post*, 4 August 1966.

[222] *South China Morning Post*, 4 August 1966; and *South China Morning Post*, 20 August 1966.

[223] *The Bangkok Post*, 31 July 1966.

[224] Thanat Khoman, Speech at the United Nations General Assembly, 27 September 1966.

[225] 'Delama Eikoku Gaimu Jikanho (Kyokutou Tantou) tono Kaidan Kiroku [The Proceedings of the Talks with Delamere, The deputy of the Subordinate Officer of the Ministry of Foreign Affairs of the United Kingdom]', Ou-A-kyoku, Eirenpou-ka [Department of the Commonwealth of Nations, Bureau of Eurasia, Ministry of Foreign Affairs of Japan], 5 July 1966, GSK File A'-410.

[226] This regional cooperation plan was later crystallised as ASEAN.

[227] *Far Eastern Economic Review*, 26 January 1967, p. 129.

ganisation was the enlarged model of the ASA.[228] This comment was intended to be a face-saver for Malaysia, so that Malaysia could participate in the new grouping without losing face. Another friendly message was conveyed to Malaysia in April by the Indonesian Ambassador to Thailand, Major General Achmad Yusuf: 'We are not opposing any groups that now exist so long as they are contributing to the development of the region'.[229]

However, the Malaysian Premier, Tunku Abdul Rahman, still stuck to the ASA, saying in April that: '[w]e already have our regional organisation…I don't see any need for setting up another. We have got to make the ASA a success and make it serve our needs before embarking on another organisation…. [Indonesia] can come in any time and make it a success'.[230] In addition, he did not entirely trust the new Indonesia, and said on his visit to Tokyo in October 1966: 'I trust Malik and Suharto's words, but it is another matter whether or not they can control Indonesia'.[231] Suharto's power had not yet completely eclipsed that of Sukarno at that stage.[232] Furthermore, Suharto's sluggish reform of Indonesia's polity and economy had been criticised at this time by members of his government, such as Adam Malik and General Abdul Haris Nasution. The latter considered that this sluggishness might allow Sukarno to seize power afresh.[233] Finally, in February 1967, Sukarno was forced to hand over all of his presidential power to Suharto. In addition, in mid-May of the same year, Sukarno was finally deprived of all of his titles, including the Chief of the Army and was expelled from the Presidential palace in Jakarta.[234]

The ruthless attitude of the Indonesian government towards Sukarno eased the Tunku's suspicion against Indonesia. Tunku Abdul Rahman soon softened his negative stance on new regional cooperation.[235] On 20-21 May 1967, Thanat Khoman held discussions with the Tunku in Tokyo regarding the new organisation and finally secured his participation.[236] Thanat explained the plan[237] to the Tunku first, among the all leaders in the region, thereby placing his status above that of other potential member countries. Thanat said to the Tunku that if the latter gave him the green light, then he would talk to other members.[238] The low-key behaviour of Malik and Thanat, and, in particular Thanat's actions, satisfied the Tunku, who had been proud of holding the leader's role in the formation of the ASA.[239] The Tunku said, 'Thanat was kind enough to sound us [out] first about this proposal'.[240] The Tunku further said, 'We agree in principle to such an association if it serves the interest of the countries in this region'.[241] In reply to the Tunku's statements, Thanat provided him with a face-saving comment at the airport

---

[228] *The Straits Times*, 18 April 1967.

[229] *The Bangkok Post*, 12 April 1967.

[230] *The Bangkok Post*, 14 April 1967.

[231] 'Shiina Gaimu Daijin, Raaman Syusyou Kaidan Youshi [The Proceedings of the talks between Japanese Foreign Minister, Shiina and Malaysian Prime Minister, Tunku Abdul Rahman]', Nansei Ajia-ka [Department of Southwest Asia, Ministry of Foreign Affairs of Japan], 22 October 1966, GSK File A'-359. Author's translation.

[232] As mentioned earlier in this chapter, at the beginning of the new government, Suharto publicly recognised Sukarno as 'the great leader of revolution' for Indonesians. (*Asahi Shimbun*, 20 April 1966.)

[233] *The Bangkok Post*, 16 January 1967.

[234] *The Straits Times*, 12 May 1967.

[235] Malik had a secret meeting with Ghazali Shafie in Bangkok on 17 April. Malik obtained Ghazali's support for the new organisation. Presumably, Malik explained to him the new government's attitude towards Sukarno at that time. See *The Straits Times*, 18 April 1967.

[236] 'Tounan Ajia Syokoku Rengou (ASEAN) no Sousetsu ni Tsuite [The Establishment of the Association of Southeast Asian Nations, ASEAN]', Nansei Ajia-ka [Department of Southwest Asia, Ministry of Foreign Affairs of Japan], 18 August 1967, GSK File B'-200.

[237] It was the plan which was designed by Indonesia and Thailand.

[238] *The Straits Times*, 22 May 1967.

[239] Ibid.

[240] Ibid.

[241] *The Straits Times*, 22 May 1967.

in the following day, '[the] new organisation will be the expansion and succession of [the] ASA'.²⁴² On 23 May, Malik and the Tunku held a short discussion on the matter at Bangkok airport, in the presence of Thanat.²⁴³ Malik was on his way to Burma and Cambodia, while the Tunku was going to Tokyo. The two had a casual conversation in Malay.²⁴⁴ During this informal meeting, the Tunku stated once again that he approved of the idea of the new organisation and the plan to promote regional cooperation for economic well-being.²⁴⁵ Indeed, as Hoang Anh Tuan describes, '[t]he very formation of ASEAN was…an indication of self-restraint by its members'.²⁴⁶

After the discussion with the Tunku in the airport setting, Malik flew on to Burma and Cambodia to invite them to join the proposed organisation.²⁴⁷ Although Malik got their broad support for his plan, he nonetheless failed to persuade them to participate directly.²⁴⁸ On 30 May 1967, Malik stopped in Manila on his way back to Indonesia. He and Philippine Foreign Secretary announced together that they would call a Foreign Ministerial Meeting for new regional cooperation in August.²⁴⁹ Malik repeated at that time that the new organisation would broaden the membership of the ASA.²⁵⁰ The foreign Ministers of five countries, Indonesia, Malaysia, the Philippines, Singapore and Thailand, gathered in Bangkok on 5 August, and began working on the final draft of the declaration. This resulted in the establishment of the Association of Southeast Asian Nations, ASEAN, on 8 August 1967.²⁵¹

From 'antagonising each other' to 'working together'
The sense of hostility between Indonesia and Malaysia (Malaya) originated in the differing views held on nation-building by Sukarno and Tunku Abdul Rahman, and over the independence process after World War II.²⁵² As Sukarno said, Indonesia was unlike other nations '…which obtained their independence as a gift from imperialists'.²⁵³ The Tunku, on the other hand, believed that the Western (British) model of modernisation was the only way to stimulate national development.²⁵⁴ Sukarno remained more sceptical about the Western style of development in this regard, and introduced the Indonesian notion democracy (Guided Democracy), based as it was on consultation and consensus.²⁵⁵ The two countries' entirely different views on nation-building had encouraged bilateral hostility. Indeed, 'Indonesian scepticism about the

---

²⁴² 'Tanatto Kouman Tai Gaisyou no Hou Ma Ni Tsuite (Houkoku) [The report for Thanat Khoman's visit to Malaysia], Zai Maleishia Asaha Rinji Dairi Taishi yori Gaimu Daijin, Dai 528 Gou [Communication from Asaha special Acting Japanese Ambassador to Malaysia to the Foreign Minister, No. 528], Ministry of Foreign Affairs of Japan, 26 May 1967, GSK File B'-200. Author's translation.
²⁴³ *The Straits Times*, 24 May 1967.
²⁴⁴ They were able to communicate in Malay because 'the Malay and Indonesian language have a common origin'. (Treaty of Friendship between Malaya and Indonesia, 17 April 1959.) Then, they changed to English for the benefit of Thai Foreign Minister who was the organiser of the meeting. (*The Straits Times*, 24 May 1967.)
²⁴⁵ *Foreign Affairs Bulletin*, 6/5 (April-May 1967), pp. 460-461.
²⁴⁶ Hoang Anh Tuan, 'ASEAN Dispute Management', p. 65.
²⁴⁷ *The Straits Times*, 24 May 1967.
²⁴⁸ Susumu Yamakage, *ASEAN*, p. 96.
²⁴⁹ *The Straits Times*, 31 May 1967.
²⁵⁰ *The Straits Times*, 31 May 1967.
²⁵¹ ASEAN Declaration, 8 August 1967.
²⁵² The difference in approach taken by the respective leaders was the process used to achieve it: 'Differences in political experience were matched by differences in political outlook and also in the form of the two regimes'. (Michael Leifer, *The Foreign Relations of the New States*, p. 57.)
²⁵³ *The Straits Times*, 20 December 1962.
²⁵⁴ Harry Miller, *Prince and Premier*, p. 207.
²⁵⁵ Sukarno, Speech at the Teachers' Union Congress, 30 October 1956.

reality of Malaysia's independence was grounded in the bitter experiences of her own fight for independence through bloody struggle and revolution'.[256]

However, the disparity of the views between the two countries reduced when Suharto came to power. The Suharto government shifted Indonesia's attitude towards world politics (anti-Communist and pro-West) and towards the affiliated countries: from aggression position to amicability. In addition, it set economic development as its top priority. It decided that Indonesia would use foreign aid from Western countries for its economic reconstruction. In this regard, Indonesia, which was isolated from the international community during the Sukarno era,[257] quickly needed to return to the international community.[258] As a first step for this, Indonesia changed its attitude towards Malaysia and abandoned its aggressive confrontation policy. Suharto's Indonesia took an anti-Communist stance, and, consequently, its policy direction became closer to that of Malaysia. This change enabled the two countries to coexist peacefully in the region for the first time in their history. In addition, Foreign Minister Adam Malik advocated that he would return to Indonesia's original foreign policy; an independent and active policy, which had been adopted before Indonesia entered the Guided Democracy period.[259] Indeed, Suharto's Indonesia re-embraced Indonesian traditional foreign policy with the spirit of tolerance and mutual respect.[260]

Indonesia and Malaysia worked well together in finally ending their long-standing conflict. The bilateral ministerial talks of May 1966 marked the beginning of frequent consultations and face-saving behaviour. Their frequent consultations and the successful settlement of two controversial issues[261] displayed a spirit of mutual concession and face-saving behaviour. Some writers criticised these ministerial talks as a 'failure' because they could only produce an incomplete agreement after the three-day talks.[262] However, considering that the Malaysian government was dissatisfied with Suharto's unwillingness to take a drastic action for the settlement of *Konfrontasi* since it first began in March 1966,[263] it was fruitful for Malaysian leaders to hear the real intentions of the new Indonesian government towards the end of the dispute, and to do so in constructive talks with the Indonesian Foreign Minister himself.[264] In addition, the visit of the army leaders of Crush Malaysia Command (KOGAM) before the bilateral talks also softened Malaysia's attitude towards a peaceful settlement of *Konfrontasi*: The Malaysian Deputy Prime Minister said after the KOGAM's courtesy visit, 'Although confrontation is still officially on, the visit of the Indonesian Army team shows that it has unofficially ended'.[265] He further said, 'I am confident that talks in Bangkok will be a success'.[266] The Malaysian Prime Minister also pointed out, 'a great demonstration of the Indonesian government's sincerity to end confrontation'.[267] If KOGAM's visit had not been realised, Malaysia would have maintained its unfavourable attitude; consequently, the following ministerial talks would have been less productive. KOGAM's visit and the following ministerial talks surely paved the way for rapprochement between the parties concerned.

---

[256] J. A. C. Mackie, *Konfrontasi*, p. 202. The similar description is in the Leifer's work. See Michael Leifer, *Indonesia's Foreign Policy*, p. 75.
[257] In particular, it was so, during the Guided Democracy period.
[258] Nicholas Turner, 'Malik Manoeuvres', *Far Eastern Economic Review*, 28 April 1966, p. 177.
[259] For the detail of Indonesia's independent and active foreign policy, see Chapter two.
[260] Mohammad Hatta, 'Indonesia's Foreign Policy', p. 445.
[261] The two issues were: (1) self-determination in Sabah and Sarawak and (2) foreign bases in Malaysia.
[262] J.A.C. Mackie, *Konfrontasi*, p. 320; and *Asahi Shimbun*, 2 June 1966.
[263] *South China Morning Post*, 23 April 1966.
[264] It is noteworthy that the talks between Malik and Tun Razak in May 1966 also promoted regional peace: diplomatic relations between the Philippines and Malaysia resumed on 3 June 1966, and Indonesia opened diplomatic relations with Singapore on 5 June.
[265] *The Straits Times*, 28 May 1966.
[266] Ibid.
[267] Ibid.

92 *The settlement of the regional problem and the formation of ASEAN*

The new atmosphere of peace and constructiveness between Indonesia and Malaysia encouraged other countries in the region to begin to build harmonious relations too. In parallel to the settlement process of *Konfrontasi*, Malaysia and the Philippines utilised this opportunity to achieve a reconciliation, and this, in turn, led to the successful resumption of full diplomatic relations on 3 June 1966. Malaysia and the Philippines effectively shelved the Sabah issue by agreeing to hold talks in the near future.[268] In late March 1966, Singaporean Prime Minister Lee Kuan Yew expressed his intention to reconcile with Malaysia, after Singapore's secession from Malaysia in August 1965 had led to mutual hostility:[269] 'I shall be happy to see the Tunku [Malaysian Prime Minister] for discussions to establish sound and good relations and find areas for cooperation'.[270]

Indonesia's refusal to join the Association of Southeast Asia (ASA), along with its proposal for a new regional organisation, was a sign of recurring antagonism towards Malaysia. However, these two countries managed to keep the harmony in the region by offering mutual concession. Firstly, there was Malaysia's strong opposition to Indonesia's leadership in the region. This stemmed from Malaysia's bitter experience with *Konfrontasi*. In addition, Malaysia had always been apprehensive of the overwhelming size of Indonesia, such as the latter's expansive territory and large population. If Suharto's Indonesia did not leave from the Sukarno era, it would have remained a large threat to Malaysia. Secondly, Malaysia's opposition also stemmed from its pride as a leading player in regional cooperation and a founding father of the ASA. Thus, the new organisation, which Indonesia was proposing, appeared as a threat to its reputation.

To ameliorate Malaysia's two main concerns, Suharto demonstrated a low-key attitude. He stated that Indonesia should abandon its arrogance and become more restrained in its manner. To relieve the Tunku's doubts about Sukarno's enduring influence in Indonesian politics and in the Indonesian Army, Suharto finally ejected Sukarno from the Presidential palace and stripped him of all titles. This publicly affirmed the new attitude towards Malaysia. In addition, Indonesia stated that the new organisation would be an enlargement of the ASA and the two organisations could coexist separately. In return, to mirror Indonesia's accommodating attitude, Malaysia acknowledged Indonesia's sensitivities by saying that it would join the new organisation. During the short meeting in Bangkok airport just after this, Adam Malik received confirmation from Tun Abdul Razak for joining the new organisation.

In the course of the formation process of the Association of Southeast Asian Nations (ASEAN), all member states recognised that peace and stability were the only means to achieve their goal of socio-economic development.[271] The main purpose of regional cooperation therefore became clear, and ASEAN seemed a natural vehicle to provide the region with a peaceful environment. As Lyon puts it, development is 'seen as the twin of security, the two together travelling hand in hand'.[272] The position of ASEAN was expressed in the ASEAN Declaration:

> To accelerate the economic growth, social progress and cultural development in the region through joint endeavours in the spirit of equality and partnership in order to strengthen the foundation for a prosperous and peaceful community of South-East Asian Nations.[273]

The ASEAN Declaration states that member countries will tolerate different views, so that they could work together in the region.[274] In this respect, the establishment of ASEAN was the

---

[268] Joint Statement between Malaysia and the Philippines on 3 June 1966.
[269] Since then, the relationship between two countries had not been worked out.
[270] *The Straits Times*, 1 April 1966.
[271] *Far Eastern Economic Review*, 24 August 1967, p. 379.
[272] Peter Lyon, *War and Peace in South-East Asia*, p. 208.
[273] ASEAN Declaration, 8 August 1967.
[274] Actually, what was reconciled through the formation of ASEAN was the ideological rift between Indonesia and Malaysia. Other issues, such as the Sabah issue between Malaysia and the Philippines and the

'landmark' of regional political achievement.²⁷⁵ The ASEAN Declaration can 'be said to represent a more sophisticated view of international affairs which subordinates dogmatic theories to practical issues'.²⁷⁶ In July 1967, a month before the establishment of ASEAN, Mohamed Khir Johani, the Malaysian delegate, expressed his idea about regional cooperation at the Second Ministerial Meeting of Asian and Pacific Council (ASPAC):²⁷⁷

> States must learn to live not merely in passive co-existence but in active co-operation with one another, fully respecting the rights of each to its own independent existence and to its own form of political and economic organisation without any external interference.²⁷⁸

The ASEAN declaration was also a proclamation that its member countries would manage regional problems by themselves. It emphasises that they will take the initiative of addressing problems in the region rather than relying on their external relations.²⁷⁹ Furthermore, the declaration stipulates that each country should strive towards socio-economic improvement as its 'primary responsibility'. In addition, the declaration underlines each country's political independence by saying that foreign bases 'are not intended to be used directly or indirectly to subvert the national independence and freedom of States'. The declaration can be said to represent the desire for self-reliance in the region; as Macapagal put it when he launched Maphilindo, 'Asian declaration of independence'.²⁸⁰

There had been Western-made organisations in Southeast Asia, such as Southeast Asia Treaty Organisation (SEATO) or the Colombo Plan. In addition, more or less all countries in ASEAN, except for Indonesia, had relied on external defence ties with the US or Britain. Nevertheless, Indonesia and Malaysia were able to settle their conflict without external help.²⁸¹ In early May 1966, when the Japanese government offered to accommodate *Konfrontasi*, the Indonesian Foreign Minister said that Indonesia and Malaysia were able to solve it without any mediator.²⁸² Two weeks later, just before the ministerial talks between Indonesia and Malaysia in Bangkok, American Secretary of State Dean Rusk also said, '[Indonesia and Malaysia] are likely to be able to resolve these matters better without us than with us, and we are perfectly prepared to cheer from the sidelines on something like this and wish them well'.²⁸³ The success of peaceful settlement encouraged neighbouring countries to solve other pending regional problems by themselves, which is represented by the oft-repeated slogan in the region: 'Asian solu-

---

ethnic tension between Malaysia and Singapore were still pending. (Yoneji Kuroyanagi, *ASEAN 35 Nen no Kiseki*, p. 33.)

²⁷⁵ Bilson Kurus, ''Understanding ASEAN: Benefits and Raison d'Etre', *Asian Survey*, 33/8 (August 1993), p. 826.

²⁷⁶ Harvey Stockwin, 'Tricky Negotiations', *Far Eastern Economic Review*, 24 August 1967, p. 379.

²⁷⁷ ASPAC was established in 1966 by nine Asia-Pacific countries: Japan, South Korea, Malaysia, the Philippines, Thailand, South Vietnam, Australia, New Zealand and Taiwan. It was set up as a consulting organisation on economic and cultural matters. It dissolved in 1975.

²⁷⁸ Mohamed Khir Johani, 'The Opening Address of the Asian and Pacific Council, The Second Ministerial Meeting, 5 July 1967', *Foreign Affairs Bulletin*, 6/6 (June-July 1967), p. 493.

²⁷⁹ 'Miki Daijin, Goorudobaagu Kaigi Roku [The Proceedings of the talks between the Foreign Minister, Takeo Miki and the US Representative to the UN, Arthur Joseph Goldberg]', Kokusai Rengou-kyoku, Seiji-ka [Department of Politics, Bureau of the United Nations, Ministry of Foreign Affairs of Japan], 25 February 1967, GSK File A'-401.

²⁸⁰ Gerald Sussman, 'Macapagal, the Sabah Claim and Maphilindo', p. 224.

²⁸¹ The settlement process also created 'mutual trust' between two countries. See *Far Eastern Economic Review*, 23 June 1966, p. 588.

²⁸² *The Straits Times*, 9 May 1966.

²⁸³ Dean Rusk, News Conference, 27 May 1966.

tions for Asian problems' which Adam Malik also advocated when he signed the peace agreement with Malaysia.[284] Indeed, as Thanat Khoman put it,

> The main motivation which has promoted Asian nations to strengthen regional co-operation lies in their common desire to assume greater responsibility in regard to Asian problems and to prevent outside Powers from interfering with and dominating the life of Asian peoples.[285]

Another element of the backdrop to regional initiative stemmed from the reaction to the frustrating standstill in Vietnam. The Philippines and Thailand sought a mediator's role to peacefully settle the Vietnam War in 1966. Philippine Foreign Secretary Narciso Ramos proposed a regional solution, according to the reiterated rally cry, 'Asian solutions by Asians' and said: 'We will now approach only Asian countries with a view of trying to find a peaceful settlement to the Vietnam War... Maybe we will create a better impression if fellow Asians approach Hanoi'.[286] Singaporean Premier Lee Kuan Yew proposed that countries in Southeast Asia should guide China to cooperate with neighbouring countries rather than sharply antagonising it; and this was supported by Malaysia and Thailand.[287] The idea of regional solutions for regional problems was inspired not only by the reconciliation of the intra-ASEAN conflict but also by insecurity in its vicinity.

Concluding remarks

Suharto's rise to power brought drastic change to Indonesia. His government drew Indonesia back to the international community by ending its confrontational attitude towards Malaysia and Britain. It also showed its willingness to work together with neighbouring countries for the sake of peace and prosperity. The Philippines, on the other hand, arrived at rapprochement with Malaysia without making any decision about the treatment of Sabah. These changes encouraged countries in Southeast Asia to form a new regional organisation, ASEAN. In this period, ASEAN countries' policies were subsumed into one: socio-economic well-being was the major objective, and peace and stability seemed essential to achieve that objective. Another major development of this period was the maintenance of a sense of regional responsibility for regional affairs, after 1963, when Indonesia, Malaya and the Philippines signed the Manila agreements. These two major issues were officially recognised and enshrined in the foundation document of ASEAN (The ASEAN Declaration) as its major objectives.

A specific form of behaviour was observed during this period: In the first half of this period, when Indonesia, Malaysia and the Philippines proceeded in the reconciliatory process, Indonesia and Malaysia had negotiations in a face-saving manner. In addition, Malaysia and the Philippines shelved the Sabah territorial issue; the latter half includes the formation process of ASEAN, consultations in a face-saving fashion, and mutual concession. The potential member states of ASEAN were encouraged to draw closer together, and do so according to these principles.

---

[284] *Asahi Shimbun*, 12 August 1966.
[285] Thanat Khoman, Speech at the United Nations General Assembly, 27 September 1966.
[286] *South China Morning Post*, 4 August 1966.
[287] 'Delama Eikoku Gaimu Jikanho (Kyokutou Tantou) tono Kaidan Kiroku [The Proceedings of the Talks with Delamere, The deputy of the Subordinate Officer of the Ministry of Foreign Affairs of the United Kingdom]', Ou-A-kyoku, Eirenpou-ka [Department of the Commonwealth of Nations, Bureau of Eurasia, Ministry of Foreign Affairs of Japan], 5 July 1966, GSK File A'-410.

5 THE CORREGIDOR AFFAIR

The so-called Corregidor affair occurred in March 1968, just seven months after the establishment of ASEAN. Contrary to the harmonious and amicable mood at the inauguration of ASEAN, Malaysia and the Philippines again plunged into a state of antagonism over the dominion of Sabah. To make matters worse, this bilateral dispute drove the Association into a dysfunctional state. However, other ASEAN member countries took a conciliatory approach and successfully prevented the disintegration of the organisation. The antagonism between the two countries was substantially soothed when Malaysia and the Philippines sat at the same table at the ASEAN ministerial dinner in Thailand in December 1968. This chapter argues that the Corregidor affair is the most significant event for the early stages of ASEAN's existence, especially because of the distinctive settlement style used to resolve the dispute. From this point of view, it elaborates on the mediation process and identifies the specific ideas and practices of ASEAN members which exemplify the 'ASEAN Way'.

The killings in the Corregidor Island

The Corregidor affair was the recurrence of the territorial dispute between Malaysia and the Philippines over Sabah, the northern part of the Island of Borneo.[1] When the two countries agreed to rapprochement in June 1966, they, in fact, shelved the dispute over the dominion of Sabah, instead of seeking a complete solution. The recurrence of the territorial dispute was triggered by killings on Corregidor, a small island in the Philippines, located at the entrance of the Manila Bay.[2] The account of the killing was published in local newspapers on 21 March 1968. Although there were no clear details of the incident,[3] at least several recruits were killed during a training of the Special Forces, according to these articles.[4] The Special Forces were formed in 1967 in order to infiltrate Sabah and were composed of Muslim recruits.[5] They were trained on the Corregidor Island, where the killings occurred.

The Liberal Party, the party in opposition to the Philippine President, Ferdinand Marcos, used this issue to attack the Marcos administration. It cross-examined Marcos in Congress re-

---

[1] The most detailed description on the progress of the affair was in Lela Garner Noble, *Philippine Policy toward Sabah*, pp. 165-205. The affair is also described in her article of 'The national Interest and the National Image', p.566-570; Amitav Acharya, *Constructing a Security Community in Southeast Asia*, pp. 49-50; Dewi Fortuna Anwar, *Indonesia in ASEAN: Foreign Policy and Regionalism* (Singapore: Institute of Southeast Asian Studies, 1994), pp. 168-170; Mely Caballero-Anthony, *Regional security in Southeast Asia*, pp. 66-67; Arnfinn Jorgensen-Dahl, *Regional Organization and Order on South-East Asia*, pp. 197-208; and Michael Leifer, 'The Philippines and Sabah Irredenta', *The World Today*, 24/10 (October 1968), pp. 421-428.

[2] As discussed in Chapter 3, the question of Sabah was one of the key issues in the regional dispute between Indonesia, Malaysia and the Philippines, which had started with the establishment of Malaysia in 1963. The settlement process helped the countries in the region to form the ASEAN cooperation. In this context, it is significant to examine how the two countries were able to settle the Corregidor affair in the framework of ASEAN. In addition, the Corregidor affair was ASEAN's first difficulty since its establishment.

[3] Lela Garner Noble, 'The National Interest and the National Image: Philippine Policy in Asia', *Asian Survey*, 13/6 (June 1973), p. 566.

[4] Michael Leifer, 'The Philippines and Sabah Irredenta', p. 423.

[5] They were from the Sulu Archipelago of the Philippines, who historically had close relationship with Muslims in Sabah. See Lela Garner Noble, 'The Moro National Liberation Front in the Philippines', *Pacific Affairs*, 49/3 (Autumn 1976), p. 408.

garding the background of the killing and the aim of the Muslim's military training on the island.[6] What actually happened, however, was controversial, as the source of information for it was a recruit who had escaped and was provided with a safe haven by the opposition Liberals. The government changed its explanation repeatedly and eventually recognised the existence of Special Forces whose purpose was to infiltrate Sabah.[7]

In addition, the Liberals were able to attract attention to the issue of the Sabah dominion. The opposition criticised Marcos for not clarifying the future of Sabah when his office had reached a rapprochement with Malaysia in June 1966.[8] At the beginning of his tenure in early 1966, President Marcos advocated the good-neighbour policy and undertook reconciliation with Malaysia.[9] He placed national development as a top priority and recognised that regional peace was essential for the country to focus its development policies.[10] In this context, he stated in February 1966 his intention to settle differences with Malaysia: 'We have, therefore, taken the first steps leading to the normalisation of our relations with Malaysia'.[11]

Marcos's new policy had been welcomed by the Malaysian government and prompted Malaysia and the Philippines to resume full diplomatic relations on 3 June 1966.[12] They did not clarify the future of Sabah in the Joint Statement at that time. Instead, they stated 'the need of sitting down together, as soon as possible, for the purpose of clarifying the claim and discussing means of settling it to the satisfaction of both parties'.[13] In the domestic realm, the Sabah claim was important for Marcos, as it was for the former President Diosdado Macapagal, because it helped the development of the Philippine identity, with an attendant symbolic and 'self-assertive Philippine nationalism'.[14] At that time, the Sabah dispute was also the significant factor influencing the result of the presidential election in the following year, at which Marcos sought to become the first re-elected Philippine president.[15]

Reaction from Kuala Lumpur

The government in Kuala Lumpur was extremely sensitive to the Philippines' claim to Sabah because Sabah was not politically stable due to smouldering dissatisfaction, mainly from Muslim groups advocating independence.[16] The Malaysian government did not want a resurfacing of the Philippines' claim to Sabah. In addition, Malaysia's general election was scheduled for the following year, and therefore the Malaysian government needed to avoid the political disturbance at home as well as with the Philippines. Nevertheless, once the issue was raised in the mass media, the Malaysian government was forced to take a strong position. It quickly sent a formal protest to Manila just two days after the news, despite the fact that the incident was not clearly identified. Malaysia's protest re-ignited the territorial dispute.

The Malaysian government maintained that the territorial dispute over Sabah had already been solved in September 1963 by the United Nations investigation, which was performed ac-

---

[6] *Far Eastern Economic Review*, 18 April 1968, p. 168.

[7] *Asahi Shimbun*, Evening edition, 2 May 1968.

[8] Harvey Stockwin, 'The Law's An Ass', *Far Eastern Economic Review*, 24 October 1968, p. 203.

[9] Richard Butwell, 'The Philippines', p. 48.

[10] Lela Garner Noble, 'The National Interest and the National Image', p. 566.

[11] Ferdinand Marcos, Foreign Policy Statement, 7 February 1966.

[12] Bernard K. Gordon, 'Regionalism in Southeast Asia', p. 509.

[13] The Joint Statement between Malaysia and the Philippines on 3 June 1966.

[14] Charles E. Morrison and Astri Suhrke, *Strategies of Survival: The Foreign Policy Dilemmas of Smaller Asian States* (St Lucia: University of Queensland Press, 1978), p. 244.

[15] In this context, filing to the ICJ would 'put the issue in a safe place for Marcos until his re-election problems were over'. See Harvey Stockwin, 'The Nude Strikes Back', *Far Eastern Economic Review*, 18 July 1968, p. 142. The Sabah issue was also important for Philippine politicians to secure Muslim votes. See *Far Eastern Economic Review*, 25 July 1968, p. 180.

[16] Andrew Tan, 'Armed Muslim Separatist Rebellion in Southeast Asia: Persistence, Prospects, and Implications', *Studies in Conflict & Terrorism*, 23 (2000), p. 272.

cording to the Manila agreements of 1963.[17] United Nations Secretary-General U Thant had, after all, announced on 14 September 1963 that the people in Sabah were in favour of joining the Federation of Malaysia. Therefore, Malaysia said that there was no room for negotiation over the matter; and it emphasised keeping harmony in the region by quoting the Manila Accord of 1963:

> [T]he Ministers agreed that in the event of North Borneo [Sabah] joining the proposed Federation of Malaysia the government of the latter and the government of the Philippines should maintain and promote the harmony and the friendly relations subsisting in their region to ensure the security and stability of the area.[18]

Tempering an international dispute

The Philippine government, on the other hand, insisted that the issue of Sabah should be solved legally because the issue had merely been 'shelved' in 1966 for the sake of regional peace and stability. It quoted paragraph 8 of the Manila Joint Statement of 1963.

> The three Heads of government take cognisance of the position regarding the Philippine claim to Sabah (North Borneo), after the establishment of the Federation of Malaysia as provided under paragraph 12 of the Manila Accord that is, that the inclusion of Sabah (North Borneo) in the Federation of Malaysia, does not prejudice either the claim or any right thereunder.[19]

Philippine Foreign Secretary Narciso Ramos said, 'We still hope that the dispute can be settled by peaceful means in accordance with the agreement reached between our two countries'.[20] According to the agreement of 3 June 1966, both governments agreed to 'abide by the Manila Accord…and with the Joint Statement accompanying it, for the peaceful settlement of the Philippines' claim to Sabah'.[21] The Philippine government proposed that the issue should be resolved in the International Court or the United Nations,[22] as directed by the Manila Joint Statement of 1963: that the Sabah claim should be solved 'by means of negotiations, conciliation and arbitration, judicial settlement, or other peaceful means of the Parties' own choice in conformity with the Charter of the United Nations'.[23]

Two months after the incident, Malaysia sought mediation through ASEAN.[24] However, as the Singaporean Foreign Minister, S. Rajaratnam, stated in opposition to this: '[I]t is important that issues not relevant to the Association are not brought in'.[25] The other ASEAN countries were reluctant to get involved in a bilateral issue for fear that the dispute might plunge the Association into crisis. When Thai Prime Minister Thanom Kttikachorn talked with Malaysian Premier Tunku Abdul Rahman on 8 June 1968,[26] Thanom promised his best efforts, but 'without being directly involved in this affair'.[27]

---

[17] The Manila agreements (the Manila Accord, the Manila Declaration and the Manila Joint Statement) were the result of a series of tripartite talks among Indonesia, Malaya and the Philippines in 1963, which were to settle the conflict over the formation of Malaysia. For details, see Chapter 3.
[18] The Manila Accord, 11 June 1963.
[19] The Manila Joint Statement, 5 August 1963.
[20] *The Bangkok Post*, 5 August 1968.
[21] The Joint Statement between Malaysia and the Philippines on 3 June 1966.
[22] *Far Eastern Economic Review*, 18 April 1968, p. 169.
[23] The Manila Joint Statement, 5 August 1963.
[24] Malaysia asked both Thailand and Indonesia to mediate in the dispute. (*Asahi Shimbun*, 8 June 1968.)
[25] *The Straits Times*, 6 August 1968.
[26] They talked in the Tunku's house in Penang.
[27] *Foreign Affairs Bulletin*, 7/6 (June-July 1968), p. 587.

Bangkok talks

Thailand organised bilateral talks in Bangkok, and these began on 17 June 1968. In the opening address, Ghazali Shafie, the Permanent Secretary of External Affairs of Malaysia, proposed a political conciliation for the sake of the development of ASEAN by saying, '[W]hatever the temporary and limited difficulties, we...are firmly resolved that larger interests and deeper ties which united our two peoples will always prevail'.[28] On the other hand, Gauttier Bisnar, the Philippine representative, stated that the Philippines would seek a definite settlement by legal means: 'We are not in this Conference Hall to find the best means of settling the Philippines' claim over Sabah. The Philippine government believes that of all the modes of settlement enumerated in the Manila Accord of 1963, judicial settlement, i.e., submittal of the case to the World Court is the most just and expeditious'.[29]

Thailand and Indonesia stressed the importance of working together in ASEAN despite their differences, and did so in the First Meeting of the Ad Hoc Committee on Civil Aviation of ASEAN, which was held during the bilateral talks between Malaysia and the Philippines. Thanat Khoman, the Thai Foreign Minister, stated in this connection that:

> [The Ad Hoc Committee on Civil Aviation] is only one aspect of regional cooperation. It is but one of the multidimensions in which we of ASEAN countries have yet to learn to live together, to work together and to prosper together. But if we put our heads together, notwithstanding the minor differences that may exist among us, we would ultimately be able to reap the benefits of our joint endeavours and to harvest and enjoy together the fruits of our common labour.[30]

The representative of the Indonesian delegation responded in the following way: '[I]nternal differences among ourselves can equally be detrimental to the future of ASEAN. It is our ardent hope and wish, that such differences, if any, could and should be solved in the ASEAN spirit as members of the same family'.[31]

However, the Bangkok talks failed to bring agreement because neither side was willing to make any significant concession to the other in the course of the month-long talks. Malaysia was in a stronger position than the Philippines because their mutual agreement was required for the dispute if the issue would be filed in the International Court of Justice (ICJ).[32] The Philippine government was irritated by the Malaysian government's obstinate questioning of the basis for its claim to Sabah.[33] Eventually, it stopped answering these questions. Consequently, on 16 July the Malaysian representatives walked out of the conference room saying that Malaysia rejected the Philippine claim to Sabah. The Philippine government was offended by Malaysia's arrogant behaviour.[34] It announced the withdrawal of all but one official from its embassy in Kuala Lumpur. The relationship between the two countries became worse than it had been before the talks.

The Jakarta agreement

The second ASEAN Ministerial Meeting (AMM) was held in early August 1968 in Jakarta. In his opening address, Tun Abdul Razak, the Malaysian Deputy Prime Minister, stressed the im-

---

[28] Ghazali Shafie, Opening Address at the Bangkok talks, 17 June 1968.
[29] Gauttier Bisnar, Opening address of the Bangkok talks, 17 June 1968.
[30] Thanat Khoman, Opening address of The First Meeting of the Ad hoc Committee on Civil Aviation of ASEAN, 25 June 1968.
[31] The representative of the Indonesian delegation (The name is unknown), Statement at the Opening Ceremony of The First Meeting of the Ad Hoc Committee on Civil Aviation of ASEAN, 25 June 1968.
[32] *Far Eastern Economic Review*, 11 July 1968, p. 103.
[33] Questions were given by Radakrishna Ramani, the former Malaysian Ambassador to the United Nations. He was a distinguished lawyer. See *Far Eastern Economic Review*, 18 July 1968, p. 141.
[34] *Asahi Shimbun*, 17 July 1968.

portance of shelving differences for the sake of ASEAN's solidarity by saying: '[L]et us not allow any differences between any of us to detract us from the more important responsibility of ensuring the peace and progress of our region'.[35] Singapore's Rajaratnam argued that '[w]e were convinced that the only alternative to regional cooperation was economic stagnation and political disaster that we decided to support the concept of ASEAN'.[36] Adam Malik, the Indonesian Foreign Minister, said, 'It is my sincere hope that by continuing this close cooperation we have started, we will attain the prosperity as well as stability in this region'.[37] While the ministers expressed their fear of possible dysfunction, or perhaps even the collapse, of ASEAN, Philippine Foreign Secretary Narciso Ramos continued to push the claim for Sabah in hope of ASEAN's mediation by arguing:

> [This meeting] provides us with the opportunity to reiterate our solidarity, our persistence and determination to make ASEAN the effective and articulate vehicle for the pursuit of our common objectives. But…we cannot and dare not ignore the fact that at the present moment, certain tensions fill the air, and certain stresses and strains agitate this organisation.[38]

In his closing remarks, Ramos reiterated his expectation of ASEAN's active engagement in the bilateral dispute: '[T]he stresses and strains between us should not be left unattended in the expectation that they will just disappear'.[39]

While the AMM was in progress, Tun Razak and Ramos had informal talks in Jakarta on the evening of 6 August 1968.[40] After the failure of the Bangkok talks, Indonesia secretly began to work for the initiation of bilateral talks without making any official announcement.[41] Although the talks were reportedly arranged by Adam Malik, it is not clear whether he himself attended.[42] After just one hour of these talks, the two countries had already reached a modest agreement.[43] Firstly, they would behave in a restrained way towards each other and maintain a diplomatically quiet relationship (the so-called 'cooling-off' period).[44] Then, after a certain period of quiet, they would begin negotiations for reconciliation.[45] Details of the negotiation process were not publicised – and no information on the negotiation process was published; not even regarding who proposed the agreement, or how the two countries had reached a common position.[46]

---

[35] Tun Abdul Razak, Opening Statement of the Second ASEAN Ministerial Meeting, Jakarta, 6 August 1968.

[36] S. Rajaratnam, Opening Statement at the Second ASEAN Ministerial Meeting, Jakarta, 6 August 1968.

[37] Adam Malik, Opening Statement of the Second ASEAN Ministerial Meeting in Jakarta, 6 August 1968.

[38] Narciso Ramos, Opening Statement at the Second ASEAN Ministerial Meeting, Jakarta, 6 August 1968.

[39] *Far Eastern Economic Review*, 22 August 1968, p. 350.

[40] *The Bangkok Post*, 7 August 1968.

[41] Dewi Fortuna Anwar, *Indonesia in ASEAN*, p. 169.

[42] *Asahi Shimbun*, 7 August 1968.

[43] Suharto was said to arrange the bilateral talks and proposed the agreement, i.e. behaving restrainedly with each other and establishing the cooling-off period. See Dewi Fortuna Anwar, *Indonesia in ASEAN*, p. 169.

[44] The idea of having a cooling-off period had already been proposed in 1963. Subandrio, the then Indonesian Foreign Minister, referred to the importance of taking a cooling-off period when Indonesia (and the Philippines) and Malaysia plunged into harsh antagonism after the establishment of Malaysia in September 1963. He said to the Japanese Ambassador to Indonesia, Takio Oda, 'If the Tunku had taken time to cool off, the situation would not have gone that way so much'. (See *The Straits Times*, 21 September 1963.) The then Philippine Foreign Secretary, Salvador Lopez, supported Subandio's suggestion at that time. (*The Straits Times*, 28 October 1963.)

[45] *The Bangkok Post*, 7 August 1968.

[46] *The Straits Times*, 8 August 1968.

The Annexation Law and the further deterioration of relations

The Jakarta agreement was soon jeopardised by the so-called Annexation Law of the Philippines. The Philippine government began to re-examine its existing Base Line Act of 1961, prompted to do so by a notification from the United Nations,[47] according to which, all waters between the islands of the Philippine archipelago were to be recognised as international waters in the existing Base Line Act.[48] Philippine Senator Arturo Tolontino, who had drawn up the draft of the Act of 1961, tabled the new bill in the upper house so that future delineation would not be prejudiced in case the Philippines should acquire Sabah.[49] The Philippines believed that it had the right '… to continue to pursue [the claim to Sabah] in accordance with international law…' even after the formation of Malaysia in 1963.[50] However, the House of Representatives amended the new bill in a more provocative fashion: Sabah was marked as a part of the Philippines. The Malaysian government warned that the amendment '…cannot but be regarded as a provocation and a hostile act and as a violation of the sovereignty and territorial integrity of Malaysia'.[51] Nevertheless, the amended bill was passed in the lower house on 26 August 1968. President Marcos finally signed it, and the Annexation Law was issued on 18 September.

On 20 September, Malaysia broke off diplomatic relations with the Philippines with the support of the United States, which announced that it would recognise Sabah as a part of Malaysia.[52] In addition, all other ASEAN members – Thailand, Indonesia and Singapore – also announced their support for Malaysia.[53] Although President Marcos strongly protested against the US's announcement, the Philippine government softened its attitude and notified several countries such as Japan, Australia and New Zealand that it did not intend to begin a war with Malaysia.[54]

While he had signed the Annexation law, Marcos nonetheless proposed Summit talks with Malaysia.[55] The Philippines sought a mediator, such as Japan or the United Nations itself, from outside of ASEAN because it could not secure sympathy from its ASEAN colleagues.[56] On 24 September 1968, the Philippine government asked the Japanese Foreign Minister, Takeo Miki, to hold bilateral talks with Malaysia in Tokyo in October.[57] Malaysia agreed to the Philippines' proposal.[58] The ministerial talks were scheduled for 22 October in Tokyo, and were to be followed by a bilateral Summit meeting. In the meantime, President Marcos requested that his

---

[47] Therefore, the Philippines' initial action was 'innocent enough'. (Lela Garner Noble, *Philippine Policy toward Sabah*, p. 179.) For details about the revision process of the base line act in the Philippine parliament, see the same book, pp. 176-196.
[48] Ibid.
[49] Ibid, p. 179.
[50] The Manila Accord, 11 June 1963.
[51] *Far Eastern Economic Review*, 10 October 1968, p. 116.
[52] *Asahi Shimbun*, Evening edition, 20 September 1968.
[53] The Soviet Union recognised Sabah as Malaysian territory. See *The Bangkok Post*, 23 October 1968. Australia also sympathised with Malaysia. See 'Dai-Nikai Nichi-Gou Seimu Kankei Jimu Reberu Kyougi [The proceedings of the 2nd Exchange of Political Views of Senior Officials between Japan and Australia]', Ministry of Foreign Affairs of Japan, 14-15 November 1968, Gaikou Shiryou Kan [hereafter GSK] File A'-394.
[54] *Asahi Shimbun*, 22 September 1968.
[55] *Asahi Shimbun*, 24 September 1968.
[56] The Japanese government saw that the Philippine government should not involve the UN in the Sabah dispute. See 'Dai-Nikai Nichi-Gou Seimu Kankei Jimu Reberu Kyougi [The proceedings of the 2nd Exchange of Political Views of Senior Officials between Japan and Australia]', Ministry of Foreign Affairs of Japan, 14-15 November 1968, Gaikou Shiryou Kan [hereafter GSK] File A'-394.
[57] The Japanese Foreign Minister, Takeo Miki, had offered assistance in mediating the issue before the Jakarta talks. See *The Straits Times*, 2 August 1968.
[58] *Asahi Shimbun*, Evening edition, 26 September 1968.

Foreign Secretary Ramos would ask U Thant, the Secretary-General of the UN, to mediate in the issue.[59]

The Philippines put the issue forward for a Plenary Meeting of the United Nations General Assembly.[60] In his speech of 15 October, Ramos raised the claim for Sabah and insisted on filing it with the ICJ declaring:

> I hereby make the reservation and put it on record that the Philippine government cannot and does not recognise the power, competence or authority of the government of the Federation of Malaysia to represent or speak for the people of the Territory of Sabah or to make any commitment for them before the United Nations or any of its organs, organisations, committees, agencies or conferences.[61]

Malaysia was outraged by this statement.[62] The following day, Radakrishna Ramani, Malaysia's permanent representative to the UN, responded to Ramos's speech: 'Both in fact and in law the Philippine claim to Sabah does not exist, is unsustainable and is…a composite of fantasy, fallacy and fiction'.[63] The Philippine government resented Ramani's statement. The heated exchange continued until 25 October in the General Assembly.

The scheduled ministerial talks in Tokyo were unilaterally cancelled by Malaysia.[64] Tun Abdul Razak said, 'If I go to Tokyo I will go as the Deputy Prime Minister of Malaysia of which Sabah is a constituent part. This is my position and my position must be recognised as such'.[65] Malaysia declared that it could not work together with the Philippines in ASEAN. It notified the Philippines on 2 November 1968 that a proposed ASEAN conference on mass media was to be suspended indefinitely.[66] This was the first case in which the integrity of the Association was jeopardised by the bilateral conflict between its member countries. Malaysia stated once again at the beginning of December that it could not work together with the Philippines in ASEAN, and it would not attend any conference in the Association because the latter did not recognise Malaysia's sovereignty in Sabah.[67] The Malaysian Premier said that ASEAN's future depended on the progress of the Sabah issue.

Towards re-establishing the Jakarta agreement

With the bilateral issue being linked to the Association, Indonesian Foreign Minister Adam Malik on 1 November formally offered to mediate the conflict between Malaysia and the Philippines. It is noteworthy that this was the first time ASEAN member countries publicly expressed their willingness to mediate an internal dispute. He suggested that it should be dealt within ASEAN by saying, '[W]e do not want to monopolise the role of mediator. We give other ASEAN members the opportunity to'.[68] However, Thailand was still reluctant to deal with the Sabah issue in the Association: 'We do not want to be involved in any way with Sabah. We do not gain anything from it'.[69]

---

[59] *The Bangkok Post*, 2 October 1968.
[60] Narciso Ramos, Speech in the 1696th Plenary Meeting of the United Nations General Assembly, 15 October 1968.
[61] Ibid.
[62] *The Bangkok Post*, 17 October 1968.
[63] Radakrishna Ramani, Speech in the 1698th Plenary Meeting of the United Nations General Assembly, 16 October 1968.
[64] *The Bangkok Post*, 17 October 1968.
[65] *Far Eastern Economic Review*, 31 October 1968, p. 227.
[66] *The Bangkok Post*, 3 November 1968.
[67] *The Bangkok Post*, 3 December 1968.
[68] *The Bangkok Post*, 3 November 1968.
[69] *The Bangkok Post*, 15 November 1968.

102 *The Corregidor affairs*

General Ali Murtopo, a personal assistant of Indonesian President Suharto, spent one day in Manila in late October 1968, after which he visited Tokyo, where the Philippine Foreign Secretary was visiting.[70] Thus, Indonesia presumably secured the Philippines' consent to shelve the claim to Sabah, on the condition of 'Manila's right to continue to pursue the claim'.[71] Two pieces of evidence support this assumption. First, on 30 October, the Philippine Foreign Minister informally told the Malaysian Deputy Prime Minister that the Philippines' claim to Sabah was a 'non-starter' and would be partitioned in the negotiation for rapprochement.[72] Second, on the following day Philippine President Marcos ordered the changing of the colour of the area of Sabah on the relief map in Luneta Park in Manila[73] so that Sabah could be shown not as Philippine territory, but as a neutral area.[74]

In late November 1968, Imron Rosjadi, the chairman of the Indonesian Parliamentary Committee on Foreign Affairs, Defence and Security, visited the ASEAN countries to ask the view on the restoration of the Jakarta agreement. He said, 'A cooling-off period is not impossible and I am not pessimistic. But of course there must be goodwill on both sides and the other three ASEAN countries must help'.[75] Imron Rosjadi also went to Manila and encouraged Ramos to withdraw the claim so that Malaysia and the Philippines could work together in ASEAN.[76] On 6 December, the Philippine government formally announced that a 'moratorium' would be placed on its claim over Sabah, until the general election in Malaysia in the following May.[77]

A series of concessions by the Philippines eased Malaysia's inflexible attitude, and facilitated the restoration of the Jakarta agreement. The Thai government, although it had earlier stated that it did not want ASEAN to be involved in the bilateral dispute, organised an informal dinner among ASEAN foreign ministers on 13 December in Bangsen, Thailand, to coincide with the Economic Commission for Asia and the Far East (ECAFE) that was being held at the same location. Both countries agreed to the restoration of the agreement in Jakarta. As such, they would behave with restraint towards each other and re-establish the 'cooling-off' period. In addition, the Philippine Foreign Secretary said that he recognised Malaysia's *de facto* sovereignty over Sabah.[78] At the end of the informal meeting, Tun Abdul Razak read a statement:

> An understanding has been reached among the ministers in regard to the differences between the Philippines and Malaysia which is being submitted for approval to the two governments concerned…Before the commencement of the talks, His Excellency Mr. Narciso Ramos, the Foreign Secretary of the Philippines, assured us in the presence of the other Ministers that he recognises me as a Deputy Prime Minister of Malaysia, a sovereign and independent state.[79]

With the Philippines temporarily dropping its claim, the agreement was kept until the Presidential election in the Philippines in November 1969. In the meantime, in late May 1969, the meeting of ASEAN Secretaries General in Bogor, Indonesia was held successfully, with the pres-

---

[70] *The Straits Times*, 29 and 30 October 1968.
[71] *South China Morning Post*, 19 December 1968.
[72] *The Straits Times*, 30 October 1968.
[73] Luneta Park (also known as Rizal Park) is one of the popular spots for the people in Manila. It is located in the heart of the city of Manila and its area is more than 50 hectares. Therefore, the act of changing the colour in the map can be recognised as the sincere desire of the Philippines for rapprochement with Malaysia.
[74] *South China Morning Post*, 1 November 1968; and *The Bangkok Post*, 1 November 1968.
[75] *The Bangkok Post*, 28 November 1968.
[76] *The Straits Times*, 30 November 1968.
[77] *The Straits Times*, 7 December 1968.
[78] *Asahi Shimbun*, 19 October 1968.
[79] Tun Abdul Razak, Mimeographed Statement at the Closure of the Informal Conference of ASEAN Foreign Ministers at Bangsen, 13 December 1968, in *Foreign Affairs Bulletin*, 8/3 (December 1968-January 1969), p. 206.

ence of all ASEAN countries. Malaysia and the Philippines resumed diplomatic relations just after the Presidential election in November, and they finally announced rapprochement on 13 December 1969 in the third ASEAN Ministerial Meeting in the Cameron Highlands, Malaysia; one year after the Bangsen talks. Ministers in ASEAN member countries reaffirmed the importance of ASEAN cooperation for peace and economic well-being in the region in its Joint Communiqué:

> [In] the course of deliberation[s], an atmosphere of cordial friendship and understanding prevailed and, cognisant of the common interests and common goal of member countries, the Ministers reaffirmed their determination to fulfil and to realise the laudable aims and purposes of the ASEAN Declaration in order to ensure peace and prosperity for all the peoples in the region. Renewed determination was expressed to strengthen further the Organisation, and to take vigorous action to implement the projects which have been approved by the Ministers.[80]

The significance of the Corregidor affair

Acharya argues that the Corregidor affair was formative to the emergence of the ASEAN Way. In his book, *Constructing a Security Community in Southeast Asia*, he writes that 'the Sabah dispute is an important milestone in ASEAN's early approach to conflict avoidance and was indicative of what was to be known later as the ASEAN Way of conflict management'.[81] Although he refers to the ministerial dinner in Bangsen, his focus is more on the ASEAN committee in May 1969. He says, 'It was an ASEAN committee meeting in Indonesia in May 1969 which brought the two countries together for the first time in eight months with the exception of an ad hoc foreign ministers meeting in December 1968'.[82] He attributes the reconciliation to the agreements reached at the ASEAN committee meeting, rather than the informal meeting in Bangsen in December 1968.

However, it should be noted that Indonesia's secret mediation, which formally re-established the Jakarta agreement at the meeting in Bangsen in December 1968,[83] contributed to easing the bilateral tension between Malaysia and the Philippines. Although the Philippine government did not formally state anything, at that stage it had substantially dropped the claim to Sabah. Furthermore, in the course of setting up the meeting in Bangsen, and also during the meeting itself, none of the ASEAN leaders did refer to the Sabah issue. This also helped the two states involved to shelve the problem. Although ASEAN's formal activity resumed on 29 May 1969, when the meeting of the Head of the ASEAN National Secretariats in Bogor of Indonesia was held,[84] the meeting in Bangsen in December 1968 did pave the way for the restoration of diplomatic relations between the two countries.

During the meeting at Bangsen, Malaysia's representatives sat at the same table as those from the Philippines, even though the former had insisted in October 1968 that it would never attend any meeting with the Philippines if the latter would keep sticking to the Sabah claim.[85] The meeting over dinner was successful because the conflict had been substantially settled beforehand through Indonesia's informal accommodation.[86]

At first, the ASEAN states did not publicly show their willingness to be involved in the bilateral dispute between Malaysia and the Philippines. They feared that such a dispute would

---

[80] Joint Communiqué of the Third ASEAN Ministerial Meeting, Cameron Highlands, 17 December 1969.
[81] Amitav Acharya, *Constructing a Security Community in Southeast Asia*, p. 50.
[82] Ibid.
[83] As described earlier, the Jakarta agreement was agreed by Malaysia and the Philippines at Jakarta in August 1968.
[84] The meeting was held in the atmosphere of 'complete cordiality, and perfect mutual understanding'. See *Foreign Affairs Bulletin*, 8/6 (June-July 1969), p. 470.
[85] *The Bangkok Post*, 3 December 1968.
[86] *The Bangkok Post*, 14 December 1968.

become a stumbling block to ASEAN's activities.[87] Thailand, the organiser of the Bangkok talks, was engaged neither in the negotiation process, nor in the talks per se. In the opening address of the talks, Chitti Sucharitkul, the Thai Under-Secretary of State for Foreign Affairs, seemed to suggest that the Thai government would remain uninvolved in the talks: 'I have the honour and pleasure…to offer you this house, Pisanuloke House, as the venue of your meeting. There will be some Ministry of Foreign Affairs officials here. If you would want the facility, it will be offered to you'.[88] In contrast to this example, after the failure of the Bangkok talks in July 1968, Indonesia started secret involvement in the bilateral issue, and provided the two countries concerned with a place for more informal discussions in Jakarta in the following month. Furthermore, Indonesia laboured secretly to persuade the Philippines to drop the claim to Sabah before the meeting in Bangsen in December 1968.

It should be noted that informality appeared as a characteristic of the process of the Jakarta agreement in August 1968, when Indonesia became secretly involved in the informal talks between the two countries.[89] Details of the formation process of the agreement as well as the bilateral talks were not published. However, considering the fact that the Jakarta agreement was reached in the course of a one-hour talk, it is wise to assume that the draft of the agreement had been negotiated before the meeting between Malaysia and the Philippines through secret negotiations.

Informality was also a characteristic of the negotiation process leading up to the meeting in Bangsen in December 1968, where Malaysia and the Philippines re-established the Jakarta agreement. Just after Indonesian emissary Ali Murtopo secretly contacted the Philippine government in the late October of 1968,[90] the latter indirectly showed a more accommodating attitude; an example of this being the earlier-mentioned recolouring of the relief map in Luneta Park, Manila.[91] Another of such an approach was the informal statement issued by Philippine Foreign Secretary Narciso Ramos that the claim to Sabah was 'non-starter'.[92] The Philippines' concessive actions were informal ones, releasing the tensions that had grown between the two countries, and providing Malaysia with a face-saving measure in order to allow it to return to the negotiating table with the Philippines at the meeting in Bangsen. The informal actions also helped the Philippines itself to substantially drop the claim to Sabah without losing face.

The Philippines' decision of one-sided concession was, as Collins points out, '[ASEAN] members [being] prepared to defer their own interests to the interests of the association'.[93] As a reward for the Philippines' act of generosity, ASEAN made no reference to the treatment of Sabah at the dinner in Bangsen.[94] There was also no reference to the future of Sabah in the statement issued at the third ASEAN Ministerial Meeting (AMM) in December 1969, which marked the formal end of the Corregidor affair: '[I]t was agreed that diplomatic relations between Malaysia and the Philippines would be normalised forthwith and that the ambassadors of their respective countries would be appointed. The Meeting warmly welcomed this happy development'.[95] Indeed, as Thanat Khoman said just before the dinner, 'Diplomatic moves have to be made without Press publicity'.[96]

---

[87] *The Straits Times*, 6 August 1968.
[88] Chitti Sucharitkul, Welcoming Address of the Bangkok Talks, 17 June 1968, in *Foreign Affairs Bulletin*, 7/6 (June-July 1968), pp. 589-591.
[89] The agreement was to establish a cooling-off period and to behave with restraint.
[90] *The Bangkok Post*, 29 October 1968.
[91] *South China Morning Post*, 1 November 1968; and *The Bangkok Post*, 1 November 1968.
[92] *The Straits Times*, 30 October 1968.
[93] Alan Collins, 'Mitigating the Security Dilemma', p. 107.
[94] *Foreign Affairs Bulletin*, 8/3 (December 1968-January 1969), p. 207.
[95] The Joint Communiqué of the Third ASEAN Ministerial Meeting, Cameron Highlands, 17 December 1969.
[96] *The Bangkok Post*, 12 December 1968.

ASEAN strengthened its solidarity through the mediation process of the Corregidor affair. During the dispute between Malaysia and the Philippines, other member countries advocated 'working together in ASEAN'.[97] As Tunku Abdul Rahman put it, the member countries' concern to 'save ASEAN from landing on the rock'.[98]

The Association was established with the agreement that peace and stability in the region should be maintained so that member countries could focus socio-economic development at home. When the summit talks between Malaysia and Thailand were held on 8 June 1968, the two leaders emphasised 'the need for the maintenance of friendship between member countries of ASEAN, and for the peace and well-being of the countries of this region'.[99] Malaysian Permanent Secretary of External Affairs Ghazali Shafie warned ASEAN not to indulge in differences by saying, 'To allow ourselves to be distracted from our tasks [nation-building and economic development] is a moral abdication of our responsibilities and will only be to the benefit of destructive and negative elements'.[100] ASEAN states were worried about the association's future throughout the Corregidor affairs, and this apprehension made them realise afresh the importance of harmonisation for the sake of their common aim. Therefore, they recognised that they should ignore small differences and work together. Indeed, Malaysia and the Philippines restored diplomatic relations 'because of the great value Malaysia and the Philippines placed on ASEAN'.[101]

It is noteworthy that ASEAN was able to manage to settle the Sabah dispute through its own actions. This dispute had been the most sensitive issue between the two countries and, to some extent, between all ASEAN countries.[102] As Acharya puts it, 'The avoidance of any further escalation of the Sabah dispute was all the more significant'.[103] Thus, ASEAN 'has served as a modest vehicle for the reduction of tension among its members. The dispute between Malaysia and the Philippines has not had the same debilitating effect on ASEAN as it had on [the] ASA.'[104] In the settlement process, member countries would recognise again the philosophy of ASEAN that they should do their best to keep peace and harmony in the Association for the sake of their own socio-economic development.

Concluding remarks

The Corregidor affair turned out to be a most significant event in the history of the ASEAN Way. It resulted in the production of a number of statements from several ASEAN members; statements which advocated the use of the now-familiar idea of 'working together beyond difference'. During the dispute, other ASEAN members emphasised the importance of 'working together in ASEAN' for the sake of peace and prosperity in the region as a whole. Considering peace and prosperity were, and remain, the major objectives of ASEAN cooperation, it became clear that the idea of 'working together' results in the promotion of regional cooperation, and it can be identified as the essence of the ASEAN Way.[105] To go on working together constructively, specific practices therefore became characteristic features of ASEAN. 'Informality' and 'consultations', and 'face-saving' were often employed in the course of making and re-establishing the Jakarta agreement. Finally, the Sabah issue, for which there was no compro-

---

[97] See Thanat Khoman, Opening address of The First Meeting of the Ad hoc Committee on Civil Aviation of ASEAN, 25 June 1968.
[98] *The Bangkok Post*, 8 June 1968.
[99] *Foreign Affairs Bulletin*, Vol. 7, No. 6 (June/July 1968), p. 587.
[100] Ghazali Shafie, Opening Address at the Bangkok talks, 17 June 1968.
[101] Joint Communiqué of the Third ASEAN Ministerial Meeting, Cameron Highlands, 17 December 1969.
[102] The bilateral dispute over Sabah, which originated in the establishment of Malaysia, had plunged the region into disturbance in 1963. For details, see Chapter 3.
[103] Amitav Acharya, *Constructing a Security Community in Southeast Asia*, p. 50.
[104] Michael Leifer, *Dilemmas of Statehood in Southeast Asia* (Vancouver: University of British Columbia Press, 1972), p. 147.
[105] *The Bangkok Post*, 3 December 1968.

mise between Malaysia and the Philippines, was shelved without the announcement of an official solution.

6 THE NATURE OF THE ASEAN WAY

This chapter explores the nature of the ASEAN way, based on the interactions between the countries in the region, discussed in the previous chapters. The chapter begins by dealing with two points: (1) whether or not traditional culture in the region is a major element in the ASEAN Way, and (2) whether or not the universal principle of non-interference is a component in it. The chapter argues that the custom of consultation was influenced by traditional cultural precepts in the region, and the cultural factor has regularly helped to alleviate tensions between member countries. The chapter also argues that the principle of non-interference does not directly form the characteristics of the ASEAN Way. Rather, it facilitated ASEAN cooperation. The chapter then goes on to argue that the ASEAN Way as a concept forged four conventions. Finally, it clarifies the relationship between the ASEAN Way and ASEAN cooperation.

The ASEAN Way and traditional culture

As reviewed in Chapter 1, the answer to the question of whether or not the ASEAN Way is strongly rooted in traditional culture remains unclear in the existing literature. Through case studies discussed in the previous chapters, here we conclude that cultural affinity helped to reduce tensions between countries in Southeast Asia. In particular, cultural commonality between the so-called Malay countries, such as Indonesia, Malaysia and the Philippines, was emphasised. In the Manila Accord in 1963, the three countries announced their willingness to work together based on 'Malay origin[s]'.[1] Malayan Prime Minister Tunku Abdul Rahman paid an informal call on Indonesian President Sukarno in the latter's hotel room just before the opening of the Manila Summit meeting (31 July 1963). The Tunku's gesture, based on Malay culture, was accepted by Sukarno and it obviously reduced the hostility between the two leaders.[2] Similar behaviour, based on the same Malay custom, could be seen in May of the same year, when the Tunku saw Sukarno off at Haneda airport in Tokyo after the two had conducted a heart-to-heart informal meeting.[3]

In the course of the settlement of the regional dispute over Malaysia in 1966, the Indonesian Army leaders of Crush Malaysia Command (KOGAM) paid a courtesy visit to the Malaysian government just before the Indonesia-Malaysia ministerial conference on reconciliation in June. Malaysian Deputy Prime Minister Tun Abdul Razak said, 'We can look confidently to the ending of confrontation [*Konfrontasi*] and building of peace and friendship with Indonesia',[4] and compared their visit with the Malay traditional custom, *kenduri*.[5]

On 23 May 1967, when the Indonesian Foreign Minister and the Malayan Deputy Prime Minister held a short meeting at the airport in Bangkok in the course of the formation of ASEAN, they first had a chat in Malay.[6] The meeting was held just after Malaysia had accepted the Indonesian plan for the new regional organisation (later taking shape as ASEAN), which Malaysia had consistently refused until then. Therefore, this informal meeting can be interpreted as a confirmation of the two countries' willingness to work together in regional cooperation. The aim of the conversation was unpublished, but it marked the end of the rivalry over the initiative to form a regional organisation. A language in common helped the reconciliation process.

---

[1] The Manila Accord, 11 June 1963.
[2] See Chapter 3.
[3] See Chapter 3.
[4] *The Straits Times*, 28 May 1966.
[5] See Chapter 4.
[6] *The Straits Times*, 24 May 1967.

Musyawarah (consultation) and *mufakat* (consensus) in Malay custom had been particularly highlighted as being the tools of conflict management.[7] The three countries of Maphilindo employed the traditional style of accommodation and named it '*Musyawarah* Maphilindo'.[8] In the Joint Statement between Indonesia and the Philippines in March 1966, issued towards the end of the three-way conflict between Indonesia, Malaysia and the Philippines,[9] the two ministers agreed to address problems by 'more frequent exchanges of visits by Indonesians and Filipinos representing all fields of activity, and of consultations on common problems in the spirit of *musyawarah* and good neighbourliness'.[10]

Just after the collapse of the reconciliation talks in Bangkok on the Sabah issue in July 1968,[11] Indonesia, as argued earlier,[12] succeeded in arranging the Jakarta agreement between Malaysia and the Philippines. Considering that their talks in Jakarta were concluded successfully in just an hour, whereas the month-long talks in Bangkok had failed to reach any agreement, it can be inferred that Indonesia, as a mediator, had informally developed the agreement plan in advance by contacting the two countries separately and secretly.[13] This mediation process reminds us of *musyawarah* and *mufakat*, which are characterised by behind-the-scenes negotiations, caring, sensitive handling of situations, and face-saving.[14] The traditional Malay custom of mediation was seen more clearly in late 1968 in the mediation process towards the talks in Bangsen: The Indonesian government, and in particular Ali Murtopo, played a significant role in this. It is highly probable that he had contacted the Philippines and had given a strong advice to its Foreign Secretary to drop the claim to Sabah, so that the bilateral issue would not affect ASEAN cooperation.[15] In order to protect the image of the Philippines, and as a way of compensation for the Philippines' concession, Indonesia did not make the result of the Sabah dispute public.[16] According to Koentjaraningrat, in the negotiation process by *musyawarah* and *mufakat*:

> Efforts are made behind the scenes to reduce the differences between conflicting viewpoints, during the discussions and gossip in the guardhouses or coffee shops. The village head, who actively participates in these operations, knows every development; at the official meeting his announcements are nothing but the final resolution of preliminary discussions, and as such are naturally acceptable to a majority of the assembled people. This system of conducting meetings is probably derived from a corresponding element in Javanese social behaviour, in which public controversy must be avoided at all costs.[17]

---

[7] For details on *musyawarah* and *mufakat*, see Chapter 1.
[8] The Manila Joint Statement, 5 August 1963. For details on Maphilindo, see Chapter 3.
[9] For a more detailed discussion of the reconciliation process of the three-way dispute, see Chapter 4.
[10] Joint Statement between Indonesia and the Philippines, 1 May 1966.
[11] The reason for the failure of the Bangkok talks can be found in the Philippines' loss of face after Malaysia withdrew from the conference. In addition, Thailand, the organiser of the conference, did not make any informal arrangements between the two countries during (or before) the talks.
[12] For the details of the Corregidor affair, see Chapter 5.
[13] Dewi Fortuna Anwar, *Indonesia in ASEAN*, p. 169.
[14] The background of Indonesia's using this type of mediation can be seen in the fact that Suharto often employed Javanese culture in Indonesian politics. See Lucian W. Pye, *Asian Power and Politics: The Cultural Dimensions of Authority* (Cambridge, Mass.: The Belknap Press, 1985), p. 115.
[15] *The Straits Times*, 29 and 30 October 1968.
[16] Other ASEAN states also did not referred to anything about Sabah during that time. Even at the time of the third ASEAN Ministerial Meeting in December 1969 when the two countries formally resumed their diplomatic relations, nothing about Sabah was mentioned.
[17] Koentjaraningrat, '*Tjelapar*: A Village in South Central Java', in Koentjaraningrat (ed.), *Villages in Indonesia* (Ithaca, NY: Cornell University Press, 1967), p. 274.

According to the above description, a dispute should be settled by the leader's decision, namely the village head. However, there was no official leader in ASEAN, which meant that the organisation did not have coercive powers over member countries, unlike the village head, who is able to force the people in a community to conform with his final decision.[18] Instead of a clear decision by the equivalent of a village head, ASEAN worked to shelve the unresolvable Sabah issue, and thus protected the organisation from disintegration.[19]

The ASEAN Way and the principle of non-interference
As reviewed in Chapter 1, there is no unified view on the question of whether or not the universal principle of non-interference is a major component of the ASEAN Way. Countries in Southeast Asia were indifferent to each other before the formation of the Association of Southeast Asia (ASA) in 1961.[20] Indonesia, which was not a member of the ASA, from 1963 aggressively intervened in the other country's business, the establishment of Malaysia, by advocating *Konfrontasi*.[21] In early September 1968, during the Corregidor affair,[22] Indonesian Foreign Minister warned the Philippines not to pass the Annexation Law, by which the Philippines could incorporate Sabah into its territory.[23] Former Indonesian Vice-President Mohammad Hatta also stated that there was no basis for the Philippines' claim. Furthermore, the Singaporean government sent its own perspective to Malaysia; namely, that it recognised Sabah as Malaysian territory.[24] In addition to these statements, Indonesia was involved in this bilateral dispute behind the scene, through the mediation between the two countries in Jakarta in August and in Bangsen in December 1968.

On the other hand, the term 'non-interference' has been used widely in ASEAN's official documents, such as in the Treaty of Amity of Cooperation (TAC) in 1976, the Declaration of ASEAN Concord in 1976, and the Hanoi Declaration of 1998.[25] How should this principle be interpreted in the context of ASEAN's activities? It can be said that ASEAN advocated the principle of non-interference beyond its intrinsic meaning.[26] As Kraft's interpretation suggests, ASEAN has advocated the principle of non-interference in order that the member states could exclude interference from powers outside the region.[27] Indeed, in the process of ending the three-way dispute in 1966,[28] Indonesia, Malaysia and the Philippines restored their diplomatic relations without the need for external mediation to take place.[29] The Corregidor affair was also settled within the region. ASEAN countries were able to manage regional matters with little, if any, involvement from external powers. This is a manifestation of their willingness to solve regional issues within the region and be free from external interference.

As Busse argues:

---

[18] In other words, the solidarity of ASEAN was fragile particularly in the formative period, whereas there is a strong sense of bond in the village having community relationship among members.
[19] It has been pointed out that reaching unanimity was difficult in ASEAN. See Hoang Anh Tuan, 'ASEAN Dispute Management', p. 77.
[20] Tunku Abdul Rahman, Letter from Tunku Abdul Rahman to President Garcia of the Philippines (Malayan Proposal for Regional Co-operation), 28 October 1959.
[21] Subandrio, Speech to Mahakarta Regiment in Jogjyakarta, 20 January 1963.
[22] For details, see Chapter 5.
[23] *Asian Almanac*, 7/2 (11 January 1969), p. 3121.
[24] Ibid, p. 3122.
[25] Treaty of Amity and Cooperation, 24 February 1976; Declaration of ASEAN Concord, 24 February 1976; and Hanoi Declaration, 16 December 1998.
[26] Simon S. C. Tay, 'Institutions and Process', p. 251.
[27] Herman Joseph S. Kraft, 'ASEAN and Intra-ASEAN relations', p. 463.
[28] The dispute was over the formation of Malaysia in 1963. For details, see Chapters 3 and 4.
[29] Although the Japanese government offered to mediate in early May 1966, the three countries concerned did not ask the former to organise any reconciliatory meetings. *The Straits Times*, 9 May 1966.

[T]he governments of the region had not forgotten the experience of colonialism and imperialism which had been their first encounters with modern international politics. The idea of sovereignty served as the legal framework for overcoming these dependency relationships and gaining equal status in the system.[30]

ASEAN countries had been troubled by external interference since the colonial period, long before the establishment of the Association. Anti-colonial sentiment merged with the threat perception of external intervention during the Cold War period. Namely, they feared intervention by big powers, such as the US, China and the Soviet Union in the region.[31] Two differing political perspectives on the formation of Malaysia show how the people in the region were worried about interference from external powers. The then Malayan Prime Minister said in the Lower House of parliament in 1961:

> If such an eventuality [grave economic unrest] should come to pass, Malayans would be fighting among themselves, goaded on and helped by forces from without. There would be bloodshed and destruction, and the country would be torn by strife and suffering, from which it would be very difficult to return to normal, if we ever get a chance to return. The same situation would develop as we have seen in the past in divided Korea, in divided Vietnam and in Laos.[32]

On the other hand, the Indonesian Communist Party (PKI) declared in the same year that:

> From their own experiences, the Indonesian people know only too well the meaning of the words "preservation of peace in Southeast Asia", the meaning of the words "international responsibilities", the word "responsibilities" towards the Commonwealth and other such words used by imperialists. Colonial practices, acts of intervention and aggression by the imperialists in South Vietnam, Laos, the Congo, as well as the plans for the landing of U.S. troops in Pakan Baru (Sumatra) [during the PRRI rebellion in 1958] which were foiled by Indonesia, and the occupation of West Irian, etc., speak clearly of this.[33]

Although the two perspectives on the formation of Malaysia were completely different, the then Malayan Prime Minister and the PKI shared the same underlying threat perception.

The bipolar rivalry in the world represented a threat for the small country's destiny under the control of large external powers. In particular, the deterioration of the situation in Indochina was the most serious concern for countries in Southeast Asia.[34] Looking at it, the countries in

---

[30] Nikolas Busse, 'Constructivism and Southeast Asian Security', *The Pacific Review*, 12/1 (1999), p. 46. Schubert argues that 'The legacy of colonialism was the most important factor behind the emergence of regionalist sentiment in Asia'. See James N. Schubert, 'Toward a "Working Peace System" in Asia: Organizational Growth and State Participation in Asian Regionalism', *International Organization*, 32/2 (Spring 1978), p. 447.
[31] See Chapter 2.
[32] Tunku Abdul Rahman, Speech in the House of Representatives in Malaya, 16 October 1961.
[33] Resolutions of the Indonesian Communist Party, December 1961.
[34] The fear was also encapsulated in the ten principles of the Asian-African Conference of 1955 in Bandung. These are:
  1. Respect for fundamental human rights and for the purposes and principles of the Charter of the United Nations.
  2. Respect for the sovereignty and territorial integrity of all nations.
  3. Recognition of the equality of all races and of the equality of all nations large and small.
  4. Abstention from intervention or interference in the internal affairs of another country.
  5. Respect for the right of each nation to defend itself singly or collectively, in conformity with the Charter of the United Nations.

Southeast Asia realised that the big external powers would promote their own national interests rather than those of countries in the region. Therefore, they recognised that they should 'rely more on neighbourly mutual support than on stronger states'.[35] The sense of regionalism in Southeast Asia was created partly because of unreliability of extra-regional powers, and it produced the idea of 'standing on their own feet'. From this point of view, 'ASEAN members value their autonomy',[36] and their ultimate goal is to be 'free from external interference'.[37]

The fear of the external military intervention was repeatedly stipulated in official documents in Southeast Asia. In the Manila Joint Statement of 1963 (Maphilindo): 'foreign bases...should not be allowed to be used directly or indirectly to subvert the national independence of any of the three countries'.[38] Furthermore, Malaysian Deputy Prime Minister Tun Abdul Razak said at the First ASEAN Ministerial Meeting in 1967,

> For many centuries, most of us have been dominated by colonial powers either directly or indirectly and even today we are not entirely free from being exposed to the struggle for domination by outside powers. ... we are all conscious of our responsibility to shape our common destiny and to prevent external intervention and interference.[39]

Indeed, as the former Thai Foreign Minister, Thanat Khoman, later said, 'ASEAN was created to prevent intervention from outside powers'.[40]

The fear of being involved in the Cold War rivalry drove ASEAN countries to become more sensitive to external interference.[41] From such a context, they advocated the principle of non-interference. At the same time, they also recognised regional responsibility for regional problems and decided to address the problems by regional cooperation. In a sense, therefore, ASEAN cooperation is maintained to protect the member states from external interference, in addition to the two explicit objectives: the furtherance of peace and prosperity.

What is the ASEAN Way?
The book embraces Ahmad's statement that: 'a spirit of "working together" forms an important feature of [ASEAN]'.[42] Then, it has examined cooperative behaviour in Southeast Asia through case studies and defines the concept of the ASEAN Way as 'working together beyond differ-

---

6. (a) Abstention from the use of arrangements of collective defence to serve the particular interests of any of the big powers.
    (b) Abstention by any country from exerting pressures on other countries.
7. Refraining from acts or threats of aggression or the use of force against the territorial integrity or political independence of any country.
8. Settlement of all international disputes by peaceful means, such as negotiation, conciliation, arbitration or judicial settlement as well as other peaceful means of the parties' own choice, in conformity with the Charter of the United Nations.
9. Promotion of mutual interests and cooperation.
10. Respect for justice and international obligations. See Final Communiqué of the Asian-African Conference, 24 April 1955.

[35] Thanat Khoman, 'ASEAN Conception and Evolution', 1 September 1992.
[36] Richard Stubbs, 'ASEAN', p. 223.
[37] Treaty of Amity and Cooperation, 24 February 1976.
[38] The Manila Joint Statement, 5 August 1963.
[39] Tun Abdul Razak, Opening Statement of the First ASEAN Ministerial Meeting, Bangkok, 8 August 1967.
[40] *Asiaweek*, 28 July 1998.
[41] The ASEAN Declaration of 1967 stated, '[ASEAN countries] are determined to ensure their stability and security from external interference'. In addition, it declared: 'all foreign bases ... are not intended to be used directly or indirectly to subvert national independence and freedom of States in the area or prejudice the orderly processes of their national development'.
[42] Zakaria Haji Ahmad, 'The World of ASEAN Decision-makers', p. 203.

ences'. The term 'working together' has encouraged ASEAN countries to create solidarity by overcoming differences. For example, different perspectives on regional security between Indonesia and the other members: Indonesia had insisted on the non-aligned position in regional security, whereas the other four countries had defence pacts with Western countries. In addition, the territorial dispute over Sabah between Malaysia and the Philippines remained outstanding business.[43] Furthermore, the underlying ethnic/cultural antagonism between Malaysia and Singapore was still strong.[44] On 8 August 1967, when the ASEAN Declaration was signed, Indonesian Foreign Minister Adam Malik said, 'I realise that differences in outlook do exist among our nations but I am convinced that we will be able to overcome those differences'.[45]

'Working together' has been iterated because countries in Southeast Asia saw that the chronic sense of crisis present in the region could be turned into a system of regional cooperation instead. As Yamakage puts it, the ASEAN Way is 'the diligent fruit of their understanding that the basis of regional cooperation was weak and mutual suspicion was deep'.[46] ASEAN members believe that if they cause the Association to break down, then the region will become insecure, and such a fear is reasonably based on historical experience. Such sentiment encourages member countries to cooperate for the sake of their prosperity. Indeed, ASEAN countries believe that working together is the most important way to overcome any rift between them.[47] They emphasise their solidarity when they cannot find the solution.[48] Indeed, ASEAN members get together at meetings 'with a disposition to agree and not to [enter into] dispute[s]'.[49] In other words, they seek 'agreement and harmony' in the talks rather than arguments.[50] The behind-the-scenes negotiation and face-saving behaviour in the process of *musyawarah* and *mufakat* have been useful in dealing with sensitive matters in member countries with a weak political basis.

The concept of 'working together' is actively demonstrated in the regional community, while the idea of 'peaceful coexistence' is also present in encouraging a soundly-based neighbourhood for ASEAN's member states. Namely, the former shows the dynamic interactions between member countries, whereas the latter shows propensity towards the maintenance of predictably positive relationship. As Thanat Khoman said in September 1966, when there was a discussion about the new regional organisation,[51] '[W]e have sought to ensure long-lasting peace in Asia

---

[43] The Sabah issue is still formally unresolved.
[44] Kuroyanagi puts it, 'just ideological antagonism was solved when ASEAN was established'. See Yoneji Kuroyanagi, *ASEAN 35 Nen no Kiseki*, p. 33. Author's translation.
[45] Adam Malik, Statement at the First ASEAN Ministerial Meeting, Bangkok, 8 August 1967.
[46] Susumu Yamakage, 'Tenkanki no ASEAN', p. 8. Author's translation.
[47] The 'ASEAN spirit' is another oft-iterated term representing the ASEAN's solidarity. The term has been in use since the early stage of ASEAN. One of the earliest usages can be traced back to the statements at the First Meeting of the *Ad Hoc* Committee on Civil Aviation of ASEAN in June 1968. The leader of the Thai delegation, Wing Commander Sanan Sangkachand said, 'I am happy and confident that with our *ASEAN spirit*, our common goals will be jointly accomplished and meet our mutual interests'. (*Foreign Affairs Bulletin*, 7/6 (June-July 1968), p. 549. Italics added.) At the same meeting, the representative of the Indonesian delegation also referred to the term: 'It is our ardent hope and wish, that such differences, if any, could and should be solved in the *ASEAN spirit* as members of the same family'. (*Foreign Affairs Bulletin*, 7/6 (June-July 1968), p. 543. Italic added.) Although there is no academic contribution to its historical argument, the term can be seen regularly in the official documents. According to the Joint Communiqué of the ASEAN Ministerial Meeting in 1971, the ASEAN spirit is based on 'cordiality and mutual understanding'. (Joint Communiqué of the Fourth ASEAN Ministerial Meeting, Manila, 13 March 1971.) However, the term has been used variously. For example, 'solidarity' was stipulated in the Declaration of ASEAN Concord in 1976 whereas 'friendship and cordiality' have appeared in its Joint Communiqué. (Declaration of ASEAN Concord, 24 February 1976; and Joint Communiqué of the First ASEAN Heads of Government Meeting Bali, 24 February 1976.)
[48] Michael Antolik, *ASEAN and the Diplomacy of Accommodation*, p. 129.
[49] Estrella D. Solidum, 'The Role of Certain Sectors in Shaping and Articulating the ASEAN Way', p. 139.
[50] Gillian Goh, 'The "ASEAN Way"', p. 114.
[51] Later it was materialised as ASEAN.

by arousing the consciousness on the part of the Asian countries not only to coexist together but also to co-operate closely for mutual benefits'.[52] The concept of 'working together' brings with it an understanding that countries in Southeast Asia would actively engage in dealing with regional matters, and in so doing maintain cooperation in a harmonious political atmosphere. Considering such behaviour, harmonisation is another word which can express the idea of countries in ASEAN.[53] They choose to collaborate with each other for the sake of their common objective, national development, despite the fact that there may be differences between member countries. Countries in Southeast Asia recognised that they had to be tolerant of each other in order to harmonise their different views.[54]

Actually, Indonesia had historically been willing to accommodate differing views. In June 1945, Sukarno introduced *Pancasila*[55] to domestic politics, so that Indonesia could survive in its ethnic and religious diversity. In the early 1950s, the then Indonesian Vice-President Mohammad Hatta applied this idea to Indonesia's foreign policy: 'The desire to put political relations with other nations on a footing of mutual respect, despite differences in the governmental structure and ideology'.[56]

Malaysia also embraced the idea of tolerance in its foreign policy. When Malayan Prime Minister Tunku Abdul Rahman was elaborating the Association of Southeast Asia (ASA), he held that peaceful coexistence among different ideologies should be realised so that countries in Southeast Asia could focus on nation-building.[57] Malaysian Deputy Prime Minister Tun Abdul Razak mentioned his view of regional cooperation at the speech in the United Nations in September 1966: '[W]e believe that the nations of the world, of whatever ideological convictions, can live together, not merely in passive coexistence but in active co-operation for the common pursuit of peace and economic and social well-being of the peoples of the world'.[58] In this context, the Tunku proposed that the People's Republic of China should be recognised and coexist with the international community rather than being politically contained: 'Communist China must be recognised as an independent sovereign nation, and as *China*. It is unrealistic to ignore the Peking regime'.[59] Tun Ismail bin Dato Abdul Rahman, the Malaysian Minister for Home Affairs and Acting Minister for Foreign Affairs, said in 1966, '[W]e call upon the People's Republic of China to keep its hands off our region and to adopt a policy of peaceful coexistence towards its fellow-Asians in South-East Asia'.[60] He continued, 'We do not oppose the communist system in Mainland China, so long as it confines itself within its own borders'.[61] Arguably, the acceptance of different views, rather than intolerance towards such, helped the idea of a regional cooperation organisation (such as the ASA, Maphilindo and ASEAN) to take shape.[62]

---

[52] Thanat Khoman, Speech at the United Nations General Assembly, 27 September 1966.

[53] In other words, '"harmonisation" of different national interests'. (Zakaria Haji Ahmad, 'The World of ASEAN Decision-makers', p. 207.)

[54] See, for example, Thanat Khoman, Opening address of The First Meeting of the Ad hoc Committee on Civil Aviation of ASEAN, 25 June 1968.

[55] For details on *Pancasila*, see Chapter 1.

[56] Mohammad Hatta, 'Indonesia's Foreign Policy', p. 445.

[57] Tunku Abdul Rahman, Interview by Kayser Sung, *Far Eastern Economic Review*, 28 July 1960, pp. 162-163.

[58] Tun Abdul Razak, Speech in the 1416th Plenary Meeting of the United Nations General Assembly, 26 September 1966.

[59] Tunku Abdul Rahman, Interview by Kayser Sung.

[60] Tun Ismail bin Dato Abdul Rahman, Address to the Foreign Correspondents Association, Johore Bahru, 23 June 1966.

[61] Ibid.

[62] Indeed, during *Konfrontasi*, Indonesia and Malaya sat at the same table and agreed with the formation of the loose cooperation plan, Maphilindo.

Four conventions for 'working together beyond difference'

The concept of 'working together beyond difference' forged four specific conventions through the process of regional cooperation (Fig. 1). These are: (1) holding consultations among member countries, (2) saving face, (3) shelving unresolvable issues and (4) emphasising informal procedure in conflict resolution. It should be noted that these four specific conventions can be a set of practices which one central concept controls.[63] However, they have not necessarily, or in practice, always been used in every specific event or crisis, but selectively so as to achieve, and maintain, an overarching regional concept of 'working together'.

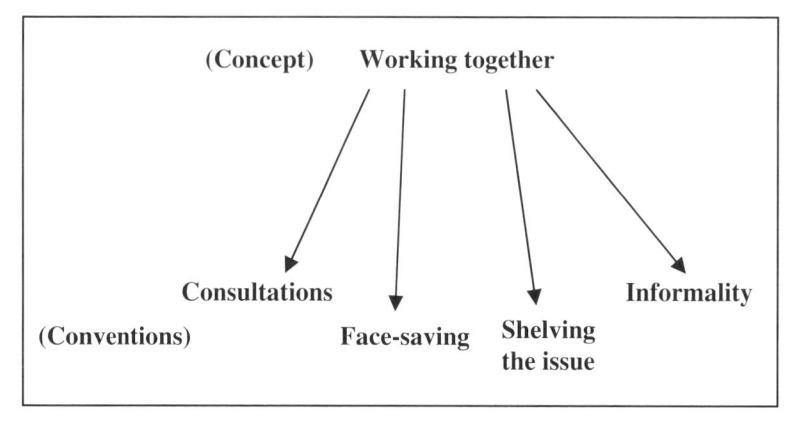

Fig. 1 The ASEAN Way (Concept and conventions)

The first convention was 'consultations', which was introduced into regional cooperation in Southeast Asia so that they could know each other.[64] Consultations contributed to the alleviation of tension and suspicion in the region during the formative period of ASEAN. Frequent meetings helped 'to crystallise a community of sentiments' as well as, in the process, building confidence.[65] The term 'consultations' first appeared during the formation of the Association of Southeast Asia (ASA). Three countries, Malaya, the Philippines and Thailand, held frequent meetings in working towards the establishment of the first regional association. Its foundation document, the Bangkok Declaration, promised to 'establish an effective machinery for friendly *consultations*' among the member countries.[66] The word 'consultations' also appeared in the

---

[63] Tay suggests that conventions of the ASEAN Way are not 'static' and can be changed. Simon S. C. Tay, 'Institutions and Process', p. 269.

[64] The term 'consultations' was highlighted in the 'Conference on Indonesia' in January 1949. The main purpose of the conference was to facilitate the independence of Indonesia. It was composed of Afghanistan, Australia, Burma, Ceylon, Egypt, Ethiopia, India (host), Iran, Iraq, Lebanon, Pakistan, the Philippines, Saudi Arabia, Syria and Yemen. China (Taiwan), Nepal, New Zealand and Thailand sent observers. The Conference also referred to cooperation among participants. One out of the three resolutions made was 'further consultations among participants for the establishment of suitable machinery for promoting regional co-operation'. However, it did not focus regional cooperation in Southeast Asia but 'within the framework of the United Nations'. See *The Conference on Indonesia, January 20-23, 1949* (Delhi: The Publications Division, Ministry of Information and Broadcasting of India, 1949), pp. 14-15.

[65] Estrella D. Solidum, *Towards a Southeast Asian Community*, p. 205. Leifer sees that ASEAN reduced tensions 'without the implementation of explicit confidence-building measures'. See Michael Leifer, *The ASEAN Regional Forum*, p. 40.

[66] The Bangkok Declaration, 31 July 1961. Italics added.

agreement of Maphilindo in 1963.[67] Thus, the practice of consultations has been recognised as important and, indeed, promoted to the status of a regional custom.

The second convention was 'face-saving' behaviour. As mentioned earlier, the practice of *musyawarah* and *mufakat* highly favours face-saving. Mohammed Hatta argued strongly, if indirectly, for recognition of this, and respect for the sensitivity of newly-independent countries: 'Nations recently become independent are strongly influenced by national sentiment and feel the need to maintain their self-respect'.[68] This is because '[i]nternal consolidation is the primary task' for the young countries.[69] The government 'must show evidence of economic and social betterment if it is to offset the influence of agitation by radical circles'.[70] Furthermore, it was essential for countries in the region to show their confidence in the area of foreign policy as well as domestic policy. Therefore, every government needed to quickly emerge from the temptation of allowing feelings of inadequacy and inferiority to remain in its dealings with other, more mature, states in the area of diplomatic relations. The importance of 'face-saving' stemmed from such political vulnerability of new countries. Such political sensitivity made member countries deal with each other with restraint, and principally in the guise of ASEAN cooperation. Hoan Anh Tuan, for example, points out that 'face-saving' is the product of frequent consultations:

> ASEAN members get to know one another, learn about each other's interests and sensitivities, and explore possibilities for expanded co-operation. Additionally, officials at different levels are encouraged to contact one another and establish personal relationships so that in the event of crisis they can pick up the telephone and call each other, thus increasing the possibility of containing any dispute.[71]

The third convention dealt with 'the shelving of difficult bilateral issues'. Such problems could also be papered over, or made more opaque, in order to lessen potential damage to bilateral ties. Indeed, the acceptable formula is not always generated through negotiations between the countries concerned. This convention was forged as a lesson drawn from the bilateral dispute between Malaya and the Philippines over Sabah, which plunged the ASA into dysfunction. The issue was shelved when the growing tendency to establish ASEAN emerged in the region. When the Sabah issue recurred a year after the establishment of the Association, it was again shelved so that ASEAN would not, and could not, experience the same fate.

The fourth convention at play was that of the importance of 'informality'. One of two aspects of informality is the institutional structure. In early 1959, when Tunku Abdul Rahman talked with Carlos P. Garcia about regional cooperation, he first resorted to a treaty-based organisation plan called the Southeast Asian Friendship and Economic Treaty (SEAFET). However, it was finally changed to the Association of Southeast Asia (ASA), by enshrining a 'practical and informal basis'.[72] Indeed, the most focused point for regional cooperation in Southeast Asia in this period was 'to acquire the habit of sitting down together' as many countries as pos-

---

[67] It also later emerged in Treaty of Amity and Cooperation (TAC) of 1976. '[T]he High Contracting Parties shall maintain regular contacts and *consultations* with one another on international and regional matters with a view to coordinating their views actions and policies'. See Treaty of Amity and Cooperation, 24 February 1976. Italics added.
[68] Mohammad Hatta, 'Indonesia's Foreign Policy', p. 445.
[69] Ibid., p. 449.
[70] Ibid. At a time when the newly-independent countries of ASEAN (and to some extent non-colonised state of Thailand) were inexperienced in nation-building, states needed to demonstrate their confidence in their ability to govern in the eyes of the people.
[71] Hoang Anh Tuan, 'ASEAN Dispute Management', p. 67.
[72] Tunku Abdul Rahman, Interview by Kayser Sung. Malaya envisaged several specific items for regional cooperation from the beginning of the plan, such as tourism, education, commodities, shipping and civil aviation, common market. See *Far Eastern Economic Review*, 14 July 1960, p. 51.

sible.[73] In this respect, the loose association plan was practicable in letting as many Southeast Asian states be involved in it as possible. Although the first regional organisation, the ASA, failed to generate a broader association of states in the region, the concept was successfully adopted by ASEAN. In addition, the foundational documents of the ASA and ASEAN – Declarations – are less legally-binding than are more formal legal documents such as Charters. This fact is more evidence of how loosely-linked the regional organisations in Southeast Asia are. As Snitwongse points out, ASEAN countries have been able to work together because there have not been so many requirements on member states.[74]

The second aspect of informality can be seen in the area of communication. Ikle points out that informal meetings took a certain role in the course of East-West negotiations during the Cold War era.[75] Therefore, it cannot always be said that the informal aspect in communication is a specific custom in Southeast Asia. What aspect, then, of such a form of communication gives ASEAN's style its distinctiveness? The specific point here, appearing in case studies throughout the book, is the importance of cultural affinity. As discussed earlier in this chapter, such cultural affinity helped to generate an atmosphere of friendship in important areas of communication between ASEAN states. The friendly gestures of Tunku Abdul Rahman towards Sukarno (in Tokyo and Manila in 1963) were a crucial factor in making a breakthrough in the bilateral crisis that had emerged between their countries. Furthermore, when Indonesia mediated between Malaysia and the Philippines during the Corregidor affair in 1968, it employed the informal negotiation style, which was based on *musyawarah* and *mufakat*. This behind-the-scenes consensus-building was accepted in both countries and successfully brought rapprochement. In this respect, informality in communication in ASEAN is based on two specific factors: respect and restraint.

The formation process of the ASEAN Way
The concept of 'working together beyond differences' originated in the above-mentioned Summit talks between Sukarno and Tunku Abdul Rahman in Tokyo on 31 May 1963. The Tokyo talks were held during the recurrence of verbal war between the two countries. In these talks, Sukarno proposed the following to the Tunku: 'I want to solve this issue with you as a friend and neighbour rather than an opponent'.[76] The result of the talks was that they successfully created a cooperative relationship. The idea for regional cooperation was therefore first written into the Manila Accord at the following Ministerial conference on 11 June 1963.[77] In the Accord, Indonesia, Malaya and the Philippines agreed to establish 'the grouping of the three nations of Malay origin *working together* in closest harmony'.[78] To do so, the three Ministers agreed to hold 'frequent and regular consultations'.[79] The subsequent Manila Summit meeting produced impressive agreements through the implementation of mutual concessions. Although, as history shows, the Manila agreements could not realise reconciliation between the three countries, this

---

[73] Daniel Wolfstone, 'Manila's Image of ASAS', *Far Eastern Economic Review*, 15 September 1960, p. 596.

[74] Kusuma Snitwongse, 'Thirty Years of ASEAN', p. 184. In particular, excluding bilateral issues from the agenda of ASEAN helped to work together among member countries. (Ibid, p. 185.)

[75] Fred Charles Ikle, *How Nations Negotiate* (New York: Harper and Row Publishers, 1964), p. 118.

[76] 'Ohira, Subandorio Kaidan (Dai Ni-kai) Youshi [The Proceedings of the Foreign Ministerial Talks between Ohira and Subandrio, The Second Session], Nantou Ajia-ka [Department of Southeast Asia, Ministry of Foreign Affairs of Japan], 1 June 1963, GSK File A'-423. Author's translation.

[77] The ASA was not able to address this issue as Indonesia did not join it. Indonesia saw that the ASA was meaningless because there was a huge gap between potential member countries. See Nicholas Tarling, 'From SEAFET and ASA', p. 10. Three member countries of the ASA (Malaya, the Philippines and Thailand) were similar in their perspective on world politics as three of them were pro-Western and anti-communist countries.

[78] The Manila Accord, 11 June 1963. Italics added.

[79] Ibid.

exercise of solving the intra-regional dispute nonetheless greatly contributed to the idea of ASEAN cooperation. When the first locally-made regional organisation was proposed in 1959, Indonesian Foreign Minister Subandrio saw that the proposed regional organisation was meaningless because there was a huge political gap between potential member countries.[80] Indonesia, at the time, did not try to express any signs of willingness for harmonisation of its relations with other countries nor to overcome political differences.

On the contrary, a series of Manila conferences in 1963 successfully made the consensus between member countries including Indonesia, and produced the concessive agreements in which the concept of 'working together beyond differences' was embodied. Indeed, Malaya was a pro-British and anti-communist country without joining the South East Asia Treaty Organisation (SEATO), and the Philippines was a pro-American and anti-communist country joining SEATO. Indonesia, on the other hand, was a non-aligned country in opposition to SEATO and tolerant of communism. These three countries, each demonstrating such distinctive perspectives in their politics, sat together and decided to collaborate with one another in shaping the framework for Maphilindo, and such a process was the first time this had occurred in the history of Southeast Asia.

In the process bringing to a close the three-way dispute over the formation of Malaysia 1966, the concept of 'working together' again appeared in the approaches taken by Indonesia, Malaysia and the Philippines. Firstly, Malaysia and the Philippines resumed diplomatic relations, overcoming their differences over the treatment of Sabah. Then, in Indonesia, General Suharto clearly showed his willingness to compromise with Malaysia by sending the Army leaders[81] to Kuala Lumpur just before the ministerial talks between Indonesia and Malaysia. Eventually, from a practical point of view, the three countries concerned succeeded in shelving issues related to the formation of Malaysia.

The Philippine government also showed its willingness to cooperate with other states in the region. It suspended the resumption of diplomatic relations with Malaysia, and did so at the request of Indonesia. In this regard, the Philippine Secretary of foreign Affairs, Narciso Ramos, said, 'The Philippines is desirous of maintaining friendly relations with Indonesia. We do not want any irreparable damage in our relations with the neighbouring country'.[82] The Philippines' decision to postpone recognition of Malaysia showed that the Philippines put the priority to regional harmonisation rather than national interest.[83]

When Tunku Abdul Rahman objected to the Indonesian plan for regional cooperation[84] by saying that the Association of Southeast Asia (ASA), an organisation formed by Malaya's initiative, already existed, Adam Malik stated that the proposed organisation was the enlargement of the ASA.[85] Malik showed restraint towards Indonesia's plan in order to protect the Tunku's

---

[80] Nicholas Tarling, 'From SEAFET and ASA', p. 10.
[81] They were the members of Crush Malaysia Command (KOGAM).
[82] *The Straits Times*, 26 March 1966.
[83] Collins points out that 'members are prepared to defer their own interests to the interests of the association' and it is 'extremely important'. See Alan Collins, 'Mitigating the Security Dilemma', pp. 107-108.
[84] It was developed by Indonesia and Thailand, and was materialised as ASEAN.
[85] 'Tounan Ajia Chiiki no Kyouryoku Taisei Soshikika ni Tsuiteno Toukoku Gaimusyou Keizai Kyokuchou no Uchiwa (Houkoku) [The Secret Report for the New Organization for Regional Cooperation in Southeast Asia by the Head of Bureau of Economy of Ministry of Foreign Affairs]', Zai Maleishia Asaha Rinji Dairi Taishi kara Gaimu Daijin, Dai-547 Gou [Communication between Asaha Special Acting Japanese Ambassador to Malaysia and Foreign Minister], Ministry of Foreign Affairs of Japan, 2 June 1967, GSK File B'-200. Narciso Ramos stated in the ASEAN Ministerial Meeting in August 1967: 'ASEAN is not intended to supplant, replace or eliminate any existing regional organization'. See Narciso Ramos, Opening Statement at the First ASEAN Ministerial Meeting, Bangkok, 8 August 1967.

prestige. Thai Foreign Minister Thanat Khoman sounded the proposed plan to the Tunku first.[86] The latter was pleased with Thanat's regard and finally accepted the new organisation plan.[87]

In the Corregidor affair, Foreign Ministers of ASEAN states called for the spirit of 'working together beyond differences' at the First Meeting of the ASEAN's Ad hoc Committee on Civil Aviation and the ASEAN Ministerial Meeting in June 1968.[88] The reconciliation was quickly brought into existence in Jakarta by the Foreign Ministers of Malaysia and the Philippines in August. After the short interruption of the harmonious atmosphere, in the course of holding the meeting in Bangsen in December 1968, the Philippines and Malaysia successfully re-established the Jakarta agreement by the Philippines' withdrawal of its claim to Sabah for the sake of ASEAN's survival. It is noteworthy that Indonesia's consultation was conducted behind the scenes to ensure that the Philippines could withdraw the claim without losing face. The spirit of 'working together beyond differences' was in full operation in the settlement process of the Corregidor affair. When the two countries made rapprochement, the third ASEAN Ministerial Meeting stated:

[I]t was a matter of paramount importance that ASEAN countries should get together and *work together* for the common good of the group in particular and of the region in general. He [Tunku Abdul Rahman] announced that as a result of a discussion between him and the Honourable Mr. Carlos P. Romulo, Secretary of Foreign Affairs of the Philippines, in the spirit of goodwill and friendship and *because of the great value Malaysia and the Philippines placed on ASEAN*.[89]

ASEAN, the ASEAN Way and the goal of ASEAN

As discussed above, the sense of primary responsibility to their regional matter has been developed in ASEAN countries, with their overarching goal being to secure being 'freedom from external interference' in their internal affairs (Fig. 2).[90] Five countries of ASEAN agreed to give national development the top priority: 'To accelerate the economic growth, social progress and cultural development in the region'.[91] They also recognised that they should maintain peace and stability so that they could focus on national development. These are arguably the major objectives of ASEAN cooperation and were stipulated in the ASEAN Declaration. The ASEAN Way, which embraces the concept of 'working together' at its very core, should be defined as the means to maintain and promote ASEAN cooperation.[92]

---

[86] *The Straits Times*, 22 May 1967.
[87] Ibid.
[88] For the details of the Corregidor affair, see Chapter 5.
[89] The Joint Communiqué of the Third ASEAN Ministerial Meeting, Cameron Highlands, 17 December 1969. Italics added.
[90] Zone of Peace, Freedom and Neutrality Declaration, 27 November 1971.
[91] The ASEAN Declaration, 8 August 1967.
[92] The ASEAN Way is 'means rather than ends' to maintain and facilitate regional cooperation. Nikolas Busse, 'Constructivism and Southeast Asian Security', p. 47. Sunitwongse sees the ASEAN Way as 'political process' of ASEAN. See Kusuma Sunitwongse, 'Thirty Years of ASEAN', p. 184. The similar view is taken by Acharya. See Amitav Acharya, *Constructing a Security Community in Southeast Asia*, p. 63.

```
┌─────────────────────────────────────────────────────────┐
│         ┌──────────────────────────────────┐            │
│         │ Freedom from external interference│───┐       │
│         └──────────────────────────────────┘   │        │
│                        ▲                        │        │
│         ┌──────────────────────────────────┐   │        │
│         │ Socio-economic development and stability │◀──┘ │
│         └──────────────────────────────────┘            │
│                        ▲                                 │
│         ┌──────────────────────┐      ┌──────────────┐   │
│         │ Regional cooperation (ASEAN) │◀····│ The ASEAN Way │
│         └──────────────────────┘      └──────────────┘   │
└─────────────────────────────────────────────────────────┘
```

Fig. 2 ASEAN, the ASEAN Way and the goal of ASEAN

The countries in the region believed that economic difficulties at home would allow external powers to encroach upon their sovereignty. As Malayan Prime Minister Tunku Abdul Rahman said in the speech of 23 October 1961:

> Neither of us [Malaya and Singapore] wants grave economic unrest, nor do we want to be subjected to external interference which would follow. We have seen this happen already elsewhere, and we do not want to see it happen here.[93]

The ASEAN states were also concerned about subversion by Communist elements at home supported by external Communists in Indochina and China.[94] Since the Southeast Asian countries lacked sufficient military power to protect themselves, an eventual Communist subversion would necessarily lead to Western, and notably US, intervention. In such a situation, these countries could become involved in bipolar antagonism; the effects of which they had already seen so vividly in Indochina. In order to avoid such a nightmare, ASEAN countries recognised that another way to protect Communist infiltration was to overcome poverty, which could provide the Communists with fertile grounds for political and military infiltration. Therefore, they focused upon economic development in order to raise the standards of living at home. Indeed, the ASEAN Declaration itself stipulated the need for such an approach:

> [T]he countries of South East Asia share a primary responsibility for strengthening the economic and social stability of the region and ensuring their peaceful and progressive national development, and that they are determined to ensure their stability and security from external interference in any form or manifestation in order to preserve their national identities in accordance with the ideals and aspirations of their peoples.[95]

National development would prevent Communist infiltration, and consequently would help prevent external interference, and another proxy war in the region. Such a situation would therefore enable ASEAN countries to further focus on their national development and secure a free hand to decide policies to their individual situations. Therefore, prosperity became the stepping-stone towards self-reliance for ASEAN countries. The path to peace and prosperity was conceptualised as 'regional resilience', which was stipulated in the following way in the Treaty of Amity and Cooperation in 1976:

---

[93] Tunku Abdul Rahman, Speech in the House of Representatives in Malaya, 16 October 1961.
[94] Susumu Yamakage, *ASEAN*, p. 109.
[95] The ASEAN Declaration, 8 August 1967.

> The High Contracting Parties in their efforts to achieve regional prosperity and security, shall endeavour to cooperate in all fields for the promotion of *regional resilience*, based on the principles of self-confidence, self-reliance, mutual respect, cooperation and solidarity which will constitute the foundation for a strong and viable community of nations in Southeast Asia.[96]

The origins of the notion of 'regional resilience' came from the idea of 'national resilience'.[97] In the Treaty of Amity and Cooperation, ASEAN countries were directed to '... endeavour to strengthen their respective national resilience in their political, economic, sociocultural as well as security fields in conformity with their respective ideals and aspirations, free from external interference as well as internal subversive activities in order to preserve their respective national identities'.

Gordon argues that Southeast Asia aimed to 'work toward the two goals simultaneously: national development *and* regional cooperation'.[98] However, considering that the main purposes of ASEAN were '[t]o accelerate the economic growth' and '[t]o promote regional peace and stability',[99] regional cooperation should be recognised as an impetus of peace and prosperity. Peace (socio-political stability) and prosperity (socio-economic well-being) are interdependent.[100] Namely, 'economic development and national security must go hand in hand'.[101] Economic development can be an impetus of bringing about social and political stability. When economic growth is achieved at a certain level, social stability is brought about. Social stability brings political stability, and political stability facilitates further policy-making for national development. This positive cycle helps to achieve self-reliance in the region. Therefore, peace and prosperity largely contribute to regional autonomy, and they are most important. As a result, ASEAN cooperation takes the role of the facilitator of 'peace, progress and prosperity in the region'.[102]

The former Thai Minister of National Development, Pote Sarasin, put these propositions in the following way: ' [Economic development] is the process that will not only bring material happiness to our people but will also contribute to the maintenance of our national security'.[103] The more peace and stability is achieved in the region, the less the region will suffer from interference from the outside. When the region gets stronger, economic well-being is brought more. Indeed, as Tunku Abdul Rahman said, '*Merdeka* [independence] has brought about the improvement of the standard of living of the people'.[104]

In the Asian-African Conference in 1955, the participants of the conference feared that the Cold War antagonism would give rise to a new World War that would deprive newly-emerging

---

[96] Treaty of Amity and Cooperation, 24 February 1976. The term 'regional resilience' can also be seen in Declaration of ASEAN Concord. Italics added.

[97] National resilience is the comprehensive approach to nation-building including economic, political, social and military development. It was originated in Indonesia. For the official explanation by the Indonesian government for national resilience, see Dewi Fortuna Anwar, 'Indonesia: *Ketahanan National, Wawasan Nusantara, Hankamrata*', in Ken Booth and Russell Trood (eds.), *Strategic Cultures in the Asia-Pacific Region* (London: Macmillan Press, 1999), p. 213.

[98] Bernard K. Gordon, *The Dimensions of Conflict in Southeast Asia*, p. 154. Italics added.

[99] The ASEAN Declaration, 8 August 1967.

[100] Countries in Southeast Asia 'are aware of the necessity of cooperation not just for political ends but for the sake of mutual development'. See Adam Malik, 'Promise of Indonesia', p. 301.

[101] Pote Sarasin, 'Economic Development and National Security', *Foreign Affairs Bulletin*, 5/3 (December 1965-January 1966), p. 249. Although these are interdepended, economic development 'must come first'. (Ibid.)

[102] The ASEAN Declaration, 8 August 1967.

[103] Pote Sarasin, 'Economic Development and National Security', p. 247.

[104] *The Straits Times*, 22 May 1967.

countries of the opportunity for nation-building.[105] The final communiqué stated: 'friendly cooperation in accordance with these [ten] principles would effectively contribute to the maintenance and promotion of international peace and security, while cooperation in the economic, social and cultural fields would help bring about the common prosperity and well-being of all'.[106] It stated that friendly cooperation would bring about peace and security to the world, but this did not suggest that peace would give rise to economic prosperity.

It should be observed that the concept of the reciprocal relationship between economic development and national security has been in practice since late 1950s.[107] Political subversion, or intimidation, in Indochina subsequently turned the eyes of countries in Southeast Asia to strengthening their own nations by greater mobilisation of resources for internal and external peace and stability. If the states devoted to great a proportion of their man-power to military activity, fewer resources would be available for economic development.[108] This idea was made clearer when the territorial dispute over Sabah recurred in 1968. Ghazali Shafie suggested at the time that the conflict should be avoided so that the two countries could concentrate on their national development program: '[W]e are united [under ASEAN] not only by ties of sentiments, but also by urgent and compelling interests, tasks of nation building, of economic development...these will require all of our money and energy, all of our sense of national and regional solidarity'.[109]

Concluding remarks

Cultural affinity helped to alleviate tensions between countries in Southeast Asia. The ASEAN Way, it might be concluded in this regard, was formed through the influence of Malay culture. However, it employed cultural practice in a necessarily weakened form. In particular, the practice of *musyawarah* and *mufakat* was introduced to ASEAN countries with some alteration, in order to compensate for the equally important absence of an exclusive and formally acknowledged ASEAN leader. Instead of coercive decision-making, ASEAN forged the convention of shelving unresolvable issues, so that the organisation itself could be preserved intact. The oft-cited principle of non-interference should be understood as the main tenet of ASEAN cooperation, rather than a specific component of the ASEAN Way. This originated from the fear of interference from external powers, particularly because of the impact of the Cold War. In order to avoid external interference, ASEAN states recognised regional responsibility for the regional problems and decided to cooperate with each other to address their problems directly, and within the context of an overarching organisation. ASEAN cooperation is to this day maintained through this, as well as for the furtherance of peace and prosperity. In this respect, the principle of non-interference contributes to maintaining, facilitating and, indeed, deepening of ASEAN cooperation.

As discussed above, the ASEAN Way is composed of both the concept and the conventions being forged by this concept. The concept is 'working together beyond differences' and it created a set of conventions. The concept was created to maintain and facilitate regional cooperation. It first emerged in 1963 when Sukarno and Tunku Abdul Rahman held talks in Tokyo, and was first written into the agreements emanating from the Manila conference that followed these talks. It came up in the ending process of the three-way dispute between Indonesia, Malaysia and the Philippines in 1966, and also emerged in the formation process of ASEAN in the fol-

---

[105] Final Communiqué of the Asian-African Conference, 24 April 1955.
[106] Ibid.
[107] As discussed in Chapter 2. Sarasin also said, 'Many a country in Asia have demonstrated the virtue of this dual policy [the interrelationship between economic development and national security], such as Thailand, Malaysia ... where unbridled economic prosperity has continued' since the latter half of 1950s. See Pote Sarasin, 'Economic Development and National Security', p. 249.
[108] Ibid., p. 248.
[109] Ghazali Shafie, Opening Address at the Bangkok talks, 17 June 1968.

lowing year. It was fully embraced among ASEAN member countries during the settlement process of the Corregidor affair in 1968. The concept created a set of conventions: holding consultations with member states, saving face, shelving the unresolvable issues, and placing the emphasis on informal procedures.

CONCLUSION

This book has demonstrated that the origins of the ASEAN Way can be traced to the period preceding the formation of ASEAN itself. It has also argued that the ASEAN Way is not just a medley of different conventions, but an idea which elicited a series of conventions, emerging in response to a variety of crises in the Southeast Asian region. At its heart, the ASEAN Way was the key to forming and maintaining ASEAN cooperation. It can be said that the ASEAN Way came to represent the philosophical basis of the Association, and beyond that cooperative relations between its member states. In demonstrating these significant perspectives, the book has explored: (1) the view of nation-building in each state in the region after World War II, (2) the formation of Western-influenced regional organisations and critical perspectives on these from countries of Southeast Asia, (3) the formation process of locally-made organisations, and (4) the process of dispute settlement in the region.

Malaya, Singapore and the Philippines undertook nation-building by receiving full support from their former colonisers after their independence. These states aimed at a Western style of national development. Indonesia, on the other hand, pointed to the limitations of Western forms of national development and pursued a nation-building process that was distinctive to its own needs and perspectives. Thailand and the Philippines stood out in another context again: they were active participants in SEATO. They therefore deeply involved themselves in bipolar ideological antagonism that underpinned the origins of this organisation, and, in return, received considerable military and financial support from the US. Malaya was not as profoundly involved in bipolar antagonisms as were Thailand and the Philippines, and instead focussed on raising living standards by receiving full support from the British government. Indonesia firmly expressed a non-aligned position and took the leadership of the third group in international politics, the so-called Non-Aligned Movement. It also rejected the military presence of SEATO in the region. But Indonesia was distinctive in its own context, because it focussed entirely on identity-building rather than purely on economic development at home.

Countries in Southeast Asia saw the brutality of a proxy war in Vietnam. The Philippines and Thailand, having realised that external superpowers did not care about the region, shifted their policy of nation-building by being away from ideological antagonism. They therefore came to concentrate on the improvement of living conditions at home; a characteristic that most of the Southeast Asian states finally came to hold as crucial to their world-views. In shifting their strategic perspective in this way, the Philippines and Thailand came to share with Malaya the emphasis on nation-building. Largely as a result of this, these three states established the first locally-fashioned regional organisation, the Association of Southeast Asia (ASA). However, Indonesia refused the invitation to join the latter, thereby limiting considerably its scope of potential efficacy. For Indonesia, the reason not to join this organisation was because its member states relied on defence agreements with Western countries, and therefore Indonesia regarded the ASA as the affiliate of SEATO. On the problematic issue of the formation of Malaysia, which emerged soon after the establishment of the ASA, Indonesia criticised Malaysia for being built by neo-colonialist. It took an uncompromising stance on the Western influence in the region and intervened directly through the launching of *Konfrontasi*.

The leadership change in Indonesia finally shifted the country's stance on nation-building. With the ouster of Sukarno, the new Indonesian government gave economic development the highest priority on the country's national agenda, shifting attention away from its former emphasis on national identity-building. In so doing, Indonesia also came to show its desire to work together with neighbouring countries; the first major signal of this being the ending of *Konfrontasi*. Such developments influenced other states in the region, with Malaysia and the Philippines achieving rapprochement by shelving the Sabah territorial issue, and Malaysia and Singapore agreeing to work together beyond the underlying ethnic antagonism that had long characterised their relations.

In sum, the countries in Southeast Asia came to recognise that peace and stability was of greatest importance to their views, and, by the end of the period of this study, the common goal of national development. They also realised that prosperity could protect them from external interference, the latter being a major concern shared by all the states of Southeast Asia, and especially so since the colonial period. This common understanding of regional politics crystallised into the establishment of ASEAN. In forming the latter association, they realised the significance of 'working together beyond difference' in order to focus on national development and prevent external interference; a set of sentiments that were, and are, embodied in the concept of the ASEAN Way. This was demonstrated very strongly through the ability of the ASEAN states to cooperate in defusing the recurrence of the Sabah territorial dispute. In the process of dealing with this dispute, Malaysia and the Philippines successfully settled the matter without impairing the centrality of ASEAN's cooperation. Such historical forms of development of regional cooperation gave rise to important conventions for the ASEAN states. The more significant examples of these were the use of frequent consultations, the recognition of the importance of face-saving, the tendency to shelve unsettled issues between member states, and, finally, the use of informal techniques in the conduct of diplomacy at bilateral and multilateral levels. Taken together, these characteristic features of regional relations, as they became consistent practice under the umbrella of ASEAN, grew into the key constituent of the ASEAN Way: the concept of 'working together beyond difference'.

BIBLIOGRAPHY

Japanese archival collections

Gaikou Shiryou Kan [The Diplomatic Record Office of the Ministry of Foreign Affairs of Japan]

'Dai-Nikai Nichi-Gou Seimu Kankei Jimu Reberu Kyougi [The proceedings of the 2nd Exchange of Political Views of Senior Officials between Japan and Australia]', Ministry of Foreign Affairs of Japan, 14-15 November 1968, Gaikou Shiryou Kan [hereafter GSK] File A'-394.

'Dai Sankai Nichi-Ei Teiki Kyougi, Shiina Daijin to Goodonwooka Gaisyo tono Kaidan Roku, Zai-Ei Taishi yori no Houkoku [The Proceedings of the Third Japan-Britain Regular Conference, the talks between Foreign Minister, Shiina and British Foreign Secretary, Gordon-Walker, The report by the Ambassador to Britain]', Oua-kyoku Eirenpou-ka [Department of Commonwealth of Nations, Bureau of Eurasia, Ministry of Foreign Affairs of Japan], 2 February 1965, GSK File A'-427.

'Dai Yon-kai Nichi-Ei Teiki Kyougi, Shiina-Stuart Ryou Gaisyou Kaidan [The fourth Japan-Britain regular conference, Foreign ministerial talks between Shina and Stewart]', Ou-A-kyoku, Eirenpou-ka [Department of the Commonwealth of Nations, Bureau of Eurasia, Ministry of Foreign Affairs of Japan], 19 October 1965, GSK File A'-427.

'Delama Eikoku Gaimu Jikanho (Kyokutou Tantou) tono Kaidan Kiroku [The Proceedings of the Talks with Delamere, The deputy of the Subordinate Officer of the Ministry of Foreign Affairs of the United Kingdom]', Ou-A-kyoku, Eirenpou-ka [Department of the Commonwealth of Nations, Bureau of Eurasia, Ministry of Foreign Affairs of Japan], 5 July 1966, GSK File A'-410.

'Ikeda Souri, Nikuson Zen Beikoku Fuku Daitouryou Kaiken Roku [The Proceedings of the talks between the Japanese Prime Minister, Ikeda and the former US Vice-President, Nixon]', Amerika-kyoku, Hokubei-ka [Department of North America, Bureau of America, Ministry of Foreign Affairs of Japan], 10 April 1964, GSK File A'-401.

'Ikeda Souri no Hou-"I" oyobi Maleishia Mondai ni Tsuite no "I"-Seifu Jyouhousuji no Kenkai Houkoku no Ken [The view of Indonesian government sources for the trip to Indonesia of the Japanese Prime Minister, Mr. Ikeda and the Malaysia issue]', Zai Indoneshia Fujiyama Rinji Dairi Taishi yori Gaisyou he [From Mr. Fujiyama, the special acting Ambassador to Indonesia to the Foreign Minister], Ministry of Foreign Affairs of Japan, 14 October 1963, GSK File A'-432.

'Ikeda Souri to Hyuumu Ei Gaisyou tono Kaidan Youshi [The proceedings of the talks of Prime Minister Ikeda with British Foreign Secretary, Earl of Hume]', Ou-A-kyoku, Eirenpou-ka [Department of the Commonwealth of Nations, Bureau of Eurasia, Ministry of Foreign Affairs of Japan], 2 April 1963, GSK File A'-411.

'Ikeda Souri to Serukaaku Eikoku Tounan Ajia Sou-benmukan tono Kaidan Naiyou [The Proceedings of the talks between Prime Minister, Ikeda and British General Commissioner for Southeast Asia, Lord Selkirk]', Ou-A-kyoku, Eirenpou-ka [Department of the Commonwealth of Nations, Bureau of Eurasia, Ministry of Foreign Affairs of Japan], 18 October 1962, File GSK A'-411.

'Indonesia Hamenku Buono Fukusyusyou to Shiina Gaimu Daijin tono Kaidan Youroku [The Proceedings of the talks between Indonesian Deputy Prime Minister, Sultan Hamenengku Buwono and Foreign Minister Shina]', Nantou Ajia-ka [Department of Southeast Asia, Ministry of Foreign Affairs of Japan], 25 May 1966, GSK File A'-396.

'Kouda Jikan to Sukarno Daitouryou tono Kaidan Youshi [The Proceedings of the talks between the subordinate officer Kouda and President Sukarno]', Kouda Jikan [The Subordinate Officer Kouda, Ministry of Foreign Affairs of Japan], 29 October 1964, GSK File A'-423.

'Miki Daijin, Goorudobaagu Kaigi Roku [The Proceedings of the talks between the Foreign Minister, Takeo Miki and the US Representative to the UN, Arthur Joseph Goldberg]', Kokusai Rengou-kyoku, Seiji-ka [Department of Politics, Bureau of the United Nations, Ministry of Foreign Affairs of Japan], 25 February 1967, GSK File A'-401.

'Ohira Gaimu Daijin to Subandorio Indoneshia Gaimu Daijin no Kaidan ni Kansuru Ken [The Proceedings of the talks between Mr. Ohira, Foreign Minister of Japan and Dr. Subandrio, Foreign Minister of Indonesia]', Ajia-kyoku, Nantou Ajia-ka [Department of Southeast Asia, Bureau of Asia, Ministry of Foreign Affairs of Japan]', 24 May 1963, GSK File A'-423.

'Ohira, Subandorio Kaidan (Dai Ni-kai) Youshi [The Proceedings of the Foreign Ministerial Talks between Ohira and Subandrio, The Second Session], Nantou Ajia-ka [Department of Southeast Asia, Ministry of Foreign Affairs of Japan], 1 June 1963, GSK File A'-423.

'Satou Souri, Nikuson Zen Bei Fuku Daitouryou Kaidan Youshi [The Proceedings of the talks between Prime Minister, Sato and the former American Vice President, Nixon]', America-kyoku, Hokubei-ka [Department of North America, Bureau of America, Ministry of Foreign Affairs of Japan], 27 August 1965, GSK File A'-401.

'Shiina Gaimu Daijin, Raaman Syusyou Kaidan Youshi [The Proceedings of the talks between Japanese Foreign Minister, Shiina and Malaysian Prime Minister, Tunku Abdul Rahman]', Nansei Ajia-ka [Department of Southwest Asia, Ministry of Foreign Affairs of Japan], 22 October 1966, GSK File A'-359.

'Shiina Gaisyou to Sir Paul Gore-Booth tono Kaidan ni Tsuite [The report of the talks between Foreign Minister, Shiina, and Sir Paul Gore-Booth], Ouei 246 Gou, Oua-kyoku, Eirennpou-ka [Department of the Commonwealth of Nations, Bureau of Eurasia, Ministry of Foreign Affairs of Japan], 18 March 1965, GSK File A'-410.

'Sukaruno Daitouryou Hounichi no Sai no Cyoutei Kousaku ni Tsuite [The memorandum of the mediation for Presudent Sukarno]', Ministry of Foreign Affairs of Japan, 23 September 1964, GSK File A'-423.

'Sukaruno Daitouryou no Tai Maleishia Kan ni Kansuru Ken [The report of President Sukarno's view on Malaysia]', Zai Indoneshia Taishi kara Gaimu Daijin he [From the Ambassador to Indonesia to Foreign Minister], Ministry of Foreign Affairs of Japan, 1 October 1963, GSK File A'-432.

'Tanatto Kouman Tai Gaisyou no Hou Ma Ni Tsuite (Houkoku) [The report for Thanat Khoman's visit to Malaysia], Zai Maleishia Asaha Rinji Dairi Taishi yori Gaimu Daijin, Dai 528 Gou [Communication from Asaha special Acting Japanese Ambassador to Malaysia to the Foreign Minister, No. 528], Ministry of Foreign Affairs of Japan, 26 May 1967, GSK File B'-200.

'Tounan Ajia Chiiki no Kyouryoku Taisei Soshikika ni Tsuiteno Toukoku Gaimusyou Keizai Kyokuchou no Uchiwa (Houkoku) [The Secret Report for the New Organization for Regional Cooperation in Southeast Asia by the Head of Bureau of Economy of Ministry of Foreign Affairs]', Zai Maleishia Asaha Rinji Dairi Taishi kara Gaimu Daijin, Dai-547 Gou [Communication between Asaha Special Acting Japanese Ambassador to Malaysia and Foreign Minister], Ministry of Foreign Affairs of Japan, 2 June 1967, GSK File B'-200.

'Tounan Ajia Syokoku Rengou (ASEAN) no Sousetsu ni Tsuite [The Establishment of the Association of Southeast Asian Nations, ASEAN]', Nansei Ajia-ka [Department of Southwest Asia, Ministry of Foreign Affairs of Japan], 18 August 1967, GSK File B'-200.

British archival collections

Cabinet (CAB)
'Cabinet Conclusions', 1 August 1963, CAB 128/37, CC51(63)4.
'Cabinet Conclusions on Discussions of the Project', 16 November 1961, CAB 128/35/2, CC 63(61)6.
'Defence in South-East Asia: memorandum by COS for Cabinet Defence Committee', 3 December 1954, CAB 131/14, D(54)41.
'Final Report of the Commonwealth Consultative Committee on South and South-East Asia about co-operative economic development', October 1950, CAB 134/226, EPC(50)105.
'Joint Cabinet Note by Mr. Eden, Mr Butler, Lord Ismay and Mr Lennox-Boyd', 20 December 1951, CAB 129/48, C(51)51.
'Joint Memorandum for Cabinet Economic Policy Committee by the Working Parties on the Sterling Area and on Development in South and South-East Asia on 18 March 1950', 22 March 1950, CAB134/225, EPC(50)40.

Colonial Office (CO)
'Despatch from Sir D White to Mr Sandys', 20 December 1962, CO 1030/1076, no 6.
'Letter from Lord Selkirk to Mr Macleod', 24 August 1961, CO 1030/982, no 498C.
'Letter from P B C Moore to W I J Wallace', 18 October 1961, CO 1030/986, no 959.
'Memorandum by Lee Kuan Yew for the Government of the Federation of Malaya', 9 May 1961, CO 1030/973, no E203.
'Memorandum by Lord Perth Recording Tunku Abdul Rahman's Proposal for Closer Association of Independent Malaya and British Dependencies in SE Asia', 10 June 1960, CO 1030/1126, no 10.
'Memorandum on the Brunei Rising by Sir D White for Lord Selkirk', 15 December 1962, CO 1030/1466, ff103-105.

Defence Committee (DC)
'CO Memorandum for Lord Perth', 9 June 1960, DC 35/10019, no 42.
'Inward Telegram SOSLON 62 from Mr Sandys to CRO', 27 August 1963, DC 169/216, no 176.
'Note by M MacDonald of his talks with Tunku Abdul Rahman on 20 December', 22 December 1958, DC 35/10019, no 12, E/3.

Foreign and Commonwealth Office (FCO)
'FCO Research Department Memorandum', 10 July 1970, FCO 51/154, no 15.

Foreign Office (FO)
'Despatch from Sir D Ormsby-Gore to Lord Home', 15 February 1963, FO 371/169908, no 18.
'Inward Telegram no 471 from Sir D Ormsby-Gore to Lord Home', 11 February 1963, FO 371/169695, no 21.
'Inward Telegram no 482 from Sir D Ormsby-Gore to Lord Home', 12 February 1963, FO 371/169695, no 23.
'Inward Telegram OCULAR 593 from T Peters to Lord Home', 3 August 1963, FO 371/169724, no 26.
'Note by M J MacDonald (Singapore)', 8 August 1954, FO 371/111852, no5.
'Outward Telegram OCULAR 1003 from Lord Home to T Peters', 2 August 1963, FO 371/169724, no 26.

Prime Minister's Office files at PRO (PMO)
'Inward Telegram No 1503 from Sir G Tory to Mr Sandys', 9 August 1963, PMO 11/4349.

'Note by Lord Selkirk for Mr Selwyn Lloyd', 17 June 1960, PMO 11/3418.
'Outward Telegram No 1946 from Mr Sandys to Sir G Tory', 10 August 1963, PMO 11/4349.
'Outward Telegram No 2459 from the FO to Lord Home', 4 August 1963, PMO 11/4349, T434/63.
'Outward Telegram No 2488 from Mr Macmillan to Lord Home', 5 August 1963, PMO 11/4349, T443B/63.
'Outward Telegram No 7462 from the FO to Washington Embassy', 4 August 1963, PMO 11/4349, T430/63.

Treasury (TR)
'Letter from Lord Selkirk to Mr Macmillan', 20 December 1962, TR 225/2551.

Official Documents

The Association of Southeast Asia (ASA)
Bangkok Declaration, 31 July 1961, in Peter Boyce (ed.), *Malaysia and Singapore in International Diplomacy: Documents and Commentaries* (Sydney: Sydney University Press, 1968), pp. 235-236.

The Association of Southeast Asian Nations (ASEAN)
ASEAN Declaration, 8 August 1967, <http://www.aseansec.org/1629.htm>, accessed 5 December 2008.
Declaration of ASEAN Concord, 24 February 1976, <http://www.aseansec.org/1216.htm>, accessed 18 November 2008.
Hanoi Declaration, 16 December 1998, <http://www.aseansec.org/2018.htm>, accessed 5 December 2008.
Joint Communiqué of the Fifteenth ASEAN Ministerial Meeting, Singapore, 16 June 1982, <http://www.aseansec.org/1245.htm>, accessed 8 December 2008.
Joint Communiqué of the First ASEAN Heads of Government Meeting Bali, 24 February 1976, <http://www.aseansec.org/1223.htm>, accessed 10 December 2008.
Joint Communiqué of the Fourth ASEAN Ministerial Meeting, Manila, 13 March 1971, <http://www.aseansec.org/1234.htm>, accessed 10 December 2008.
Joint Communiqué of the Sixteenth ASEAN Ministerial Meeting, Bangkok, 25 June 1983, <http://www.aseansec.org/1246.htm>, accessed 8 December 2008.
Joint Communiqué of the Third ASEAN Ministerial Meeting, Cameron Highlands, 17 December 1969, <http://www.aseansec.org/1233.htm>, accessed 22 October 2008.
Joint Communiqué of the Thirteenth ASEAN Ministerial Meeting, Kuala Lumpur, 25-26 June 1980, <http://www.aseansec.org/1243.htm>, accessed 31 October 2008.
Joint Communiqué of the Twenty-Sixth ASEAN Ministerial Meeting, Singapore, 24 July 1993, < http://www.aseansec.org/2009.htm>, accessed 15 January 2009.
Joint Press Statement of the ASEAN Foreign Ministers Meeting to Assess the Agreement on Ending the War and Restoring Peace in Vietnam and to Consider its Implications for Southeast Asia, Kuala Lumpur, 15 February 1973, <http://www.aseansec.org/1255.htm>, accessed 31 October 2008.
Treaty of Amity and Cooperation, 24 February 1976, <http://www.aseansec.org/1217.htm>, accessed 18 November 2008.
Zone of Peace, Freedom and Neutrality Declaration, 27 November 1971, <http://www.aseansec.org/1215.htm>, accessed 19 September 2008.

The ASEAN Regional Forum
Chairman's Statement at the First Meeting of ASEAN Regional Forum, 25 July 1994, <http://www.aseanregionalforum.org/PublicLibrary/ARFChairmansStatementsandReports/ChairmansStatementofthe1stMeetingoftheASE/tabid/201/Default.aspx>, accessed 02 February 2009.

The British Government
Federation of Malaya, Annual Report, 1952 (London: Her Majesty's Stationery Office, 1954).
Federation of Malaya, Annual Report, 1955 (Kuala Lumpur: B. T. Fudge, Acting Government Printer, 1956).
New Horizons in the East: The Colombo Plan for Co-operative Economic Development in South and South-East Asia (London: His Majesty's Stationery Office, 1950).
Report of the Commission of Enquiry, North Borneo and Sarawak, August 1962, in Department of Foreign Affairs, Australia (ed.), *Malaysia, Select Documents on International Affairs, No. 1 of 1963* (Canberra, 1963), pp. 61-102.

The Indian Government
The Conference on Indonesia, January 20-23, 1949 (Delhi: The Publications Division, Ministry of Information and Broadcasting of India, 1949).

The Indonesian Government
The Birth of *Pancasila*, 1 June 1945, in Herbert Feith and Lance Castles (eds.), *Indonesian Political Thinking, 1945-1965* (Ithaca and London: Cornell University Press, 1970), pp. 40-49.

The Indonesian Communist Party (PKI)
Resolutions of the Indonesian Communist Party, December 1961, in Peter Boyce (ed.), *Malaysia and Singapore in International Diplomacy: Documents and Commentaries* (Sydney: Sydney University Press, 1968), pp. 68-69.

The Malaysian Government
Background to Indonesia's Policy Towards Malaysia: The Territory of The Indonesian State in 1945 (Discussion in the meeting of Investigating Committee for Preparation of Indonesia's Independence,) (Kuala Lumpur: The Federal Department of Information of Malaysia, 1964.
Indonesian Intentions towards Malaysia (Kuala Lumpur: The Federal Department of Information of Malaysia, 1964).
Malaya /Indonesia Relations: 31st August, 1957 to 15th September, 1963 (Kuala Lumpur: The Government of Malaysia, 1963).
Malaya/Philippine Relations: 31st August, 1957 to 15th September, 1963 (Kuala Lumpur: The Government of Malaysia, 1963).

The Philippine Government
Philippine Claim to North Borneo (Sabah) Volume I, (First reprint, Manila: Bureau of Printing, 1968).

Southeast Asia Treaty Organization (SEATO)
Final Communiqué of Third Meeting of the Council of the SEATO, 13 March 1957, in *Department of State Bulletin*, 36/927 (1 April 1957), pp. 527-529.
Manila Pact, 8 September 1954, in *Department of State Bulletin*, 31/795 (20 September 1954), pp. 393-395.

The United Nations

Final Conclusions of the Secretary-General Regarding Malaysia, Doc. SG/1583, 13 September 1963, in Peter Boyce (ed.), *Malaysia and Singapore in International Diplomacy: Documents and Commentaries* (Sydney: Sydney University Press, 1968), pp. 74-78.

The United States Government

'Chronology of Principal Events Relating to the Korean Conflict, Research Project No. 244, April 1951', Foreign Policies Branch, Division of Historical Policy Research, Department of State of the United States of America, in Dennis Merrill (ed.), *Documentary History of the Truman Presidency, Volume 19* (University Publications of America, 1997), pp. 789-851.

'Committee on Foreign Relations, United States Senate 88th Congress, 1st Session, Vietnam and Southeast Asia', Report of Senators Mike Mansfield, J. Caleb Beggs, Claiborne Pell, Benjamin A. Smith, Washington, U.S. Government Printing Office 1963, p. 17, in Peter Boyce (ed.), *Malaysia and Singapore in International Diplomacy: Documents and Commentaries* (Sydney: Sydney University Press, 1968), p. 159.

'Meeting, The White House, February 4, 1950', Memorandum of Conversation, Department of State, 4 February 1950, in Dennis Merrill (ed.), *Documentary History of the Truman Presidency, Volume 5* (University Publications of America, 1997), pp. 407-411.

International agreements and joint statements

Agreement between the Government of the United Kingdom of Great Britain and Northern Ireland and the Government of the Federation of Malaya on External Defence and Mutual Assistance, 12 October 1957, in Department of Foreign Affairs, Australia (ed.), *Malaysia, Select Documents on International Affairs, No. 1 of 1963* (Canberra, 1963), pp. 204-206.

Agreement Relating to Malaysia in London, 9 July 1963, in Department of Foreign Affairs, Australia (ed.), *Malaysia, Select Documents on International Affairs, No. 1 of 1963* (Canberra, 1963), pp. 143-145.

Agreement to Normalize Relations between the Republic of Indonesia and Malaysia, 11 August 1966, in Peter Boyce (ed.), *Malaysia and Singapore in International Diplomacy: Documents and Commentaries* (Sydney: Sydney University Press, 1968), pp. 108-109.

Aide Me moiré Dated 2nd August 1962 Handed by Philippine Vice-President Emmanuel Pelaez to H. M. M. Ambassador in Malaya, in *Malaya/Philippine Relations: 31st August, 1957 to 15th September, 1963* (The Government of Malaysia, 1963), pp. 19-20.

Aide Me moiré Dated 3rd October 1962 Handed by Permanent Secretary for External Affairs to Philippine Ambassador in Kuala Lumpur, in *Malaya/Philippine Relations: 31st August, 1957 to 15th September, 1963* (The Government of Malaysia, 1963), pp. 21-22.

Final Communiqué of the Asian-African Conference, 24 April 1955, in George McT. Kahin, *Asian-African Conference, Bandung, Indonesia, April, 1955* (Ithaca, NY: Cornell University Press, 1956), pp. 76-85.

Joint Communiqué between Indonesia, Malaya and the Philippines, 17 April 1963, in *The Straits Times*, 18 April 1963.

Joint Ministerial Statement between Indonesia and Malaysia, 1 June 1966, in Peter Boyce (ed.), *Malaysia and Singapore in International Diplomacy: Documents and Commentaries* (Sydney: Sydney University Press, 1968), p. 107.

Joint Public Statement Issued by the British and Malayan Governments, 1 August 1962, in Department of Foreign Affairs, Australia (ed.), *Malaysia, Select Documents on International Affairs, No. 1 of 1963* (Canberra, 1963), pp. 104-105.

Joint Statement after the Tokyo talks between Sukarno and Tunku Abdul Rahman, 1 June 1963, in *Malaya /Indonesia Relations: 31st August, 1957 to 15th September, 1963* (Kuala Lumpur, 1963), p. 44.

Joint Statement between Indonesia and Thailand, 31 August 1966, in *Foreign Affairs Bulletin*, 6/1 (August-September 1966), p. 22-23.

Joint Statement between Indonesia and the Philippines, 1 May 1966, in *The Bangkok Post*, 2 May 1966.

Joint Statement between Malaysia and the Philippines on 3 June 1966, in Peter Boyce (ed.), *Malaysia and Singapore in International Diplomacy: Documents and Commentaries* (Sydney: Sydney University Press, 1968), p. 128.

Joint Statement by the Governments of the United Kingdom and the Federation of Malaya, 23 November 1961, in Department of Foreign Affairs, Australia (ed.), *Malaysia, Select Documents on International Affairs, No. 1 of 1963* (Canberra, 1963), pp. 38-39.

Manila Accord, 11 June 1963, in Department of Foreign Affairs, Australia (ed.), *Malaysia, Select Documents on International Affairs, No. 1 of 1963* (Canberra, 1963), pp. 140-142.

Manila Declaration, 5 August 1963, in Department of Foreign Affairs, Australia (ed.), *Malaysia, Select Documents on International Affairs, No. 1 of 1963* (Canberra, 1963), pp. 195-196.

Manila Joint Statement, 5 August 1963, in Department of Foreign Affairs, Australia (ed.), *Malaysia, Select Documents on International Affairs, No. 1 of 1963* (Canberra, 1963), pp. 196-198.

Treaty of Friendship between Malaya and Indonesia, 17 April 1959, in Avrahm G. Mezerick (ed.), *Malaysia-Indonesia Conflict* (New York: International review Service, 1965), pp. 97-99.

Speeches

Bisnar, Gauttier, Opening address of the Bangkok talks, 17 June 1968, in *Foreign Affairs Bulletin*, 7/6 (June-July 1968), p. 591.

Sucharitkul, Chitti, Welcoming Address of the Bangkok Talks, 17 June 1968, in *Foreign Affairs Bulletin*, 7/6 (June-July 1968), p. 589.

Dillon, Douglas, Address made before the Advertising club of New Jersey at Newark, N. J.: 'Encouraging Economic Growth in Less Developed Countries of the Free World', on 4 June 1957, in *Department of State Bulletin*, 37/940 (1 July 1957), pp. 31-33.

--------, Address made before the American Assembly, at Harriman, N. Y., on 2 May 1957: 'A New Approach to Mutual Security', *Department of State Bulletin*, 36/934 (20 May 1957), pp. 800-804.

--------, Address made before the Virginia State Chamber of Commerce at Roanoke, Va.: 'Some Economic Aspects of U.S. Foreign Policy', on 15 April 1960, in *Department of State Bulletin*, 42/1088 (2 May 1960), pp. 679-683.

Dulles, John Foster, Address made before the House Foreign Affairs Committee: 'Major Purposes of the Mutual Security Programs (Press release on 10 June 1957)', *Department of State Bulletin*, 37/940 (1 July 1957), pp. 3-8.

--------, Statement in the Closing Session at the Southeast Asia Conference at Manila, 8 September 1954, in *Department of State Bulletin*, 31/795 (20 September 1954), pp. 392-393.

Eisenhower, Dwight D., Cable to Winston Spencer Churchill, 4 April 1954, in Louis Galambos and Daun Van Ee (eds.), *The Papers of Dwight David Eisenhower, The Presidency: The Middle Way XV* (Baltimore: The John Hopkins University Press, 1996), pp. 1002-1006.

--------, Speech: 'Peace in Freedom' at the American Jewish Tercentenary Dinner at New York, 20 October 1954, in *Department of State Bulletin*, 31/802 (8 November 1954), pp. 675-676.

--------, The President's News Conference, 7 April 1954, in US Presidential Library (ed.), *Public Papers of the Presidents of the United States, Eisenhower, Dwight, D., 1954*, pp. 381-390.

Garcia, Carlos P., Address before the American Congress, on 18 June 1958, in *Department of State Bulletin*, 39/995 (21 July 1958), pp.120-126.

Hatta, Mohammad, Opening Address before an All-Indonesian Cultural Congress, January 1952, in Herbert Feith and Lance Castles (eds.), *Indonesian Political Thinking, 1945-1965* (Ithaca and London: Cornell University Press, 1970), pp. 286-291.

Johani, Mohamed Khir, Opening Address of the Asian and Pacific Council, The Second Ministerial Meeting, 5 July 1967, in *Foreign Affairs Bulletin*, 6/6 (June-July 1967), pp. 492-494.

Khoman, Thanat, Address: 'Prospects of a New Pax Asiana', at the East-West Center in Hawaii, 9 October 1969, in *Foreign Affairs Bulletin*, 9/2 (October-November 1969), pp. 141-155.

--------, Opening address of The First Meeting of the Ad hoc Committee on Civil Aviation of ASEAN, 25 June 1968, in *Foreign Affairs Bulletin*, 7/6 (June-July 1968), pp. 540-541.

--------, Opening Statement of the Second ASEAN Ministerial Meeting in Jakarta, 6 August 1968, in ASEAN Secretariat (ed.), *Statements by the ASEAN Foreign Ministers at ASEAN Ministerial Meetings 1967-1987* (Jakarta: ASEAN, 1987), pp. 55-56.

--------, Speech at the United Nations General Assembly, 27 September 1966, in *The United Nations General Assembly, Twenty-first Session, Official Records, 1418th Plenary Meeting, 27 September 1966* (New York: The United Nations), pp. 3-9.

King Bhumidol Adulyadej, Address to the Congress, on 29 June 1960, in *Department of State Bulletin*, 42/1100 (25 July 1960), pp. 143-146.

Lee, Kuan Yew, Speech to the National Press Club at Canberra, 16 March 1965, in Peter Boyce (ed.), *Malaysia and Singapore in International Diplomacy: Documents and Commentaries* (Sydney: Sydney University Press, 1968), pp. 25-26.

Macapagal, Diosdado, Address before the Joint Session of the Congress of the Philippines, 28 January 1963, in *Malaya/Philippine Relations: 31st August, 1957 to 15th September, 1963* (The Government of Malaysia, 1963), pp. 22-23.

--------, Statement at the Veterans' Memorial Hospital, 11 March 1963, in Department of Foreign Affairs, Australia (ed.), *Malaysia, Select Documents on International Affairs, No. 1 of 1963* (Canberra, 1963), p. 132.

--------, Statement of President Macapagal Proposing the Formation of a Malayan Confederation, 27 July 1962, in Department of Foreign Affairs, Australia (ed.), *Malaysia, Select Documents on International Affairs, No. 1 of 1963* (Canberra, 1963), pp. 102-104.

MacArthur, Douglas II, Address before the Naigai Josei Chosakai (Research Institute of Japan) of 26 February 1959, in *Department of State Bulletin*, 40/1034 (20 April 1959), p. 559-562.

Malik, Adam, Opening Statement of the Second ASEAN Ministerial Meeting in Jakarta, 6 August 1968, in ASEAN Secretariat (ed.), *Statements by the ASEAN Foreign Ministers at ASEAN Ministerial Meetings 1967-1987* (Jakarta: ASEAN, 1987), pp. 57-59.

--------, Statement at the First ASEAN Ministerial Meeting, Bangkok, 8 August 1967, in ASEAN Secretariat (ed.), *Statements by the ASEAN Foreign Ministers at ASEAN Ministerial Meetings 1967-1987* (Jakarta: ASEAN, 1987), p. 35.

Marcos, Ferdinand, Address in the 1411th Plenary Meeting of the United Nations General Assembly, 21 September 1966, in *Official Records of the United Nations General Assembly, Twenty-First Session, 1411th Plenary Meeting, 21 September 1966* (New York: The United Nations), pp. 1-5.

--------, Foreign Policy Statement, 7 February 1966, in Peter Boyce (ed.), *Malaysia and Singapore in International Diplomacy: Documents and Commentaries* (Sydney: Sydney University Press, 1968), p. 127.

Merchant, Livingston T., 'Notes on the Wake Conference', on 18 October 1950, Department of State, the United States of America, pp. 1-4, in D. Merrill (ed.), *Documentary History of the Truman Presidency, Vol. 18*, (University Publications of America, 1997), pp. 591-594.

Murphy, Robert, Address: 'The Defence of Asia' before the National Foreign Trade Council at New York, on 16 November 1954, in *Department of State Bulletin*, 31/805 (29 November 1954), pp. 799-803.

Murtopo, Ali, Opening Address at the First Conference of ASEAN Students of Regional Affairs (ASEAN I), Jakarta, 22 October 1974, in Centre for Strategic and International Studies (ed.), *Regionalism in Southeast Asia, Papers Presented at the Fist Conference of ASEAN Students of Regional Affairs (ASEAN I), 22-25 October 1974, Jakarta* (Jakarta, 1975), pp. 11-16.

Pelaez, Emmanuel, Speech in the 1134th Plenary Meeting of the United Nations General Assembly, 27 September 1962, in *Official Records of the United Nations General Assembly, Seventeenth Session, 1134th Plenary Meeting, 27 September 1962* (New York: The United Nations), pp. 165-168.

Phitsuwan, Surin, Opening Statement at the 32nd ASEAN Ministerial Meeting, Singapore, 23 July 1999, in *BBC Monitoring Service: Asia-Pacific*, 26 July 1999.

Rajaratnam, S., Opening Statement at the Second ASEAN Ministerial Meeting, Jakarta, 6 August 1968, in ASEAN Secretariat (ed.), *Statements by the ASEAN Foreign Ministers at ASEAN Ministerial Meetings 1967-1987* (Jakarta: ASEAN, 1987), pp. 51-54.

Ramani, Radakrishna, Speech in the 1698th Plenary Meeting of the United Nations General Assembly, 16 October 1968, in *Official Records of the United Nations General Assembly, Twenty-third Session, 1698th Plenary Meeting, 16 October 1968* (New York: The United Nations), pp. 21-27.

Ramos, Narciso, Opening Statement at the First ASEAN Ministerial Meeting, Bangkok, 8 August 1967, in ASEAN Secretariat (ed.), *Statements by the ASEAN Foreign Ministers at ASEAN Ministerial Meetings 1967-1987* (Jakarta: ASEAN, 1987), pp. 33-34.

--------, Opening Statement at the Second ASEAN Ministerial Meeting, Jakarta, 6 August 1968, in ASEAN Secretariat (ed.), *Statements by the ASEAN Foreign Ministers at ASEAN Ministerial Meetings 1967-1987* (Jakarta: ASEAN, 1987), pp. 48-50.

--------, Speech in the 1696th Plenary Meeting of the United Nations General Assembly, 15 October 1968, in *Official Records of the United Nations General Assembly, Twenty-third Session, 1696th Plenary Meeting, 15 October 1968* (New York: The United Nations), pp. 1-8.

Romuro, Carlos P., Address at University of Seattle, on June 1954, in *Congressional Record: Proceedings and Debates of the Congress, 9 June 1954* (Washington D. C.: U.S.G.P.O.), pp. 7972-7973.

Rusk, Dean, News Conference, 27 May 1966, in *Department of State Bulletin*, 54/1407 (13 June 1966), p. 923.

Sangkachand, Sanan, Statement at the Opening Ceremony of the First Meeting of the Ad Hoc Committee on Civil Aviation of ASEAN, 25 June 1968, in *Foreign Affairs Bulletin*, 7/6 (June-July 1968), p. 549.

Sarasin, Pote, Speech to the Thai Council of World Affairs and International Law: 'Economic Development and National Security', 26 January 1966, in *Foreign Affairs Bulletin*, 5/3 (December 1965-January 1966), pp. 247-256.

Shafie, Ghazali, Opening Address at the Bangkok talks, 17 June 1968, in *Foreign Affairs Bulletin*, 7/6 (June-July 1968), pp. 589-591.

Subandrio, Speech in the United Nations General Assembly on 20 November 1961, in Peter Boyce (ed.), *Malaysia and Singapore in International Diplomacy: Documents and Commentaries* (Sydney: Sydney University Press, 1968), p. 67.

--------, Speech to Mahakarta Regiment in Jogjyakarta, 20 January 1963, in Peter Boyce (ed.), *Malaysia and Singapore in International Diplomacy: Documents and Commentaries* (Sydney: Sydney University Press, 1968), pp. 69-70.

Sucharitkul, Chitti, Welcoming Address of the Bangkok Talks, 17 June 1968, in *Foreign Affairs Bulletin*, 7/6 (June-July 1968), pp. 589-591.

Sukarno, Executive Order of 11 March, 11 March 1966, in David Bouchier and Vedi R. Hadiz (eds.), *Indonesian Politics and Society: A Reader* (London and New York: RoutledgeCurzon, 2003), p. 32.

--------, President's Independence Day Speech, 17 August 1959, in Herbert Feith and Lance Castles (eds.), *Indonesian Political Thinking, 1945-1965* (Ithaca and London: Cornell University Press, 1970), pp. 99-109.

--------, President's Independence Day Speech, 17 August 1963, in Herbert Feith and Lance Castles (eds.), *Indonesian Political Thinking, 1945-1965* (Ithaca and London: Cornell University Press, 1970), pp. 392-395.

--------, President's Independence Day Speech, 17 August 1965, in Peter Boyce (ed.), *Malaysia and Singapore in International Diplomacy: Documents and Commentaries* (Sydney: Sydney University Press, 1968), pp. 105-106.

--------, Speech at the Closing Ceremonies of the Conference of Heads of Government of the Federation of Malaya, Republic of Indonesia and the Republic of the Philippines, in Manila, 5 August 1963, in George Modelski (ed.), *The New Emerging Forces: Documents on the Ideology of Indonesian Foreign Policy, Documents and Data Paper No. 2* (Canberra: Department of International Relations, Research School of Pacific Studies, Institute of Advanced Studies, The Australian National University, 1963), pp. 77-79.

--------, Speech at the Conference of Non-Aligned Countries in Belgrade, 1 September 1961, in George Modelski (ed.), *The New Emerging Forces: Documents on the Ideology of Indonesian Foreign Policy, Documents and Data Paper No. 2* (Canberra: Department of International Relations, Research School of Pacific Studies, Institute of Advanced Studies, The Australian National University, 1963), pp. 33-43.

--------, Speech at the Constituent Assembly, 22 April 1959, in Bedi, B. P. I. (ed.), *Guided Democracy: A Volume of Basic Speeches and Documents* (New Delhi: Unity Book Club of India, 1959), pp. 64-108.

--------, Speech at the Opening of the Conference of National Front Committees in Jakarta, 13 February 1963, in George Modelski (ed.), *The New Emerging Forces: Documents on the Ideology of Indonesian Foreign Policy, Documents and Data Paper No. 2* (Canberra: Department of International Relations, Research School of Pacific Studies, Institute of Advanced Studies, The Australian National University, 1963), pp. 74-77.

--------, Speech at the State Banquet in Jakarta, 13 April 1963, in George Modelski (ed.), *The New Emerging Forces: Documents on the Ideology of Indonesian Foreign Policy, Documents and Data Paper No. 2* (Canberra: Department of International Relations, Research School of Pacific Studies, Institute of Advanced Studies, The Australian National University, 1963), pp. 69-72.

--------, Speech at the Teachers' Union Congress, 30 October 1956, in Herbert Feith and Lance Castles (eds.), *Indonesian Political Thinking, 1945-1965* (Ithaca and London: Cornell University Press, 1970), pp. 82-83.

--------, Speech before the Investigating Committee for the Preparation of Independence, 1 June 1945, in Herbert Feith and Lance Castles (eds.), *Indonesian Political Thinking, 1945-1965* (Ithaca and London: Cornell University Press, 1970), pp. 40-49.

--------, Speech to the Investigating Committee for the Preparation of Indonesia's Independence, 11 July 1945, in *Background To Indonesia's Policy Towards Malaysia: The Territory of The Indonesian State in 1945 (Discussion in the meeting of Investigating Committee for Preparation of Indonesia's Independence)* (Kuala Lumpur: The Federal Department of Information of Malaysia, 1964), pp. 19-22.

Suwito, Kusmowidadjo, Interview by K. Krishna Moorthy, in *Far Eastern Economic Review*, 13 July 1961, pp. 54-55.

The Representative of the Indonesian Delegation (The name is unknown), Statement at the Opening Ceremony of The First Meeting of the Ad Hoc Committee on Civil Aviation of ASEAN, 25 June 1968, in *Foreign Affairs Bulletin*, 7/6 (June-July 1968), pp. 542-543.

Tun Abdul Razak, Mimeographed Statement at the Closure of the Informal Conference of ASEAN Foreign Ministers at Bangsen, 13 December 1968, in *Foreign Affairs Bulletin*, 8/3 (December 1968-January 1969), p. 206.

--------, Opening Statement of the Second ASEAN Ministerial Meeting, Jakarta, 6 August 1968, in ASEAN Secretariat (ed.), *Statements by the ASEAN Foreign Ministers at ASEAN Ministerial Meetings 1967-1987* (Jakarta: ASEAN, 1987), pp. 45-47.

--------, Opening Statement of the First ASEAN Ministerial Meeting, Bangkok, 8 August 1967, in ASEAN Secretariat (ed.), *Statements by the ASEAN Foreign Ministers at ASEAN Ministerial Meetings 1967-1987* (Jakarta: ASEAN, 1987), pp. 36-37.

--------, Speech in the 1416th Plenary Meeting of the United Nations General Assembly, 26 September 1966, in *Official Records of the United Nations General Assembly, Twenty-First Session, 1416th Plenary Meeting, 26 September 1966* (New York: The United Nations), pp. 12-16.

Tun Ismail bin Dato Abdul Rahman, Address to the Foreign Correspondents Association, Johore Bahru, 23 June 1966, in Peter Boyce (ed.), *Malaysia and Singapore in International Diplomacy: Documents and Commentaries* (Sydney: Sydney University Press, 1968), pp. 236-237.

Tunku Abdul Rahman, Address Given to the Foreign Correspondents Association of Southeast Asia, 27 May 1961, in Peter Boyce (ed.), *Malaysia and Singapore in International Diplomacy: Documents and Commentaries* (Sydney: Sydney University Press, 1968), pp. 8-9.

--------, Interview by Kayser Sung, in *Far Eastern Economic Review*, 28 July 1960, pp. 162-163.

--------, Letter from Tunku Abdul Rahman to President Garcia of the Philippines (Malayan Proposal for Regional Co-operation), 28 October 1959, in Peter Boyce (ed.), *Malaysia and Singapore in International Diplomacy: Documents and Commentaries* (Sydney: Sydney University Press, 1968), pp. 234-235.

--------, Press Statement, 25 September 1964, in Peter Boyce (ed.), *Malaysia and Singapore in International Diplomacy: Documents and Commentaries* (Sydney: Sydney University Press, 1968), pp. 42-43.

--------, Speech at the Malaysian Alliance Convention, 17th April 1965, in *Tunku's Call for Unity :Extracts from the Speech by the Hon'ble the Prime Minister at the Malaysian Alliance Convention on 17th April 1965* (Kuala Lumpur?: Federal Department of Information, Malaysia, 1965?).

--------, Speech at the Opening of the Commonwealth Prime Ministers' Conference, 6 September 1966, in Peter Boyce (ed.), *Malaysia and Singapore in International Diplomacy: Documents and Commentaries* (Sydney: Sydney University Press, 1968), p. 201.

--------, Speech in the House of Representatives in Malaya, 16 October 1961, in Department of Foreign Affairs, Australia (ed.), *Malaysia, Select Documents on International Affairs, No. 1 of 1963* (Canberra, 1963), pp. 18-28.

--------, Statement in Malayan Legislative Council, 11 December 1958, in Peter Boyce (ed.), *Malaysia and Singapore in International Diplomacy: Documents and Commentaries* (Sydney: Sydney University Press, 1968), p. 42.

Yamin, Muhammad, Address at the Investigating Committee for the Preparation of Indonesia's Independence, 31 May 1945, in Herbert Feith and Lance Castles (eds.), *Indonesian Political Thinking, 1945-1965* (Ithaca and London: Cornell University Press, 1970), pp. 438-441.

Yudhoyono, Susilo Bambang, Keynote Speech by H.E. Susilo Bambang Yudhoyono President of Indonesia at the ASEAN Regional Forum: Rethinking ASEAN Towards the ASEAN Community 2015, Jakarta, 7 August 2007, <http://www.aseansec.org/20812.htm>, accessed 26 October 2008.

Unpublished Theses

Babineau, Derek, 'Analysing Security Policy: Southeast Asia, Australia and the Concept of a Regional Security Community During the Years of the Howard Government – 1996 to 2007' (MA Thesis, University of Adelaide, Australia, 2008).

Turner, Sean Matthew, 'Containment and Engagement: U.S. China Policy in the Kennedy and Johnson Administrations' (PhD Thesis, University of Adelaide, Australia, 2008).

Yingxi, Wang, 'ASEAN in China's Embrace: An Assessment of the Evolving Relationship between China and ASEAN' (MA Thesis, University of South Australia, 2008).

Secondary Sources

Acharya, Amitav, *Constructing a Security Community in Southeast Asia: ASEAN and the Problem of Regional Order* (London: Routledge, 2001).

--------, 'Ideas, Identity and Institution-building: the "Asia-Pacific Way"', *The Pacific Review*, 10/3 (1997), pp. 319-346.

--------, *Regionalism and Multilateralism: Essays on Cooperative Security in the Asia-Pacific* (2nd edn., Singapore: Eastern Universities Press, 2003).

--------, 'The Association of Southeast Asian Nations: "Security Community" or "Defence Community"?', *Pacific Affairs*, 64/2 (1991), pp. 159-178.

Ahmad, Zakaria Haji, 'The World of ASEAN Decision-makers: A Study of Bureaucratic Elite Perceptions in Malaysia, the Philippines and Singapore', *Contemporary Southeast Asia*, 8/3 (1986), pp. 192-212.

Akagi, Kanji, 'Reisen to Senryaku no Henyo [The Transformation of Strategies in the Cold War]', in Masao Okonogi and Kanji Akagi (eds.), *Reisenki no Kokusai Seiji [International Politics in the Cold War Era]* (5th edn., Tokyo: Keio Tsushin, 1995), pp. 416-432.

Alagappa, Muthiah, 'Asian Practice of Security: Key Features and Explanations', in Muthiah Alagappa (ed.), *Asian Security Practice: Material and Ideational Influences* (Stanford, CA: Stanford University Press, 1998), pp. 611-676.

--------, 'Regionalism and the Quest for Security: ASEAN and the Cambodian Conflict', *Journal of International Affairs*, 46/2 (1993), pp. 439-467.

Almonte, Jose T., 'Ensuring Security the "ASEAN Way"', *Survival*, 39/4 (Winter 1997), pp. 80-92.

Ambrose, Stephen E., 'The Presidency and Foreign Policy', *Foreign Affairs*, 70/5 (Winter 1991), pp. 120-137.

Amer, Ramses, 'Conflict Management and Constructive Engagement in ASEAN's Expansion', *Third World Quarterly*, 20/5 (1999), pp. 1031-1048.

Anderson, Benedict O., *Imagined Communities: Reflections on the Origin and Spread of Nationalism* (Revised edn., London and New York: Verso, 1991).

--------, 'Languages of Indonesian Politics', in Benedict O. Anderson (ed.), *Language and Power: Exploring Political Culture in Indonesia* (Ithaca and London: Cornell University Press, 1990).

--------, *The Spectre of Comparisons: Nationalism, Southeast Asia and the World* (London and New York: Verso, 1998).

Antolik, Michael, *ASEAN and the Diplomacy of Accommodation* (Armonk, NY: M. E. Sharpe, 1990).

Anwar, Dewi Fortuna, 'Indonesia: Domestic Priorities Define National Security' in Muthiah Alagappa (ed.), *Asian Security Practice: Material and Ideational Influences* (Stanford, CA: Stanford University Press, 1998), pp. 477-512.

--------, *Indonesia in ASEAN: Foreign Policy and Regionalism* (Singapore: Institute of Southeast Asian Studies, 1994).

--------, 'Indonesia: *Ketahanan National, Wawasan Nusantara, Hankamrata*', in Ken Booth and Russell Trood (eds.), *Strategic Cultures in the Asia-Pacific Region* (London: Macmillan Press, 1999), pp. 199-224.

--------, 'National Versus Regional Resilience?: An Indonesian Perspective', in Derek da Cunha (ed.), *Southeast Asian Perspectives on Security* (Singapore: Institute of Southeast Asian Studies, 2000), pp. 81-97.

Askandar, Kamarulzaman, Jacob Bercovitch and Mikio Oishi, 'The ASEAN Way of Conflict Management: Old Patterns and New Trends', *Asian Journal of Political Science*, 10/2 (December 2002), pp. 21-42.

Ball, Desmond, *Strategic Culture in the Asia-Pacific Region (With Some Implications for Regional Security Cooperation)* (Canberra: Strategic and Defence Centre in Australian National University, 1993).

Beeson, Mark, 'Sovereignty under Siege: Globalisation and the State in Southeast Asia', *Third World Quarterly*, 24/2 (2003), pp. 357-374.

Berger, Mark T., 'Decolonizing Southeast Asia: Nationalism, Revolution and the Cold War' in Mark Beeson (ed.), *Contemporary Southeast Asia: Regional Dynamics, National Differences* (Basingstoke, NY: Palgrave Macmillan, 2004), pp. 30-49.

--------, '(De)constructing the New Order: Capitalism and the Cultural Contours of the Patrimonial state in Indonesia', in Yao Souchou (ed.). *House of Glass: Culture, Modernity, and the State in Southeast Asia* (Singapore: Institute of Southeast Asian Studies, 2001), pp. 192-212.

--------, 'Post-Cold War Indonesia and the Revenge of History: The Colonial Legacy, Nationalist Visions and Global Capitalism', in Mark T. Berger and Douglas A. Borer (eds.), *The Rise of East Asia: Critical Visions of the Pacific Century* (London: Routledge, 1997), pp.169-192.

--------, 'The New Asian Renaissance and Its Discontents: National Narratives, Pan-Asian Visions and the Changing Post-Cold War Order', *International Politics*, 40 (2003), pp. 195-221.

Berger, Peter L., 'An East Asian Development Model?', in Peter L. Berger and Michael H. H. Hsiao (eds.), *In Search of An East Asian Development Model* (New Brunswick, NJ: Transaction Publishers, 1993), pp. 3-11.

Bessho, Koro, *Identities and security in East Asia*, (Adelphi Papers, London: Oxford University Press, 1999).

Boden, Ragna, 'Cold War Economics: Soviet Aid to Indonesia', *Journal of Cold War Studies*, 10/3 (Summer 2008), pp. 110-128.

Bourchier, David, 'The 1950s in New Order: Ideology and Politics' in David Bourchier and John Legge (eds.), *Democracy in Indonesia: 1950s and 1990s* (Monash Papers on Southeast Asia, No. 31, Clayton: Centre of Southeast Asian Studies, Monash University, 1994), pp. 50-62.

Bowen, John R., 'On the Political Construction of Tradition: *Gotong Royong* in Indonesia', *The Journal of Asian Studies,* 45/3 (May 1986), pp. 545-561.

Boyce, Peter, 'The Machinery of Southeast Asian Regional Diplomacy', in Lau Teik Soon (ed.), *New Directions in the International Relations of Southeast Asia: Global Powers and Southeast Asia* (Singapore: Singapore University Press, 1973), pp. 173-185.

Brackman, Arnold C., *Indonesia, the Gestapu affair* (New York: American-Asian Educational Exchange, 1969).

--------, *Southeast Asia's Second Front: The Power Struggle in the Malay Archipelago* (London: Pall Mall Press, 1966).

Bull, Hedley and Adam Watson (eds.), *Expansion of International Society* (Oxford: Oxford University Press, 1984).

Bunnell, Frederick P., 'Guided Democracy Foreign Policy: 1960-1965, President Sukarno Moves from Non-Alignment to Confrontation', *Indonesia*, 2 (October 1966), pp. 37-76.

Buss, Claude A., *The United States and the Philippines: Background for Policy* (AEI-Hoover policy Studies 23/ Hoover Institute Studies 59, Washington D.C.: American Enterprise Institute for Public Policy Research and Stanford: Hoover Institution on War, Revolution and Peace, Stanford University, 1977).

Busse, Nikolas, 'Constructivism and Southeast Asian Security', *The Pacific Review*, 12/1 (1999), pp. 39-60.

Buszynski, Leszek, 'ASEAN's New Challenges', *Pacific Affairs*, 70/4 (Winter 1997-98), pp. 555-577.

--------, 'Thailand: The Erosion of a Balanced Foreign Policy', *Asian Survey*, 22/11 (November 1982), pp. 1037-1055.

--------, 'Thailand's Foreign Policy: Management of a Regional Vision', *Asian Survey*, 34/8 (August 1994), pp. 721-737.

Butwell, Richard, 'Malaysia and Its Impact on the International Relations of Southeast Asia', *Asian Survey*, 4/7 (July 1964), pp. 940-946.

--------, *Southeast Asia Today – And Tomorrow: A Political Analysis* (Revised edn., New York and London: Frederick A. Praeger, 1964).

--------, 'The Philippines: Changing of the Guard', *Asian Survey*, 6/1 (January 1966), pp. 43-48.

Buzan, Barry, 'Security Architecture in Asia: The Interplay of Regional and Global Levels', *The Pacific Review*, 16/2 (2003), pp. 143-173.

Caballero-Anthony, Mely, 'Mechanisms of Dispute Settlement: The ASEAN Experience', *Contemporary Southeast Asia*, 20/1 (April 1998), pp. 38-66.

-------, *Regional Security in Southeast Asia: Beyond the ASEAN Way* (Singapore: Institute of Southeast Asian Studies, 2005).

Callister, Ronda Roberts and James A. Wall Jr., 'Thai and U.S. Community Mediation', *Journal of Conflict Resolution*, 48/4 (August 2004), pp. 573-598.

Camroux, David, *'Looking East'...and Inwards: Internal Factors in Malaysian Foreign Relations During the Mahathir Era, 1981-1994* (Australia-Asia Papers, No. 72, Nathan, Queensland: Centre for the Study of Australia-Asia Relations, Faculty of Asian and International Studies, Griffith University, 1994).

--------, 'The Asia-Pacific Policy Community in Malaysia', *The Pacific Review*, 7/4 (1994), pp. 421-433.

Canonica-Walangitang, Resy, *The End of Suharto's New Order in Indonesia* (Frankfurt am Main: Peter Lang, 2003).

Carothers, Thomas, 'Democracy without Illusions', *Foreign Affairs*, 76/1 (January-February 1997), pp. 85-99.

Charrier, Philip, 'ASEAN's Inheritance: The Regionalization of Southeast Asia, 1941-61', *The Pacific Review*, 14/3 (2001), pp. 313-338.

Chi-Ching, Edith Yuen, 'Social-Cultural Context of Perceptions and Approaches to Conflict: The Case of Singapore', in Kwok Leung and Dean Tjosvold (eds.), *Conflict Management in the Asia Pacific: Assumptions and Approaches in Diverse Cultures* (Singapore: John Wiley and Sons (Asia), 1998), pp. 123-145.

Chin, Kin Wah, 'ASEAN: Consolidation and Institutional Change', *The Pacific Review*, 8/3 (1995), pp. 424-439.

Chinyong Liow, Joseph, *The Politics of Indonesia-Malaysia Relations: one kin, two nations* (Asia paperback edn., Oxford: Routledge, 2008).

--------, 'Tunku Abdul Rahman and Malaya's Relations with Indonesia, 1957-1960', *Journal of Southeast Asian Studies*, 36/1 (February 2005), pp. 87-109.

Collins, Alan, 'Mitigating the Security Dilemma, the ASEAN Way', *Pacifica Review*, 11/2 (June 1999), pp. 95-114.

Colvert, Evelyn, *Southeast Asia in International Politics, 1941-1956* (Ithaca, NY: Cornell University Press, 1977).

Corpuz, Onofre D., 'Realities of Philippine Foreign Policy', in Frank H. Golay (ed.), *The United States and the Philippines* (Englewood Cliffs, NJ: Prentice-Hall, 1966), pp. 50-66.

Crouch, Harold, 'Another Look at the Indonesian "Coup"', *Indonesia*, 15 (April 1973), pp. 1-20.

--------, 'Generals and Business in Indonesia', *Pacific Affairs*, 48/4 (Winter 1975-1976), pp. 519-540.

--------, 'Malaysia: Neither Authoritarian nor Democratic', in Kevin Hewson, Richard Robinson and Garry Rodan (eds.), *Southeast Asia in the 1990s: Authoritarianism, Democracy and Capitalism* (Sydney: Allen and Unwin, 1993), pp. 133-157.

--------, 'Part II State Control: Introduction', in Arief Budiman (ed.), *State and Civil Society in Indonesia* (Monash Papers on Southeast Asia No. 22, Clayton: Centre of Southeast Asian Studies, Monash University, 1990), pp. 115-120.

--------, *The Army and Politics in Indonesia* (Ithaca, NY: Cornell University Press, 1978).

Damian, Eddy and Robert Hornick, 'Indonesia's Formal Legal System', *The American Journal of Comparative Laws*, 20/3 (Summer 1972), pp. 492-530.

Darling, Frank C., *Thailand and the United States* (Washington D. C.: Public Affairs Press, 1965).

--------, 'Thailand: Stability and Escalation', *Asian Survey*, 8/2 (February 1968), pp. 120-126.

Darmaputera, Eka, *Pancasila and the Search for Identity and Modernity in Indonesian Society: A Cultural and Ethical Analysis* (Leiden, New York, Copenhagen and Koln: E. J. Brill, 1988).

Davidson, Jamie S. and Douglas Kammen, 'Indonesia's Unknown War and the Lineages of Violence in West Kalimantan', *Indonesia*, 73 (April 2002), pp. 53-87.

De Bary, Wm. Theodore, *Asian Values and Human Rights: a Confucian Communitarian Perspective* (Cambridge, Mass. and London: Harvard University Press, 1998).

Doeppers, Daniel F., 'An Incident in the PRRI/PERMESTA Rebellion of 1958', *Indonesia*, 14 (October 1972), pp. 182-195.

Easter, David, *Britain and the Confrontation with Indonesia, 1960-1966* (London and New York: Tauris Academic Studies, 2004).

Eaton, Sarah and Richard Stubbs, 'Is ASEAN Powerful?, Neo-realist Versus Constructivist Approaches to Power in Southeast Asia', *The Pacific Review*, 19/2 (June 2006), pp. 135-155.

Edwards, Peter G., *Crises and Commitments: The Politics and Diplomacy of Australia's Involvement in Southeast Asian Conflicts 1948-1965* (North Sydney: Allen and Unwin, 1992).

Elson, Robert, 'Reinventing a Region: Southeast Asia and the Colonial Experience', in Mark Beeson (ed.), *Contemporary Southeast Asia: Regional Dynamics, National Differences* (Basingstoke; NY: Palgrave Macmillan, 2004), pp. 15-29.

Emmer, Ralf, *Cooperative Security and the Balance of Power in ASEAN and the ARF* (London: Routledge, 2003).

Emmerson, Donald K., 'Indonesia, Malaysia, Singapore: A Regional Security Core?', in Richard J. Ellings and Sheldon W. Simon (eds.), *Southeast Asian Security in the New Millennium* (Armonk, NY: M.E. Sharpe, 1996).

Feith, Herbert, 'Dynamics of Guided Democracy', in Ruth T. McVey (ed.), *Indonesia* (Southeast Asia Studies, Yale University, New Haven, CT: Hraf Press, 1963), pp. 309-409.

--------, 'President Soekarno, the Army and the Communists: The Triangle Changes Shape', *Asian Survey*, 4/8 (August 1964), pp. 969-980.

--------, 'Suharto's Search for a Political Format', *Indonesia*, 6 (October 1968), pp. 88-105.

Feith, Herbert and Daniel S. Lev, 'The End of the Indonesian Rebellion', *Pacific Affairs*, 36/1 (Spring 1963), pp. 32-46.

Fernandez, Alejandro M., *The Philippines and The United States: The Forging of New Relations* (Quezon City: NSDB-UP Integrated Research Program, 1977).

Fifield, Russell H., *The Diplomacy of Southeast Asia: 1945-1958* (New York: Harper and Brothers, 1958).

Fukami, Sumio and Shinzou Hayase, 'Datsu Syokuminchika no Michi' [The Road to Decolonization], in Setsuho Ikehata (ed.), *Tounan Ajia Shi II [The History of Southeast Asia II]* (Tokyo: Yamakawa Syuppan-sya, 1999), pp. 366-405.

Fukuyama, Francis, 'Re-Envisioning Asia', *Foreign Affairs*, 84/1 (January-February 2005), pp. 75-87.

--------, *The End of History and the Last Man* (London and New York: Penguin Books, 1992).

--------, 'The Primacy of Culture', *Journal of Democracy*, 6/1 (1995), pp. 7-14.

Funabashi, Yoichi, 'The Asianization of Asia', *Foreign Affairs*, 72/5 (November-December 1993), pp. 75-85.

Funston, John, 'ASEAN: Out of Its Depth?', *Contemporary Southeast Asia*, 20/1 (April 1998), pp. 21-37.

Ganesan, N., 'ASEAN's Relations with Major External Powers', *Contemporary Southeast Asia*, 22/2 (August 2000), pp. 258-278.

--------, *Bilateral Tensions in Post-Cold War ASEAN* (Singapore: Institute of Southeast Asian Studies, 1999).

Garofano, John, 'Power, Institutions, and the ASEAN Regional Forum: A Security Community for Asia?', *Asian Survey*, 42/3 (2002), pp. 502-521.

Gerschenkron, Alexander, *Economic Backwardness in Historical Perspective* (Cambridge, Mass.: Harvard University Press, 1962).

Goh, Gillian, 'The "ASEAN Way": Non-intervention and ASEAN's Role in Conflict Management', *Stanford Journal of East Asian Affairs*, 3/1 (Spring 2003), pp. 113-118.

Golay, Frank H., Ralph Anspach, M. Ruth Pfanner and Eliezer B. Ayal, *Underdevelopment and Economic Nationalism in Southeast Asia* (Ithaca, NY: Cornell University Press, 1969).

Goldsworthy, David (ed.), *The Conservative Government and the End of Empire, 1951-1957, Parts I-III* (British Documents on the End of Empire, Series A, Vol. 3, London: Her Majesty's Stationery Office, 1994).

Gomez, Edmund Terence and Jomo K. S., *Malaysia's Political Economy: Politics, Patronage and Profits* (Cambridge: Cambridge University Press, 1997).

Gordon, Bernard K., 'Problems of Regional Cooperation in Southeast Asia', *World Politics*, 16/2 (January 1964), pp. 222-253.

--------, 'Regionalism in Southeast Asia' in Robert O. Tilman (ed.), *Man, State, and Society in Contemporary Southeast Asia* (London: Pall Mall Press, 1969), pp. 506-522.

--------, *The Dimensions of Conflict in Southeast Asia* (Englewood Cliffs, NJ: Prentice-Hall, 1966).

--------, 'The Potential for Indonesian Expansionism', *Pacific Affairs*, 36/4 (Winter 1963-64), pp. 378-393.

Green, Marshall, *Indonesia: Crisis and Transformation, 1965-1968* (Washington D.C.: The Compass Press, 1990).

Gunn, Geofrrey C., 'Ideology and the Concept of Government in the Indonesian New Order', *Asian Survey*, 19/8 (August 1979), pp. 751-769.

Haacke, Jurgen, *ASEAN's Diplomatic and Security Culture: Origins, Development and Prospects* (London and New York: Routledge Curzon, 2003).

--------, 'The concept of flexible engagement and the practice of enhanced interaction: Intramural challenges to the "ASEAN way"', *The Pacific Review*, 12/4 (1999), pp. 581-611.

Haas, Michael, *The Asian Way to Peace: A Story of Regional Cooperation* (New York: Praeger Publishers, 1989).

Hack, Karl, *Defence and Decolonisation in Southeast Asia: Britain, Malaya and Singapore 1941-1968* (Richmond, VA: Curzon, 2001).

Harriman, W. Averell, 'Leadership in World Affairs', *Foreign Affairs*, 32/4 (July 1954), pp. 525-540.

Harris, Stuart, 'Asian Multilateral Institutions and Their Response to the Asian Economic Crisis: The Regional and Global Implications', *The Pacific Review*, 13/3 (2000), pp. 495-516.

Hatta, Mohammad, 'Indonesia's Foreign Policy', *Foreign Affairs*, 31/3 (April 1953), pp. 441-452.

--------, 'One Indonesian View of the Malaysia Issue', *Asian Survey*, 5/3 (March 1965), pp. 139-143.

Hau, Caroline S., 'Rethinking History and "Nation-Building" in the Philippines', in Wang Gungwu (ed.), *Nation-Building: Five Southeast Asian Histories* (Singapore: Institute of Southeast Asian Studies, 2005), pp. 39-67.

Hemmer, Christopher and Peter J. Katzenstein, 'Why is There No NATO in Asia? Collective Identity, Regionalism, and the Origins of Multilateralism', *International Organization*, 56/3 (Summer 2002), pp. 575-607.

Henderson, Jeannie, *Reassessing ASEAN* (Adelphi Papers, Oxford: Oxford University Press, 1999).

Higgott, Richard, 'Ideas, Identity and Policy Coordination in the Asia-Pacific', *The Pacific Review*, 7/4 (1994), pp. 367-379.

Hill, Hal, *Indonesia's New Order* (Sydney: Allen and Unwin, 1994).

Hilley, John, *Malaysia: Mahathirism, Hegemony and The New Opposition* (London and New York: Zed Books, 2001).

Hilsman, Roger, *To Move A Nation: The Politics of Foreign Policy in the Administration of John F. Kennedy* (Garden City, NY: Doubleday, 1967).

Hindley, Donald, 'Indonesia's Confrontation with Malaysia: A Search for Motives', *Asian Survey*, 4/6 (June 1964), pp. 904-913.

Hoang Anh Tuan, 'ASEAN Dispute Management: Implications for Vietnam and an Expanded ASEAN', *Contemporary Southeast Asia*, 18/1 (June 1996), pp. 61-80.

Huat, Chua Beng, 'Asian Values: Is an Anti-authoritarian Reading Possible?' in Mark Beeson (ed.), *Contemporary Southeast Asia: Regional Dynamics, National Differences* (Basingstoke, NY: Palgrave Macmillan, 2004), pp. 98-117.

Hughes, John, *Indonesian Upheaval* (New York: D. McKay, 1967).

Hund, Markus, 'ASEAN Plus Three: Towards a New Age of Pan-East Asian Regionalism? A Skeptic's Appraisal', *The Pacific Review*, 16/3 (2003), pp. 383-417.

--------, 'From "Neighbourhood Watch Group" to Community?', *Australian Journal of International Affairs*, 56/1 (2002), pp. 99-122.

Huntington, Samuel P., *The Clash of Civilizations and the Remaking of World Order* (New York: Simon and Schuster, 1996).

--------, 'The West: Unique, Not Universal', *Foreign Affairs*, 75/6 (November-December 1996), pp. 28-46.

Hyam, Ronald (ed.), *The Labour Government and the End of Empire, 1945-1951, Part II* (British Documents on the End of Empire, Series A, Vol. 2, London: Her Majesty's Stationery Office, 1992).

Hyam, Ronald and Wm Roger Louis (eds.), *The Conservative government and the end of empire 1957-1964, Part I* (British Documents on the End of Empire, Series A, Vol. 4, London: The Stationery Office, 2000).

Ikle, Fred Charles, *How Nations Negotiate* (New York: Harper and Row Publishers, 1964).

Irvine, David, 'Making Haste Less Slowly: ASEAN from 1975', in Alison Broinowki (ed.), *Understanding ASEAN* (London and Basingsloke: MacMillan Press, 1982), pp. 37-69.

Jacobini, H. B., 'Fundamentals of Philippine Policy towards Malaysia', *Asian Survey*, 4/11 (November, 1964), pp. 1144-1151.

Jain, Purnendra, Greg O'Leary and Felix Patrikeeff (eds.), *Crisis and Conflict in Asia: Local, Regional and International Responses* (Huntington, NY: Nova Science Publishers, 2002).

Jenkins, David, *Suharto and His Generals: Indonesian Military Politics 1975-1983* (Cornell Modern Indonesia Project No. 64, Ithaca, NY: Southeast Asia Program, Cornell University, 1984).

Jetly, Rajshree, 'Conflict Management Strategies in ASEAN: Perspectives for SAARC', *The Pacific Review*, 16/1 (2003), pp. 53-76.

Johnston, Alastair Iain, *Cultural Realism* (Princeton, NJ: Princeton University Press, 1995).

--------, 'The Myth of the ASEAN Way?: Explaining the Evolution of the ASEAN Regional Forum', in Helga Haftendorn, Robert O. Keohane and Celeste A. Wallander (eds.), *Imperfect Unions: Security Institutions over Time and Space* (Oxford: Oxford University Press, 1999), pp. 287-324.

Jones, David Martin and Michael L. R. Smith, 'ASEAN's Imitation Community', *Orbis*, 46/1 (Winter 2002), pp. 93-109.

Jones, Howard Palfrey, *Indonesia: The Possible Dream* (New York: Harcourt Brace Jovanovich, 1971).

Jorgensen-Dahl, Arnfinn, *Regional Organization and Order on South-East Asia* (London and Basingstoke: Macmillan Press, 1982).

Kahin, Audrey R. and George McT. Kahin, *Subversion as Foreign Policy: The Secret Eisenhower and Dulles Debacle in Indonesia* (New York: The New Press, 1995).

Kahin, George McT., *Asia-African Conference, Bandung, Indonesia, April 1955* (Ithaca, NY: Cornell University Press, 1956).

--------, 'Malaysia and Indonesia', *Pacific Affairs*, 37/3 (Autumn 1964), pp. 253-270.

--------, *Nationalism and Revolution in Indonesia* (Ithaca, NY: Cornell University Press, 1952).

--------, *Southeast Asia: A Testament* (London: Routledge Curzon, 2003).

-------- (ed.), *Governments and Politics of Southeast Asia* (2nd edn., Ithaca, NY: Cornell University Press, 1964).

Kahler, Miles, 'Legalization as Strategy: The Asia-Pacific Case', *International Organization*, 54/3 (Summer 2000), pp. 549-571.

Katsumata, Hiro, 'Establishment of the ASEAN Regional Forum: Constructing a "Talking Shop" or a "Norm Brewery"?', *The Pacific Review*, 19/2 (2006), pp. 181-198.

Katzenstein, Peter J., 'Regionalism and Asia', in Shaun Breslin, Christopher W. Houghes, Nicola Phillips and Ben Rosamond (eds.), *New Regionalisms in the Global Political Economy: Theories and Cases* (London and New York: Routledge, 2002), pp. 104-118.

Kennan, George F., 'Peaceful Coexistence: A Western View', *Foreign Affairs*, 38/2 (January 1960), pp. 171-190.

Khoman, Thanat, 'A Policy of Regional Cooperation', *Foreign Affairs Bulletin*, 8/1 (August-September 1968), pp. 1-4.

--------, 'ASEAN Conception and Evolution', 1 September 1992, <http://www.aseansec.org/thanat.htm>, accessed 4 October 2008.

--------, 'Reconstruction of Asia', *Foreign Affairs Bulletin*, 9/1 (August-September 1969), pp. 7-15.

--------, 'The Founding of ASEAN', 8 August 1997, <http://www.aseansec.org/7071.htm>, accessed 24 October 2008.

--------, 'Which Road For Southeast Asia?', *Foreign Affairs*, 42/4 (July 1964), pp. 628-639.

Khoo, How San, 'ASEAN as a "Neighbourhood Watching Group"', *Contemporary Southeast Asia*, 22/2 (August 2000), pp. 279-301.

Khrushchev, Nikita S., 'On Peaceful Coexistence', *Foreign Affairs*, 38/1 (October 1959), pp. 1-18.

Kimura, Hirotsune, *Indonesia: Gendai Seiji no Kouzou [Indonesia: The Contemporary Political Structure]* (Tokyo: San-ichi Syobo, 1989).

Kingsbury, Damien, *The Politics of Indonesi,* (2nd edn., South Melbourne: Oxford University Press, 2002).

Kivimaki, Timo, 'The Long Peace of ASEAN', *Journal of Peace Research*, 38/1 (2001), pp. 5-25.

Koentjaraningrat, '*Tjelapar*: A Village in South Central Java', in Koentjaraningrat (ed.), *Villages in Indonesia* (Ithaca, NY: Cornell University Press, 1967), pp. 244-280.

Kraft, Herman Joseph S., 'ASEAN and Intra-ASEAN relations: Weathering the Storm?', *The Pacific Review*, 13/3 (2000), pp. 453-472.

Kuhonta, Erik Martinez, 'Walking a tightrope: democracy versus sovereignty in ASEAN's illiberal peace', *The Pacific Review*, 19/3 (2006), pp. 337-358.

Kuroyanagi, Yoneji, 'ASEAN Syokoku no Anzen Hosyō Mondai: Furui Taishitsu to Aratana Cyosen [The Security Issue among ASEAN Countries: The Conflict between Conservative and Progressive Views]' in Tatsumi Okabe (ed.), *ASEAN no 20 Nen: Sono Jizoku to Hatten [ASEAN in Twenty Years on: Its Vitality and Development]* (Tokyo: Nihon Kokusai Mondai Kenkyujyo [The Japan Institute of International Affairs], 1987), pp. 61-80.

--------, '"ASEAN Way" Saikou [Rethinking the "ASEAN Way"]', in Yoneji Kuroyanagi (ed.), *Ajia Chiiki Chitsujyo to ASEAN no Tyousen [Asia Regional Order and the Challenge of ASEAN: Seeking the East Asian Community]* (Tokyo: Akashi Syoten, 2005), pp. 15-37.

--------, *ASEAN 35 Nen no Kiseki: 'ASEAN Way' no Koyo to Genkai [The Trajectory for 35 Years of ASEAN: The Good and the Limit of the 'ASEAN Way']* (Tokyo: Yushindo Kobun Sha, 2003).

--------, '"Jinken Gaiko tai "Eijian Wei" – Nan Chakuriku wo Motomete ["Human Rights Diplomacy" and the "Asian Way" – Seeking the Soft Landing]', *Kokusai Mondai*, 422 (May 1995), pp. 31-45.

Kurus, Bilson, 'The ASEAN Triad: National Interest, Consensus-seeking, and Economic Co-operation', *The Contemporary Southeast Asia*, 16/4 (1995), pp. 404-420.

--------, 'Understanding ASEAN: Benefits and Raison d'Etre', *Asian Survey*, 33/8 (August 1993), pp. 819-831.

Lawson, Stephanie, 'Regional Integration, Development and Social Change in the Asia-Pacific', *Global Change, Peace and Security*, 17/ 2 (June 2005), pp. 107-122.

-------- (ed.), *Europe and the Asia-Pacific: Culture, Identity and Representations of Region* (London and New York: Routledge Curzon, 2003).

Lehmann, Jean-Pierre, 'Dictatorship and Development in Pacific Asia: Wider Implications', *International Affairs*, 61/4 (1985), pp. 591-606.

Leifer, Michael, *ASEAN and the Security of Southeast Asia* (London: Routledge, 1989).

--------, 'Continuity and Change in Indonesian Foreign Policy', *Asian Affairs* (Journal of the Royal Central Asian Society), 60/II (June 1973), pp. 173-180.

--------, *Dilemmas of Statehood in Southeast Asia* (Vancouver: University of British Columbia Press, 1972).

--------, *Indonesia's Foreign Policy*, London (Boston and Sydney: George Allen and Unwin, 1983).

--------, 'Indonesia and Malaysia: The Changing Face of Confrontation', *The World Today*, 22/9 (September 1966), pp. 395-405.

--------, 'Some South-East Asian Attitudes', *International Affairs*, 42/2 (April 1966), pp. 219-229.

--------, 'The ASEAN Peace Process: A Category Mistake', *The Pacific Review*, 12/1 (1999), pp. 25-38.

--------, *The ASEAN Regional Forum* (Adelphi Papers, London: Oxford University Press, 1996).

--------, 'The Changing Temper of Indonesian Nationalism', in Michael Leifer (ed.), *Asian Nationalism* (New York: Routledge, 2000), pp.153-169.

--------, *The Foreign Relations of the New States* (Camberwell, Vic: Longman Australia, 1974).

--------, *The Philippine Claim to Sabah* (Hull Monographs on South-East Asia, No. 1, Centre for South-east Asian Studies, University of Hull, Zug, Switzerland: Inter Documentation, 1968).

--------, 'The Philippines and Sabah Irredenta', *The World Today*, 24/10 (October 1968), pp. 421-428.

Liddle, William R., 'Politics and Culture in Indonesia', in William R. Liddle (ed.), *Leadership and Culture in Indonesian Politics* (St. Leonards, NSW: Allen and Unwin, 1996), pp. 63-106.

Liow, Joseph Chinyong, 'Tunku Abdul Rahman and Malaya's Relations with Indonesia, 1957-1960', *Journal of Southeast Asian Studies*, 36/1 (February 2005), pp. 87-109.

Luhulima, C. P. F., *Scope of ASEAN's Security Framework for the 21st Century* (Singapore: Institute of Southeast Asian Studies, 2000).

Loong Wong, 'Cultural Claims on the New World Order: Malaysia as a Voice from the Third World?', in Yao Souchou (ed.), *House of Glass: Culture, Modernity, an the State in Southeast Asia* (Singapore: Institute of Southeast Asian Studies, 2001), pp. 173-190.

Lyon, Peter, *War and Peace in South-East Asia* (London: Oxford University Press, 1969).

Mackie, J. A. C., *Konfrontasi: The Indonesia-Malaysia Dispute, 1963-1966* (Kuala Lumpur: Oxford University Press, 1974).

------, 'The Political Economy of Guided Democracy', *The Australian Outlook*, 13/4 (1959), pp. 285-292.

Mahbubani, Kishore, 'The Pacific Impulse', *Survival*, 37/1 (Spring 1995), pp. 105-120.

Malik, Adam, 'Promise of Indonesia', *Foreign Affairs*, 46/2 (January 1968), pp. 292-303.

--------, 'Regional Cooperation in International Politics', in Centre for Strategic and International Studies (ed.), *Regionalism in Southeast Asia, Papers presented at the First Conference of ASEAN Students of Regional Affairs (ASEAN I)* (Jakarta, 22-25 October 1974), pp. 157-169.

Mansor, Norma, 'Managing Conflict in Malaysia: Cultural and Economic Influences', in Kwok Leung and Dean Tjosvold (eds.), *Conflict Management in the Asia Pacific: Assumptions and Approaches in Diverse Cultures* (Singapore: John Wiley and Sons (Asia)), pp. 147-166.

Mazarr, Michael J., 'Race and Culture: A World View', *The Washington Quarterly*, 19/2 (Spring 1996), pp. 177-198.

McIntyre, Angus, 'The "Greater Indonesia" Idea of Nationalism in Malaya and Indonesia', *Modern Asian Studies*, 7/1 (1973), pp. 75-83.

McVey, Ruth T., 'In Memoriam: Adam Malik (1917-1984)', *Indonesia*, 39 (April 1985), pp. 144-148.

Means, Gordon P., 'Soft Authoritarianism in Malaysia and Singapore', *Journal of Democracy*, 7/4 (1996), pp. 103-117.

Mesquita, Bruce Bueno de and George W. Downs, 'Development and Democracy', *Foreign Affairs*, 84/5 (September-October 2005), pp. 77-86.

Miller, Harry, *Prince and Premier: A Biography of Tunku Abdul Rahman Putre Ali-Haj, First Prime Minister of the Federation of Malaya* (London: George G. Harrap, 1959).

Milne, R. S., 'Malaysia', *Asian Survey*, 4/2 (February 1964), pp. 695-701.

--------, 'Malaysia, Confrontation and Maphilindo', *Parliamentary Affairs*, 16/4 (May 1963), pp. 404-410.

--------, 'The New Administration and the New Economic Program in the Philippines', *Asian Survey*, 2/7 (September 1962), pp. 36-42.

Milne, R. S. and Diane K. Mauzy, *Malaysian Politics under Mahathir* (London and New York: Routledge, 1999).

Modelski, George, 'Indonesia and the Malaysia Issue', *The Year Book of World Affairs*, 1964, pp. 128-149.

--------, 'International Relations and Area Studies: The Case of South-East Asia', *International Relations*, 2/3 (April 1961), pp. 143-155.

--------, *The New Emerging Forces: Documents on the ideology of Indonesian foreign policy* (Canberra, Department of International Relations, Research School of Pacific Studies, Institute of Advanced Studies, The Australian National University, 1963).

Mohamad, Mahathir bin, *Malaysia on Track for 2020 Vision*, 2000?, <http://nupanl.un.org/intradoc/groups/public/documents/apcity/unpan003222.pdf.> , accessed on 14 June 2006.

--------, *The Malay Dilemma* (Singapore: Donald Moore for Asia Pacific Press, 1970).

Mohamad, Mahathir bin and Ishihara Shintaro, *The Voice of Asia: Two Leaders Discuss the Coming Century* (New York: Kodansha International, 1995).

Moller, Kay, 'Cambodia and Burma: The ASEAN Way Ends Here', *Asian Survey*, 38/12 (December 1998), pp. 1087-1104.

Moorthy, K. Krishna, 'Soviet Aid to Indonesia', *Far Eastern Economic Review*, 27 July 1961, pp. 183-185.

Morgner, Aurelius, 'The American Foreign Aid Program: Costs, Accomplishments, Alternatives?', *The Review of Politics*, 28/4 (October 1966), pp. 65-75.

Morrison, Charles E. and Astri Suhrke, *Strategies of Survival: The Foreign Policy Dilemmas of Smaller Asian States* (St Lucia: University of Queensland Press, 1978).

Mortimer, Rex, *Indonesian Communism under Sukarno: Ideology and Politics, 1959-1965* (Ithaca and London: Cornell University Press, 1974).

Muhammad Ghazali bin Shafie, 'ASEAN's Response to Security Issues in Southeast Asia', in Centre for Strategic and International Studies (ed.), *Regionalism in Southeast Asia, Papers Presented at the First Conference of ASEAN Students of Regional Affairs (ASEAN I)* (Jakarta, 22-25 October 1974), pp. 17-37.

--------, *The Pattern of Indonesian Aggression* (Kuala Lumpur, The Federal Department of Information of Malaysia, 1965).

Murakami, Yasusuke, *An Anticlassical Political-economic Analysis: A Vision for the Next Century* (Stanford, CA: Stanford University Press, 1996).

Narine, Shaun, 'ASEAN and ARF: The Limits of the "ASEAN Way"', *Asian Survey*, 37/10 (October 1997), pp. 961-978.

--------, 'ASEAN and the Management of Regional Security', *Pacific Affairs*, 71 (1998), pp. 195-214.

--------, 'Forty Years of ASEAN: A Historical Review', *The Pacific Review*, 21/4 (December 2008), pp. 411-429.

--------, 'State Sovereignty, Political Legitimacy and Regional Institutionalism in the Asia-Pacific', *The Pacific Review*, 17/3 (2005), pp. 423-450.

Neher, Clark D., 'Asian Style Democracy', *Asian Survey*, 34/11 (November 1994), pp. 949-961.

Nielsen, Waldemar A. and Zoran S. Hodjera, 'Sino-Soviet Bloc Technical Assistance – Another Bilateral Approach', *Annals of American Academy of Political and Social Science*, 323 (May 1959), pp. 40-49.

Nischalke, Tobias Ingo, 'Does ASEAN Measure Up?, Post-Cold War Diplomacy and the Idea of Regional Community', *The Pacific Review*, 15/1 (2002), pp. 89-117.

--------, 'Insights from ASEAN's Foreign Policy Co-operation: The "ASEAN Way", A Real Spirit or a Phantom?', *Contemporary Southeast Asia*, 22/1 (April 2000), pp. 89-112.

Nishihara, Masashi, *The Japanese and Sukarno's Indonesia: Tokyo-Jakarta Relations, 1951-1966* (Honolulu: The University Press of Hawaii, 1976).

Nixon, Richard M., 'Asia after Viet Nam', *Foreign Affairs*, 46/1 (October 1967), pp. 111-125.

Noble, Lela Garner, *Philippine Policy toward Sabah: A Claim to Independence* (Tucson, AZ: The University of Arizona Press, 1977).

--------, 'The Moro National Liberation Front in the Philippines', *Pacific Affairs*, 49/3 (Autumn 1976), pp. 405-424.

--------, 'The National Interest and the National Image: Philippine Policy in Asia', *Asian Survey*, 13/6 (June 1973), pp. 560-576.

Okabe, Tatsumi, 'ASEAN no Kihonteki Seikaku to sono Kokusaiteki Igi [The Basic Character of ASEAN and Its Meaning in the International Arena]', in Tatsumi Okabe (ed.), *ASEAN no 20 Nen: Sono Jizoku to Hatten [ASEAN in Twenty Years On: Its Vitality and Development]* (Tokyo: Nihon Kokusai Mondai Kenkyujyo [The Japan Institute of International Affairs], 1987), pp. 15-35.

--------, *Posuto Kanbojia no Tounan Ajia [Southeast Asia after the Cambodian Conflict]* (Tokyo: Nihon Kokusai Mondai Kenkyujyo [The Japan Institute of International Affairs], 1992).

Ott, Marvin C., 'Foreign Policy Formation in Malaysia', *Asian Survey*, 12/3 (March 1972), pp. 225-241.

--------, 'Mediation as a Method of Conflict Resolution: Two Cases', *International Organization*, 26 (1972), pp. 595-618.

Ovendale, Richie, 'Britain, the United States, and the Cold War in South-East Asia, 1949-1950', *International Affairs*, 58 (Summer 1982), pp. 447-464.

Pabottingi, Mochtar, 'Indonesia: Historicizing the New Order's Legitimacy Dilemma', in Muthiah Alagappa (ed.), *Political Legitimacy in Southeast Asia: The Quest for Moral Authority* (Stanford, CA: Stanford University Press, 1995), pp. 224-256.

Palmujoki, Eero, *Regionalism and Globalism in Southeast Asia* (New York: Palgrave, 2001).

Pauker, Guy J., 'Indonesia: Internal Development or External Expansion?', *Asian Survey*, 3/2 (February 1963), pp. 69-75.

Paauw, Douglas S., 'From Colonial to Guided Economy', in Ruth T. McVey (ed.), *Indonesia* (New Haven, CT: Human Relations Area Files, 1963), pp. 155-247.

Patrikeeff, Felix and Purnendra Jain, 'The Pacific Century and the Post-Cold War World', in Purnendra Jain, Felix Patrikeeff and Gerry Groot (eds.), *Asia-Pacific and a New International Order: Responses and Options* (Hauppauge, NY: Nova Science Publishers, 2006), pp. 3-12.

Pauker, Guy J., 'Indonesia: Internal Development or External Expansion?', *Asian Survey*, 3/2 (February 1963), pp. 69-75.

--------, 'Toward a New Order in Indonesia', *Foreign Affairs*, Vol. 45, No. 3 (April 1967), pp. 503-519.

Peffer, Nathaniel, 'Regional Security in Southeast Asia', *International Organization*, 8/3 (August 1954), pp. 311-315.

--------, *The Far East: A Modern History* (Ann Arbor: The University of Michigan Press, 1958).

Pelaez, Emmanuel, *Government by the People*, Quezon City: published privately by the author, 1964, in Roger M. Smith (ed.), *Southeast Asia: Documents of Political Development and Change* (Ithaca and London: Cornell University Press, 1974), p. 527.

Pluvier, Jan, *South-East Asia from Colonialism to Independence* (Kuala Lumpur: Oxford University Press, 1974).

Pollard, Vincent K., 'ASA and ASEAN, 1961-1967: Southeast Asian Regionalism', *Asian Survey*, 10/3 (March 1970), pp. 244-255.

Polomka, Peter, *Indonesia Since Sukarno* (Ringwood, Vic: Penguin Books Australia, 1971).

Poulgrain, Greg, *The Genesis of Konfrontasi: Malaysia, Brunei and Indonesia, 1945-1965* (Bathurst, NSW: Crawford House Publishing, 1998).

Poon-Kim, Shee, 'A Decade of ASEAN, 1967-1977', *Asian Survey*, 17/8 (August 1977), pp. 753-770.

Prawiranegara, Sjafruddin, 'Pancasila as the Sole Foundation', *Indonesia*, 38 (October 1984), pp. 74-83.

Pye, Lucian W., *Asian Power and Politics: The Cultural Dimensions of Authority* (Cambridge, Mass.: The Belknap Press, 1985).

--------, 'Civility, Social Capital, and Civil Society: Three Powerful Concepts for Explaining Asia. (Patterns of Social Capital: Stability and Change in Comparative Perspective, part 2)', *Journal of Interdisciplinary History*, 29/4 (1999), pp. 763-772.

--------, 'Culture and Political Science: Problems in the Evaluation of the Concept of Political Culture', *Social Science Quarterly*, 53/2 (1972), pp. 285-296.

--------, 'Southeast Asia', in Robert E. Ward and Roy C. Macridis (eds.), *Modern Political Systems: Asia* (Englewood Cliffs, NJ: Prentice-Hall, 1963), pp. 297-364.

Ramage, Douglas E., *Politics in Indonesia: Democracy, Islam and the Ideology of Tolerance* (London and New York: Routledge, 1995).

Ramcharan, Robin, 'ASEAN and Non-interference: A Principle Maintained', *Contemporary Southeast Asia*, 22/1 (April 2000), pp. 60-88.

Rees, David, *The Age of Containment: The Cold War 1945-1965* (London: Macmillan, 1967).

Reeves, Julie, *Culture and International Relations: Narratives, Natives and Tourists* (London: Routledge, 2004).

Robinson, Richard, 'Culture, Politics and Economy in the Political History of the New Order', *Indonesia*, 31 (April 1981), pp. 1-29.

--------, (ed.), *Pathways to Asia: The Politics of Engagement* (St Leonards, NSW: Allen and Unwin, 1996).

Rostow, W. W., 'The Third Round', *Foreign Affairs*, 42/1 (October 1963), pp. 1-10.

--------, *The United States and the Regional Organization of Asia and the Pacific* (Austin, TX: University of Texas, 1986).

Ruland, Jurgen, 'ASEAN and the Asian Crisis: Theoretical Implications and Practical Consequences for Southeast Asian Regionalism', *The Pacific Review*, 13/3 (2000), pp. 421-451.

Runder, Martin, *Malaysian Development: A Retrospective* (Ottawa: Carlton University Press, 1994).

Sakurai, Yumio, 'Senjyou kara Shijyou he: Gekidou no Indoshina [From the Battle Field to the Market: Indochina in Turbulence]', in Yoneo Ishii and Yumio Sakurai (eds.), *Tounan Ajia Shi I [History of Southeast Asia I]* (Tokyo: Yamakawa Syuppan, 1999), pp. 442-483.

Samad, Paridah Abd., and Darusalam Abu Bakar, 'Malaysia-Philippines Relations: The Issue of Sabah', *Asian Survey*, 32/6 (June 1992), pp. 554-567.

SarDesai, D. R., *Southeast Asia: Past & Present* (5th edn., Boulder, CO: Westview Press, 2003).

Sato, Kouichi, *ASEAN Rejimu: ASEAN ni okeru Kaigi Gaikou no Hatten to Kadai [ASEAN Regime: Success and Problem of Conference Diplomacy in ASEAN]* (Tokyo: Keisou Syobou, 2003).

--------, 'Chiiki Funsou to ASEAN no Kinou [The Regional Conflict and the Role of ASEAN]', in Susumu Yamakage (ed.), *Tenkanki no ASEAN: Aratana Kadai heno Cyousen [ASEAN in the Turning Point: The Challenge for New Issues]* (Tokyo: Nihon Kokusai Mondai Kenkyujyo [The Japan Institute of International Affairs], 2001), pp. 177-207.

Scalapino, Robert A., 'Asia's Future', *Foreign Affairs*, 66/1 (Fall 1987), pp. 77-108.

--------, *The Politics of Development: Perspectives on Twentieth-century Asia* (Cambridge, Mass. and London: Harvard University Press, 1989).

Schubert, James N., 'Toward a "Working Peace System" in Asia: Organizational Growth and State Participation in Asian Regionalism', *International Organization*, 32/2 (Spring 1978), pp. 425-462.

Scott, Peter Dale, 'The United States and the Overthrow of Sukarno, 1965-1967', *Pacific Affairs*, 58/2 (Summer 1985), pp. 239-264.

Sen, Amartya, *Beyond the Crisis: Development Strategies in Asia* (Singapore: Institute of Southeast Asian Studies, 1999).

----------, *Development as Freedom* (New York: Knopf, 1999).

----------, 'Minsyusyugi to Seigi [Democracy and Social Justice]', *Sekai*, June 1999, pp. 130-147.

Severino, Rodolfo C., *Southeast Asia in Search of an ASEAN Community: Insights from the Former ASEAN Secretary-General* (Singapore: Institute of Southeast Asian Studies, 2006).

Shaplen, Robert, 'Southeast Asia – Before and After', *Foreign Affairs*, 53/3 (1975), pp. 533-557.

Sharpe, Samuel, 'An ASEAN Way to Security Cooperation in Southeast Asia?', *The Pacific Review*, 16/2 (2003), pp. 231-250.

Shee, Poon-Kim, 'A Decade of ASEAN, 1967-1977', *Asian Survey*, 17/18 (August 1977), pp. 753-770.

Shibusawa, Masahide, Zakaria Hadi Ahmad and Brian Bridges, *Pacific Asia in the 1990s* (London: Routledge, 1992).

Simon, Sheldon W., 'ASEAN Security in the 1990s', *Asian Survey*, 29/6 (June 1989), pp. 580-600.

--------, 'Security Prospects in Southeast Asia: Collaborative Efforts and the ASEAN Regional Forum', *The Pacific Review*, 11/2 (1998), pp. 195-212.

Simone, Vera and Anne T. Feraru, *The Asian Pacific: Political and Economic Development in a Global Context* (New York: Longman Publishers, 1995).

Singh, L. P., 'Thai Foreign Policy: The Current Phase', *Asian Survey*, 3/11 (November 1963), pp. 535-543.

Smith, Anthony, 'Indonesia's Role in ASEAN: The End of Leadership?', *Contemporary Southeast Asia*, 21/2 (1999), pp. 238-260.

--------, *Strategic Centrality: Indonesia's Changing Role in ASEAN*, Pacific Strategic Papers No.10 (Singapore: Institute of Southeast Asian Studies, 2000).

--------, 'Theory of Nationalism', in Michael Leifer (ed.), *Asian Nationalism* (New York: Routledge, 2000), pp. 1-20.

Smith, Roger M., *The Philippines and the Southeast Asia Treaty Organization* (Data Paper No. 38, Ithaca, NY: Southeast Asia Program, Cornell University, 1959).

Snitwongse, Kusuma, 'Indonesia: Domestic Priorities Define National Security', in Muthiah Alagappa (ed.), *Asian Security Practice: Material and Ideational Influences* (Stanford, CA: Stanford University Press, 1998), pp. 477-512.

--------, 'National Versus Regional Resilience? An Indonesian Perspective', in Derek da Cunha (ed.), *Southeast Asian Perspectives on Security* (Singapore: Institute of Southeast Asian Studies, 2000), pp. 81-97.

--------, 'Thai Foreign Policy in the Global Age: Principle or Profit?', *Contemporary Southeast Asia*, 23/2 (August 2001), pp. 189-212.

--------, 'Thirty Years of ASEAN: Achievements through Political Cooperation', *The Pacific Review*, 11/2 (1998), pp. 183-194.

Soesastro, Hadi, 'ASEAN in 2030: The Long View', in Simon S. C. Tay, Jesus P. Estanislao and Hadi Soesastro (eds.), *Reinventing ASEAN* (Singapore: Institute of Southeast Asian Studies, 2001), pp. 273-310.

--------, *Indonesia's Role in ASEAN and Its Impact on US-Indonesia Economic Relationship, Testimony at a Hearing of the Senate Foreign Relations Subcommittee on East Asia and the Pacific, U.S. Senate, September 15, 2005 at 2:00 p.m.*, <http://foreign.senate.gov/testimony/2005/SoesastroTestimony050915.pdf>, accessed 3 December 2008.

Solidum, Estrella D., 'Philippine Perceptions of Crucial Issues Affecting Southeast Asia', *Asian Survey*, 22/6 (June 1982), pp. 536-547.

--------, 'The Role of Certain Sectors in Shaping and Articulating the ASEAN Way', in R. P. Anand and Purificacion V. Quisumbing (eds.), *ASEAN: Identity, Development and Culture* (Quezon City: University of the Philippines Law Center and Honolulu: East-West Center Culture Leaning Institute, 1981), pp. 130-148.

--------, *Towards a Southeast Asian Community* (Quezon City: University of the Philippines Press, 1974).

Solingen, Etel, 'ASEAN, Quo Vadis? Domestic Coalitions and Regional Co-operation', *Contemporary Southeast Asia*, 21/1 (April 1999), pp. 30-53.

Sopiee, Noordin, 'The "Newtralisation" of South-East Asia', in Hedley Bull (ed.), *Asia and the Western Pacific: Towards a New International Order* (West Melbourne, VIC: Thomas Nelson, 1975), pp. 132-158.

Stockwell, Anthony J., 'Britain and Brunei, 1945-1963: Imperial Retreat and Royal Ascendancy', *Modern Asian Studies*, 38/4 (2004), pp. 785-819.

--------, 'Forging Malaysia and Singapore: Colonialism, Decolonization and Nation-Building', in Wang Gungwu (ed.), *Nation-Building: Five Southeast Asian Histories* (Singapore: Institute of Southeast Asian Studies, 2005), pp. 191-219.

--------, 'Introduction' in A J Stockwell (ed.), *Malaysia* (British Documents on the End of Empire, Series B, Vol. 8, London: The Stationery Office, 2004), pp. xxxv-xcv.

Stockwell, A J (ed.), *Malaysia* (British Documents on the End of Empire, Series B, Vol. 8, London: The Stationery Office, 2004).

Stockwin, Harvey, 'Filipinos in a Frenzy', *Far Eastern Economic Review*, 1 August 1968, pp. 217-218.

--------, 'The Law's An Ass', *Far Eastern Economic Review*, 24 October 1968, pp. 200-204.

--------, 'The Nude Strikes Back', *Far Eastern Economic Review*, 18 July 1968, pp. 141-142.

--------, 'Tricky Negotiations', *Far Eastern Economic Review*, 24 August 1967, pp. 378-381.

Stubbs, Richard, 'ASEAN: Building Regional Cooperation', in Mark Beeson (ed.), *Contemporary Southeast Asia: Regional Dynamics, National Differences* (Basingstoke; New York: Palgrave Macmillan, 2004), pp. 222-224.

--------, 'ASEAN Plus Three: Emerging East Asian Regionalism?', *Asian Survey*, 42/3 (May-June 2002), pp. 440-455.

Subandrio, *Indonesia's Foreign Policy* (Jakarta: The Government of the Republic of Indonesia, 1964?).

Subritzky, John, *Confronting Sukarno: British, American, Australian and New Zealand Diplomacy in the Malaysian-Indonesian Confrontation, 1961-5* (Basingstoke, Hampshire and London: Macmillan Press, 2000).

Sudarsono, Yuwono, 'Problems of Internal Stability in the ASEAN Countries', in Hedley Bull (ed.), *Asia and the Western Pacific: Towards a New International Order* (West Melbourne, VIC: Thomas Nelson, 1975), pp. 77-86.

Suharto, *Soeharto: My Thoughts, Words and Deeds (An Autobiography)* (Jakarta: PT. Citra Lamtoro Gung Persada, 1991).

Suhrke-Goldstein, Astri, 'Thailand: Trapped in the Bamboo Image', *Australian Outlook*, 22/3 (December 1968), pp. 334-346.

Stubbs, Richard, 'ASEAN: Building Regional Cooperation' in Mark Beeson (ed.), *Contemporary Southeast Asia: Regional Dynamics, National Differences* (Basingstoke, NY: Palgrave Macmillan, 2004), pp. 216-233.

--------, 'ASEAN Plus Three: Emerging East Asian Regionalism?', *Asian Survey*, 42/3 (2002), pp. 440-455.

Sukma, Rizal, 'Indonesia's *Bebas-Aktif* Foreign Policy and the "Security Agreement" with Australia', *Australian Journal of International Affairs*, 51/2 (1997), pp. 231-241.

--------, *Islam in Indonesian Foreign Policy* (London and New York: Routledge Curzon, 2003).

Sussman, Gerald, 'Macapagal, the Sabah Claim and Maphilindo: The Politics of Penetration', *Journal of Contemporary Asia*, 13/2 (1983), pp. 210-228.

Sutter, John O., 'Two Faces of *Konfrontasi*: "Crush Malaysia" and the *GESUTAPU*', *Asian Survey*, 6/10 (October 1966), pp. 523-546.

Suryohudojo, Supomo, 'Rebellion in the *Kraton* World as seen by the *Puhangga*' in Ross Garnaut, Peter McCawley and J. A. C. Mackie (eds.), *Indonesia: Australian Perspectives* (Canberra: Research School of Pacific Studies, The Australian National University, 1980), pp. 563-575.

Sutter, O. John, 'Two Faces of *Konfrontasi*: "Crush Malaysia" and the *GESTAPU*', Asian Survey, 6/10 (October 1966), pp. 523-546.

Tamaki, Kazunori, 'ARF Kouiki Anzen Hosyou, ASEAN Way no Kanousei [The ARF, Expanding Regional Security Cooperation: The Possibility of Introducing the ASEAN Way]', in Yoneji Kuroyanagi (ed.), *Ajia Chiiki Chitsujyo to ASEAN no Tyōsen: 'Higashi Ajia Kyoudoutai' wo Mezashite [Regional order in Asia and the Challenge of ASEAN: 'Seeking the East Asia Community']* (Tokyo: Akashi Syoten, 2005), pp. 237-258.

Tan, Andrew, 'Armed Muslim Separatist Rebellion in Southeast Asia: Persistence, Prospects, and Implications', *Studies in Conflict & Terrorism*, 23 (2000), pp. 267-288.

Tanter, Richard, 'The Totalitarian Ambition: Intelligence Organizations in the Indonesian State', in Arief Budiman (ed.), *State and Civil Society in Indonesia* (Monash Papers on Southeast Asia No.22, Clayton, VIC: Centre of Southeast Asian Studies, Monash University, 1990), pp. 213-288.

Tarling, Nicholas, 'From SEAFET and ASA: Precursors of ASEAN', *International Journal of Asia-Pacific Studies*, 3/1 (May 2007), pp. 1-14.

--------, *Regionalism in Southeast Asia: To Foster the Political Will* (Oxford: Routledge, 2006).

Tay, Simon S. C., 'Institutions and Process: Dilemmas and Possibilities', in Simon S. C. Tay, Jesus P. Estanislao and Hadi Soesastro (eds.), *Reinventing ASEAN* (Singapore: Institute of Southeast Asian Studies, 2001), pp. 243-272.

Taylor, George E., 'The Challenge of Mutual Security', in Frank H. Golay (ed.), *The United States and the Philippines* (Englewood Cliffs, NJ: Prentice-Hall, 1966), pp. 67-94.

--------, *The Philippines and the United States: Problems of Partnership* (New York and London: Frederick A. Praeger, 1964).

Taylor, Milton C., 'South Vietnam: Lavish Aid and Limited Progress', *Pacific Affairs*, 34/3 (Autumn, 1961), pp. 242-256.

Terada, Takashi, 'Constructing an "East Asian" Concept and Growing Regional Identity: from EAEC to ASEAN+3', *The Pacific Review*, 16/2 (2003), pp. 251-277.

Thambipillai, Pushpa, 'The ASEAN growth areas: Sustaining the dynamism', *The Pacific Review*, 11/2 (1998), pp. 249-266.

Thambipillai, Pushpa and J. Saravanamuttu, *ASEAN Negotiations: Two Insights* (Singapore: Institute of Southeast Asian Studies, 1985).

Tiwon, F. W. M., 'Pantjasila (Birth and Development)', Lecture Delivered at Ghaziabad Rotary Club on 19th October, 1954, in Information Service Indonesia, Embassy of the Republic of Indonesia in India (ed.), *The National Struggle (Past and Present)* (New Delhi: The Information Service Indonesia, Embassy of the Republic of Indonesia in India, 1954?).

Tokyo Daigaku Shakai Kagaku Kenkyujo [Institute of Social Science, The University of Tokyo] (ed.), *20-seiki Shisutemu, Dai-4-kan, Kaihatsu Shugi [The 20th-Century Global System Vol. 4, Developmentalism]* (Tokyo: Tokyo Daigaku Syuppan Kai [The University of Tokyo Press], 1998).

Trood, Russell and Ken Booth, 'Strategic Culture and Conflict Management in the Asia-Pacific', in Ken Booth and Russell Trood (eds.), *Strategic Cultures in the Asia-Pacific Region* (London: Macmillan Press, 1999), pp. 339-361.

Tuan, Hoang Anh, 'ASEAN Dispute Management: Implications for Vietnam and an Expanded ASEAN', *Contemporary Southeast Asia*, 18/1 (June 1996), pp. 61-80.

Tunku Abdul Rahman, 'Malaysia: Key Area in Southeast Asia', *Foreign Affairs*, 43/4 (July 1965), pp. 659-670.

Turner, Nicholas, 'Malik Manoeuvres', *Far Eastern Economic Review*, 28 April 1966, pp. 177-178.

Vandenbosch, Amry and Richard Butwell, *The Changing Face of Southeast Asia* (Lexington, KY: University of Kentucky Press, 1966).

Van der Kroef, Justus M., 'ASEAN Security and Development: Some Paradoxes and Symbols', *Asian Affairs*, 9/2 (1978), pp. 143-160.

--------, 'Indonesia, Malaya, and the North Borneo Crisis', *Asian Survey*, 3/4 (April 1963), pp. 173-181.

--------, 'Sukarno: The Ideologue: A Review Article', *Pacific Affairs*, 41/2 (Summer 1968), pp. 245-261.

Vatikiotis, Michael R. J., *Indonesian Politics under Suharto: The Rise and Fall of the New Order* (3rd edn., London and New York: Routledge, 1998).

--------, 'Resolving Internal Conflicts in Southeast Asia: Domestic Challenges and Regional Perspectives', *Contemporary Southeast Asia*, Vol. 28, No. 28/1 (2006), pp. 27-47.

Vellut, J. L., *The Asian Policy of the Philippines, 1954-1961* (Working Paper No. 6, Canberra: Department of International Relations, Research School of Pacific Studies, Institute of Advanced Studies, The Australian National University, 1965).

Vogel, Ezla F., *The Four Little Dragons: The Spread of Industrialization in East Asia* (Cambridge, Mass. and London: Harvard University Press, 1991).

Wallerstein, Immanuel, 'After Developmentalism and Globalization, What?', *Social Forces*, 83/3 (2005), pp. 1263-1278.

--------, 'Development: Lodestar or Illusion', in Leslie Sklair (ed.), *Capitalism and Development* (London and New York: Routledge, 1994), pp. 3-20.

Wanandi, Yusuf, 'ASEAN's Domestic Political Developments and Their Impact on Foreign Policy', *The Pacific Review*, 8/3 (1995), pp. 440-458.

--------, 'Politico-security Dimensions of Southeast Asia', *Asian Survey*, 17/8 (August 1977), pp. 771-792.

Watson Jr., Richard L., *The United States in the Contemporary World, 1945-1962* (New York: The Free Press, 1965).

Weatherbee, Donald E., *Approaches to the Interpretation of Gestapu: the Indonesian Coup Attempt of 1 October, 1965* (Columbia: University of South Carolina, 1968).

--------, *Ideology in Indonesia: Sukarno's Indonesian Revolution* (Monograph Series No. 8, New Haven, CT: Southeast Asia Studies, Yale University, 1966).

Webber, Douglas, 'Two Funerals and a Wedding? The Ups and Downs of Regionalism in East Asia and Asia-Pacific after the Asian Crisis', *The Pacific Review*, 14/3 (2001), pp. 339-372.

Weinstein, Franklin B., *Indonesia Abandons Confrontation: An Inquiry Into the Functions of Indonesian Foreign Policy* (Modern Indonesia Project, Interim Reports Series No.45, Ithaca, NY: Southeast Asia Program, Department of Asian Studies, Cornell University, 1969).

--------, *Indonesian Foreign Policy and the Dilemma of Dependence: From Sukarno to Soeharto* (Ithaca, NY: Cornell University Press, 1976).

--------, 'The Second Asian-African Conference: Preliminary Bouts', *Asian Survey*, 5/7 (July 1965), pp. 359-373.

Wesley, Michael, 'The Asian Crisis and the Adequacy of Regional Institutions', *Contemporary Southeast Asia*, 21/1 (April 1999), pp. 54-73.

White, Nicholas J., 'The Beginning of Crony Capitalism: Business, Politics and Economic Development in Malaysia, 1955-70', *Modern Asian Studies*, 38/2 (2004), pp. 389-417.

Wilson, David, 'Thailand: A New Leader', *Asian Survey*, 4/2 (February 1964), pp. 711-715.

Wolfstone, Daniel, 'Colombo Plan Issues', *Far Eastern Economic Review*, 2 November 1961, pp. 267-268.

--------, 'Manila's Image of ASAS', *Far Eastern Economic Review*, 15 September 1960, pp. 596-600.

World Bank, *The East Asian Miracle* (Oxford: Oxford University Press, 1993).

Wurfel, David, 'A Changing Philippines', *Asian Survey*, 4/2 (February 1964), pp. 702-710.

Yahuda, Michael, *The International Politics of the Asia-Pacific* (2nd and revised edn., Oxford: Routledge Curzon, 2004).

--------, *The Post Cold War Order in Asia and the Challenge to ASEAN* (Singapore: Institute of Southeast Asian Studies, 2006).

Yamakage, Susumu, *ASEAN: Shinboru kara Shisutemu he [ASEAN: From Symbol to System]* (Tokyo: Tokyo Daigaku Syuppan [University of Tokyo Press], 1991).

--------, 'Chiiki Tougou Kara Mita ASEAN no Kinou [The Function of ASEAN in View of the Regional Integration]', in Tatsumi Okabe (ed.), *ASEAN no 20 Nen: Sono Jizoku to Hatten [ASEAN in Twenty Years on: Its Vitality and Development]* (Tokyo: Nihon Kokusai Mondai Kenkyujyo [The Japan Institute of International Affairs], 1987), pp. 185-211.

--------, 'Chiiki Tougou Ron Saikou: Aratana Tenbou wo Motomete [Rethinking Regional Integration Theory: Seeking a New View]', *Kokusai Seiji*, 74 (August 1983), pp. 93-116.

--------, 'Tenkanki no ASEAN: Kakudai, Shinka, Aratana Kadai [ASEAN in the Turning Point: Expansion, Deepening and New Issues]', in Susumu Yamakage (ed.), *Tenkanki no ASEAN: Aratana Kadai heno Cyousen [ASEAN in the Turning Point: The Challenge for New Issues]* (Tokyo: Nihon Kokusai Mondai Kenkyujyo [The Japan Institute of International Affairs], 2001), pp. 1-19.

--------, 'Tounan Ajia ni okeru Jinken Mondai no Tayousei [A Diversity of Human Rights issues in Southeast Asia]', in Akio Watanabe (ed.), *Ajia no Junken: Kokusai Seiji no Shiten Kara [Human Rights in Asia: From the Perspective of International Politics]* (Tokyo: Nihon Kokusai Mondai Kenkyujyo [Japan Institute of International Affairs], 1997), pp. 53-72.

Newspapers & periodicals

Asahi Shimbun
Asian Almanac
Asian Week
BBC Monitoring Service: Asia-Pacific
Far Eastern Economic Review
Manila Times
New York Times
South China Morning Post
The Australian
The Age
The Bangkok Post
The Straits Times
The Sun

INDEX

Anglo-Malaysian Defence Agreement 56, 58
ASA 10, 13, 16, 33-35, 45, 55, 84-86, 88-90, 92, 109, 113-117
ASEAN Ministerial Meeting 7, 12, 98, 103-104, 111, 118
ASEAN Way 6-9, 14-17, 118-121
Asian-African Conference 31, 85, 121,
ASAS 31
Australia 9, 20-21, 37, 49, 70, 81, 83, 85, 100

Bangkok declaration 34, 115
Bangsen 102-104, 108-109, 118
behind-the-scene 11, 14, 108-109, 112, 116, 118
Borneo 33, 36-39, 41-43, 45, 47, 50, 54, 56, 59-62, 95, 97
British government 25, 36, 38, 40, 49, 59-61, 63, 66-67, 79, 123
Brunei 33, 36-38, 41-42, 45-48, 73

Cambodia 10, 21, 29, 40, 86, 90,
China 20-22, 35, 39-40, 50, 94, 110, 113, 119
Cold War 9, 19-20, 22-23, 25, 27, 40, 50, 110-111, 116, 121
Colombo Plan 19-22, 70, 93
Communist 19-26, 29-31, 34-35, 39-40, 49-50, 86-87, 117, 119
consultation 7-8, 11-15, 17, 29, 32-34, 36, 54-56, 63, 65-68, 90-91, 94, 105, 107-108, 114-115, 117-118, 122, 124
Corregidor affair 95-105, 109, 116, 118, 122
Corregidor Island 95

Dulles, John Foster 21, 25

Eisenhower, Dwight D. 24
ethnic Malay 68, 72
external power 9-10, 20, 34-35, 40, 67, 79, 109-111, 119, 121

face-saving 7-8, 11-12, 14-15, 66, 68, 89, 91, 94, 104-105, 108, 112, 115, 124

Garcia, Carlos P. 26-29, 32, 43, 55, 85, 115
Geneva Conference 22, 24-25, 40

harmonisation 17, 64, 66-67, 74, 86, 88, 105, 113, 117
harmony 8, 15, 54, 62, 65, 80, 88, 92, 97, 105, 112, 117
Hatta, Mohammad 19, 30, 32, 36-37, 68, 91, 109, 113, 115

Indonesia 9, 16-17, 19-23, 29-34, 36-38, 40, 42-68, 70-94, 98-100, 102-104, 107-110, 112, 116-118
Indonesian Communist Party (PKI) 42, 46, 72-74, 110
Informality 8-9, 13, 68, 104-105, 114-116

Jones, Howard Palfrey 42

Kennedy, John F. 49, 60,
Khoman, Thanat 6-7, 25, 34, 64, 84, 86-90, 94, 98, 104, 111-112, 118
Khrushchev, Nikita S. 23
Konfrontasi (Confrontation) 33, 47, 49, 64, 67, 73-77, 79-80, 82-83, 91-93, 107, 109, 123
Kttikachorn, Thanom 97
Kusumowidagdo, Suwito 32, 50-52, 65

Lee, Kuan Yew 39, 62, 67, 73, 92, 94
Leifer, Michael 12
Lopez, Salvador P. 50, 62-63, 71
Lord Cobbold 42
Lord Selkirk 39-41
Luneta Park 102, 104

Macapagal, Diosdado 43-44, 47-48, 50-51, 54-55, 63, 66, 68, 70-71, 78, 85, 93, 96
MacDonald, Malcom 22, 36, 38
Macmillan, Harold 41, 60
Mahmud, Azahari bin Sheikh 33, 45, 48, 73
Malaya 19-20, 22, 27-29, 32-34, 36-42, 44-60, 62-68, 84, 115-117, 119
Malaysia 6, 9, 14, 17, 33-34, 36-68, 70-73, 75-86, 88-94, 95-98, 100-105, 107-113, 116-118
Manila Accord 54-55, 63, 65, 97-98, 107, 116
Manila agreements 55, 57, 60-68, 71, 76-77, 80, 82, 94, 97, 117
Manila Joint Statement 65, 97, 111
Maphilindo 6, 10, 16, 36, 54-55, 62, 64-69, 71, 85, 93, 108, 111, 114-115, 117
Marcos, Ferdinand 78-79, 86, 88, 95-96, 100, 102

Modelski, George 16, 67
Murtopo, Ali 7, 102, 104, 108
Musyawarah 13-17, 29, 55, 68, 108, 112, 115-116
mufakat 13-14, 16-17, 108, 112, 115-116
Musyawarah Maphilindo 55, 108

Nasution, Abdul Haris 30, 45, 80, 89
Netherlands 19, 31, 43
non-interference 8-11, 17, 107, 109, 111
North Vietnam 20, 24, 35, 40, 86

Pancasila 16, 22-23, 113
Pelaez, Emmanuel 44-45, 47, 55
Philippines 6, 14, 16-17, 19-22, 25-28, 33-34, 38, 43-44, 47-49, 51-52, 54-56, 58-59, 61-68, 70-71, 78-79, 84-88, 90, 92, 95-105, 107-109, 112, 114-118,
Phitsuwan, Surin 7
Pye, Lucian W. 22

Rajaratnam, S. 97, 99
Ramos, Narciso 79-80, 84, 86-87, 94, 97, 99, 101-102, 104, 117
Regionalism 9, 35, 111

Sabah 6, 17, 33, 36, 37-38, 40-48, 54-58, 63-64, 70-71, 76, 81-83, 112, 115, 117-118
Sandys, Duncan 59-60, 62, 66-67
Sarasin, Pote 120
Sarawak 36-38, 40-43, 45, 52, 54-58, 62-64, 70-71, 76, 81-83
SEATO 9, 16, 19-22, 24-28, 32, 34-35, 41-42, 44, 87, 93, 117
Shafie, Ghazali 62, 82-83, 98, 105, 121
Singapore 9, 14-15, 36-37, 39, 41-42, 55-56, 58, 61-64, 73, 77-80, 86, 90, 92, 94, 97, 99-100, 112
South Vietnam 20-22, 24-25, 40, 78, 110
Southeast Asian Friendship and Economic Treaty (SEAFET) 29, 115
Soviet Union 20, 23, 31, 40, 49-50, 72, 110
Stalin, Joseph 23
Subandrio 40, 42-43, 46-48, 50-51, 53, 56-58, 61-62, 66-67, 72, 74, 78, 117
Suharto 73-74, 76-78, 80-83, 88-89, 91-92, 94, 102, 117
Sukarno 16, 19, 23, 29-32, 38, 42, 45-46, 48, 50, 52-53, 56-60, 63, 65-68, 70-77, 79-80, 82-83, 89-92, 107, 113, 116

Thailand 9, 14-17, 19-22, 25-28, 32-35, 70, 78, 81, 84-85, 87-90, 94-95, 98, 100-102, 104-105, 114
Treaty of Amity of Cooperation (TAC) 12-13, 16, 20, 22, 25-27, 30-32, 34-35, 37, 40, 53, 56-57, 59, 61-62, 64-65, 67, 70-71, 74, 80-81, 86, 95-97, 104, 108-110, 115, 120
Treaty of Friendship 32, 66
Tun Abdul Razak (Tun Razak) 49-51, 57, 62, 80-81, 83-84, 86, 92, 98-99, 101-102, 107, 111, 113
Tunku Abdul Rahman (the Tunku) 22, 26-29, 32, 34, 36-41, 44, 46-53, 56-60, 62-68, 70-72, 77-79, 84-85, 88-90, 92, 97, 105, 107, 113, 115-120

U Thant 57, 61, 63-64, 97, 101
United Nations 8-10, 20, 31, 42, 45, 49, 54, 56-57, 61-64, 72, 75, 88, 96-97, 100-101, 113
United States of America (US, America) 11, 20, 22-27, 30-31, 34-35, 40, 43, 49, 72, 75, 79, 87, 93, 100, 110

working together 8, 13-14, 54, 65, 68, 70, 86, 90, 98, 105, 111-115, 117-118
World War II 9, 18-19, 34, 88, 90

■ About Author

Kazuhisa Shimada is Associate Professor at Okayama University, Japan, and Visiting Research Fellow in School of History and Politics at the University of Adelaide, Australia.

"Working Together"
for Peace and Prosperity of Southeast Asia, 1945–1968
The Birth of the ASEAN Way

2013年10月30日 初版第1刷発行

■著　者────島田和久
■発 行 者────佐藤　守
■発 行 所────株式会社　大学教育出版
　　　　　　　〒700-0953　岡山市南区西市855-4
　　　　　　　電話 (086)244-1268㈹　FAX (086)246-0294
■印刷製本────モリモト印刷㈱

© Kazuhisa Shimada 2013, Printed in Japan
検印省略　　落丁・乱丁本はお取り替えいたします。
無断で本書の一部または全部を複写・複製することは禁じられています。

ISBN978-4-86429-244-3